PRESIDENTIAL LEGISLATION IN INDIA

India has a parliamentary system. Yet the president has authority to occasionally enact legislation (or ordinances) without involving parliament. This book is a study of ordinances at the national level in India, centred around three themes. First, it tells the story of how an artifact of British constitutional history, over time, became part of India's legislative system. Second, it offers an empirical account of the ways in which presidents have resorted to ordinances in post-independence India. Third, the book analyses a range of ordinance-related questions, including some that are yet to be judicially adjudicated. In the process, the book explains why much of the Indian Supreme Court's jurisprudence is mistaken and what should take its place. Overall, the book explains why the fate of parliamentary reforms in India may be tied to the reform of this provision for ordinances. Standing at the intersection of constitutional law and political science, *Presidential Legislation in India* offers a new frame through which to assess executives' legislative powers in both parliamentary and presidential systems.

Shubhankar Dam is an Assistant Professor of Law at Singapore Management University School of Law. He received his BCL from University of Oxford and the LLM from Harvard Law School. He specialises in the fields of law and governance in India and comparative constitutional law, and has held visiting positions at universities in Australia, India and Germany.

COMPARATIVE CONSTITUTIONAL LAW AND POLICY

Series Editors:

Tom Ginsburg
University of Chicago

Zachary Elkins
University of Texas at Austin

Ran Hirschl
University of Toronto

Comparative constitutional law is an intellectually vibrant field that encompasses an increasingly broad array of approaches and methodologies. This series collects analytically innovative and empirically grounded work from scholars of comparative constitutionalism across academic disciplines. Books in the series include theoretically informed studies of single constitutional jurisdictions, comparative studies of constitutional law and institutions, and edited collections of original essays that respond to challenging theoretical and empirical questions in the field.

Volumes in the Series:

Comparative Constitutional Design edited by Tom Ginsburg (2012)

Consequential Courts: Judicial Roles in Global Perspective edited by Diana Kapiszewski, Gordon Silverstein and Robert A. Kagan (2013)

Social and Political Foundations of Constitutions edited by Denis Galligan and Mila Versteeg (2013)

Constitutions in Authoritarian Regimes edited by Tom Ginsburg and Alberto Simpser (2014)

Presidential Legislation in India: The Law and Practice of Ordinances by Shubhankar Dam (2014)

Presidential Legislation in India

THE LAW AND PRACTICE OF ORDINANCES

Shubhankar Dam
Singapore Management University School of Law

CAMBRIDGE
UNIVERSITY PRESS

CAMBRIDGE
UNIVERSITY PRESS

32 Avenue of the Americas, New York, NY 10013-2473, USA

Cambridge University Press is part of the University of Cambridge.

It furthers the University's mission by disseminating knowledge in the pursuit of education, learning and research at the highest international levels of excellence.

www.cambridge.org
Information on this title: www.cambridge.org/9781107039711

First published 2014

Printed in the United States of America

A catalog record for this publication is available from the British Library.

Library of Congress Cataloging in Publication data
Dam, Shubhankar, 1981–
Presidential legislation in India : the law and practice of ordinances / Shubhankar Dam, Singapore Management University School of Law.
pages cm. – (Comparative constitutional law and policy)
Includes bibliographical references and index.
ISBN 978-1-107-03971-1 (hardback)
1. Orders in council – India. 2. Executive orders – India. I. Title.
KNS2220.D36 2013
328.54'077–dc23 2013028338

ISBN 978-1-107-03971-1 Hardback

To my teacher, Professor N. R. Madhava Menon

गुरुर्ब्रह्मा गुरुर्विष्णुर्गुरुर्देवो महेश्वरः।
गुरुरेव परं ब्रह्म तस्मै श्रीगुरवे नमः॥

(श्री गुरुगीता : ५८)

Contents

List of Tables

List of Abbreviations

BJP	Bharatiya Janata Party
BNO	Bank Nationalisation Ordinance
CVC	Central Vigilance Commission
ESMO	Essential Services Maintenance Ordinance
JD	Janata Dal
JS	Jana Sangh
NAC	National Advisory Council
NDA	National Democratic Alliance
NF	National Front
NHRC	National Human Rights Commission
OBC	Other Backward Classes
POTO	Prevention of Terrorism Ordinance
SEBI	Securities and Exchange Board of India
SP	Swatantra Party
ST	Scheduled Tribes
TDP	Telegu Desam Party
UF	United Front
UPA	United Progressive Alliance

Acknowledgements

Books, even sole-authored ones, are rarely written by single authors. Almost always, writing a book involves many people, and this one is no different in that regard. This project has been in the works for more than four years, and several people have directly and indirectly made this possible, and I want to acknowledge their contributions. At the very top of this list is the Founding Dean of SMU School of Law, Michael P. Furmston. Without his counsel, support and encouragement, this book would not have happened. Parts of the manuscript were completed in Australia, Germany and India, and the dean generously approved those research visits. Peter Cane and Armin von Bogdandy kindly hosted me in Canberra and Heidelberg, respectively, and made available a wide array of resources that eventually proved crucial to this project. I thank them for their support and hospitality. Not all materials necessary for the book were available at the Li Ka Shing Library at SMU. Two librarians, Charlotte Gill and Lim Siew Khim, went out of their way to source for materials, both locally and internationally. Charlotte Gill also made a few databases available to me, which proved rather important in the ultimate scheme of things. Two students – Tania Sebastian and Teng Lee Hong – provided valuable research assistance in preparing the manuscript. I could not have asked for better research assistants, and this book benefitted a great deal from their meticulous efforts. Both have since graduated; Tania is an academic in her own right in India, and Lee Hong has joined the ranks of the civil service providers in Singapore.

Various parts of this book have been presented at a number of conferences and seminars, and I gained valuable feedback on every occasion. Vrinda Dalmiya, Michael Furmston, Maximo Langer, Jacqueline Ross, Richard Ross, Kim Lane Scheppele, Mitra Sharafi and M. P. Singh, among others, offered feedback on parts of the manuscript. Also, in November

2011, M. P. Singh, then Vice Chancellor of the National University of Juridical Sciences (NUJS), India, invited me to present some of the materials to the faculty and students at NUJS. I benefitted from that exercise too.

My thanks to John Berger, my editor at Cambridge University Press, as well as to the series editors for their interest in this project. The editors offered useful suggestions at different stages; Ran Hirschl in particular patiently read through several drafts and offered detailed comments. I also wish to thank Wendy Bedenbaugh, David Jou and Paul Smolenski in their various capacities at Cambridge University Press for guiding the manuscript through publishing stages, as well as Adrian Pereira at Aptara Corp. for capably managing production and Dalene Bickel at PETT Fox, Inc., for excellent copyediting. Suneethi Raja helped prepare the index.

Finally, a word about my teacher, N. R. Madhava Menon, to whom this book is dedicated. The National University of Juridical Sciences opened its doors to its first batch of students in 2000. Many students chose to join this new law school; some others joined because they had no other choice. But as members of the pioneering cohort, all of us, it is safe to say, shared a belief that NUJS was worth the risk simply because of the towering presence of Professor Menon. In the next four years, he almost single-handedly built the institution, set high standards and inspired the faculty and students to attempt to achieve those standards. My academic career almost certainly would not have taken off without his advice, support and encouragement. Words are all I have to thank him with, and I dedicate these 90,000-odd words to him.

The law discussed in this book is current as of 15 August 2013.

Shubhankar Dam
Singapore, 2013

Introduction: Alternatives to Parliamentary Legislation

INDIA'S OTHER PARLIAMENT

The legislative process in India's parliamentary system, like elsewhere, is a shared exercise: the executive and the legislature partake in it. Ordinarily, proposals for legislation originate in the cabinet. If the cabinet decides that a law is necessary, a bill is drafted, on occasions, with external inputs. After it is introduced in the two houses, the bill goes through several 'readings', committee hearings and amendments. The final draft is debated and voted on. If a bill secures the requisite majority in both houses of parliament, it is sent to the president for assent, upon which the bill becomes an Act.[1] Parliament, in this formal view, is central to the legislative process, and legislation are products of – amongst other things – a rational-legal scrutiny and vote.[2]

In practice, parliament is less than central; the legislative process rarely confirms to the constitutional-ideal type. Take, for example, political parties and their influence on the legislative process. The party to which a

[1] For a description of the legal process, A. R. Mukherjea, *Parliamentary Procedure in India* 232–276 (Oxford University Press, New Delhi, 1983). Subhas Kashyap, *Our Parliament* (National Book Trust, New Delhi, 2004).

[2] Constitution of India, Article 107(2) ('. . . a Bill shall not be deemed to have been passed by the Houses of Parliament unless it has been agreed to by both Houses, either without amendment or with such amendments only as are agreed to by both Houses'). The suggestion that legislation are products of 'rational-legal' scrutiny must be understood in a normative sense. I take the view that all public officials including legislators *should* assess the constitutionality (or legality) of their actions, and not make decisions merely because it is politically expedient to do so. In other words, the question of constitutionality is not for judges only. Even though the latter are supposed to have special expertise in dealing with questions of constitutionality, it is not their exclusive province. Parliamentarians too, in my view, are required to take the Constitution seriously.

government belongs can have a disproportionate say in policy and legislative matters. Indeed, depending on the personalities involved, legislative proposals may even originate and take shape in party headquarters.[3] Or consider a coalition government. A cabinet's decision to introduce a bill may be evidence of compulsion, not necessity. It may be a price for keeping the coalition together or a political manoeuvring to secure new allies.[4] Also, consider the influence of non-representative actors and their ability to direct legislative proposals. A cabinet's decision to introduce a bill may be a grudging response to a populist outcry or a concession to a caste, religious or trade lobby.[5] In each of these situations, 'cabinet', 'parliament' and 'voting' are less central than in the Constitution's idealised process. The party chief may matter more than the prime minister. Debates occur, but rarely in parliament. And backroom deals rather than the formal vote may decide the fate of legislative proposals. Coupled with the general decline in members' interest and performance, these surrogates diminish, to a large extent, parliament's representative – and deliberative – relevance to the legislative process in India.[6]

[3] The National Advisory Council (NAC) is obviously the most recent example of this phenomenon. Set up by an order of the Union Cabinet in 2004 (No. 631/2/1/2004-Cab) and later reconstituted in 2010, the NAC often drafts legislation to be 'considered' by the cabinet. See Anon, 'Sonia as NAC Head Is Pseudo-Constitutional Power Centre: BJP' *Indian Express*, 30 March 2010. For an early, but contrary, view on the matter, see W. H. Morris-Jones, *Parliament in India* 166–185 (Longmans, Green and Co., London, 1957). Based on his analysis of the relationship between the former Indian National Congress and the cabinet led by Jawaharlal Nehru, Morris-Jones came to the 'unmistakable' conclusion that 'for the parties, for political life as a whole, parliament [had] become the focus of attention'. *Id.* at 185. For an account of the changing relationship between prime ministers and the parties to which they belonged, especially the Congress Party, see Robin Jeffrey, 'The Prime Minister and the Ruling Party' in James Manor (ed.), *Nehru to the Nineties: The Changing Office of Prime Minister in India* 161–185 (Hurst and Co., London, 1994).

[4] Arun Shourie, *The Parliamentary System* 36–49 (ASA Rupa, New Delhi, 2007); V. Ramkrishnan, 'All for Survival' *Frontline*, 15(8), (11–24 April) 1998; Sukumar Muralidharan, 'BJP and Friends' *Frontline*, 15(1), (10–23 January) 1998. For an overview of coalitions and coalition-building in India, see Bidyut Chakrabarty, *Forging Power: Coalition Politics in India* 19–63 (Oxford University Press, New Delhi, 2006).

[5] See Asghar Ali Engineer, *The Shah Bano Controversy* (Ajanta Publishers, Delhi, 1987); Prem Shankar Jha, 'Coalition Politics and Economic Decision-Making' in Mahendra Prasad Singh and Anil Mishra (eds.), *Coalition Politics in India: Problems and Prospects* 285–292 (Manohar, New Delhi, 2004). See also, *id.* Shourie, at 58–63.

[6] For assessments of India's parliament, see Vernon Hewitt and Shirin M. Rai, 'Parliament' in Niraja Jayal and Pratap Mehta (eds.), *Oxford Companion to Politics in India* 28–42 (Oxford University Press, New Delhi, 2010); Arun Agarwal, 'The Indian Parliament' in Devesh Kapur and Pratap Mehta (eds.), *Public Institution in India*, 77–104 (Oxford University Press, New Delhi, 2007); Gail Omvedt, 'Parliamentary System in India: Issues and Suggestions', 33(3–4) *Indian Journal of Political Science* 4–16 (1999); Nand Lal and Urmila Lal, 'Decline of Indian

Although these political surrogates compromise parliament's prominence, they are 'non-institutional' in nature; they can complicate but not derogate from the constitutional requirements. The real work behind legislation may happen elsewhere rather than in the two houses, and it may be done by people other than parliamentarians. However, cabinet, parliament and voting are nonetheless present: they matter, even if in form only.

However, articled in India's Constitution is a legislative process that compromises parliament and voting both in form *and* substance. This is because the Constitution authorises the president, under certain circumstances, to enact legislation without parliamentary involvement. With such legislation, or 'ordinances', parliament does not matter even in form; initially, the president surrogates for it. This book is an empirical and analytical account of ordinances – a form of institutionalised surrogacy that reduces the legislative process to a 'private' affair.[7] The book grapples with three broad sets of questions: Where did this mechanism originate, and how did it become part of India's legislative design? How has it been used thus far? What do judicial opinions tell us about the law and practice of federal ordinances in India?

ORDINANCES: THE BASICS

Article 123(1) provides for ordinances at the federal level: 'If at any time, except when both Houses of Parliament are in session, the President is satisfied that circumstances exist which render it necessary for him to take

Parliament: How and Why It Has Happened?' in K. S. Saxena and Anil Gupta (eds.), *Indian Democracy: Recent Trends and Issues* 192–201 (Anmol Publications, New Delhi, 1985). See also Surya Prakash, *What Ails India's Parliament* (Harper Collins, New Delhi, 1995). For assessments of parliament's performance in terms of debates and utilization of time, PRS Legislative Research offers the best data. See, e.g., Anon, 'Utilisation of Time by Parliament: Monsoon Session 2007' *available at*: http://www.prsindia.org/administrator/uploads/general/1241757849~~Vital%20Stats%20Monsoon%202007.pdf (visited on 22 April 2012); Anon, 'Legislative Activity in Parliament' *available at*: http://www.prsindia.org/administrator/uploads/general/1241757164~~Legislative%20activity%20in%20Parliament.pdf (visited on 23 April 2012).

[7] The claim that ordinances are 'private affairs' can only be understood in the light of arguments in Chapter 3. For the sake of clarity, let me mention three ways in which the reference should be understood here. First, ordinances are private in the sense that *reasons* for promulgating them are usually not made public. Second, they are private in the sense that ordinances, by definition, exclude the possibility of parliamentary involvement initially. Third, and perhaps most egregiously, ordinances are private in the sense that, under current law, they take effect even before being made available to the public.

immediate action, he may promulgate such ordinances as the circumstances appear to him to require'. Article 213(1) confers similar powers on governors at the state level: 'If at any time, except when the Legislative Assembly of a State is in session . . . the Governor is satisfied that circumstances exist which render it necessary for him to take immediate action, he may promulgate such ordinances as the circumstances appear to him to require'. Even though some additional limitations apply to ordinances at the state level, by and large, they are structurally similar. First, the power to promulgate ordinances, in practice, is exercised by the relevant council of ministers. The council of ministers decides if an ordinance is necessary and the president (or governor) gives assent to it. The latter has some discretion in the matter, but the scope of that discretion remains untested. Second, ordinances, at the national level, for example, may be promulgated 'except when *both* Houses of Parliament are in session'. That is, it may be done even if either the Lower House or the Upper House is still in session. Similar rules apply to state legislative chambers. Third, the maximum duration of ordinances is not directly provided for. Under both Articles 123 and 213, ordinances remain in force until the expiry of six weeks from the commencement of the next legislative session. Ordinarily, this means that ordinances may be in force for a period of little more than seven months. This is because the Constitution requires both houses at the federal level, for example, to meet at least once every six months.[8] Also, because ordinances require approval after they come into effect, legislative chambers have no ex ante control over ordinances. Objections, if any, may be recorded only after promulgation. Fourth, ordinances are like parliamentary legislation; they have the 'same force and effect'. They are not rules, orders, by-laws or delegated legislation of some other kind commonly associated with the exercise of executive power. Rather, they are legislation proper. When presidents and governors promulgate them, they act as legislative surrogates; they are to ordinances what both houses of parliament or state assemblies are to legislation. Fifth, and most importantly, ordinances are, at least textually, limited to circumstances when it is necessary to take 'immediate action'. They are predicated on some form of legislative urgency and, unlike Acts, require additional justifications. Taken together, these features make ordinances an exceptional arrangement. They authorise a non-deliberative, non-majoritarian and 'private'

[8] Constitution of India, Article 85(1) ('The President shall from time to time summon each House of Parliament to meet at such time and place as he thinks fit, but six months shall not intervene between its last sitting in one session and the date appointed for its first sitting in the next session').

legislative method – one that reduces legislation to fiats. And this heightened executive ownership of legislation calls into question, not without reason, India's parliamentary credentials.[9]

Although constitutionally limited to circumstances when it is necessary to take immediate action, ordinances, in practice, have an expansive presence in India's parliamentary annals. After six decades, they are neither exceptional nor limited. Rather, they are a convenient and – distressingly at times – the *preferred* legislative method.[10] Take, for example, two ordinance-related controversies – experiences that are emblematic of this widespread 'preferential' attitude. In October 2001, the Vajpayee-led National Democratic Alliance (NDA) government promulgated the Prevention of Terrorism Ordinance, 2001 (POTO) to deal with what it claimed were Indian modules of a global terror network.[11] Introduced just weeks before the winter session of parliament, both the ordinance and the method of bringing it into existence, the Indian National Congress-led opposition argued, were undemocratic.[12] The cabinet had neither majority support for the law nor any interest in its public scrutiny. It was, the opposition felt, designed to undermine parliament. Some coalition partners of the NDA government also shared the opposition's scepticism: The 'draconian' provisions and the potential targeting of minority communities worried them.[13] None of this mattered to members of Vajpayee's cabinet. To them, ordinances were a constitutional alternative to ordinary legislation, including those that did not enjoy majority support in parliament.[14] POTO, incidentally, was only one of the thirty-three

[9] For a defence of India's parliamentary credentials, B. L. Shankar and Valerian Rodrigues, *The Indian Parliament: A Democracy at Work* 371–386 (Oxford University Press, New Delhi, 2011).

[10] I should point out that 'preference' here does not refer to numbers. It is not to suggest that there are more ordinances than legislation in India. Rather, the word must be understood in its *qualitative* sense. To say that ordinances have become the 'preferred' method is to suggest that cabinets prefer to promulgate ordinances even in situations when legislation is entirely possible. The claim can be fully understood only in the light of the empirical analysis in Chapter 2.

[11] Anon, 'Police Get Sweeping Powers to Fight Terror' *Times of India*, 17 October 2001.

[12] Kapil Sibal, 'Politics of POTO: Nothing Anti-national about Dissent' *Times of India*, 16 November 2001.

[13] Sidharth Varadarajan, 'Reject POTO in Toto' *Times of India*, 14 November 2001.

[14] Arun Jaitley, 'POTO Pin-Up' *Times of India*, 13 December 2001. It must be added that the ordinance lapsed, and was re-promulgated for a second time. Eventually it was formally enacted into law an extraordinary procedure providec for in Article 108 in the Constitution. Anon, 'Govt. Powers POTO through Joint Session' *Times of India*, 27 March 2002.

ordinances promulgated into law by the Vajpayee cabinet between October 1999 and May 2004.

In March 2006, the ordinance controversy returned, but this time the roles were reversed. The NDA-led opposition started an agitation against Mrs Sonia Gandhi, the leader of the Congress Party, and her alleged 'office of profit' – something, they argued, disqualified her from the membership to the Lower House.[15] Parliament was in session at that point. But the Congress-led United Progressive Alliance (UPA) government decided to put a lid on the controversy through an ordinance. A plan was secretly drawn up to adjourn the two houses sine die. That would have provided the cabinet with an excuse to promulgate an ordinance removing Mrs Gandhi's disqualification under the relevant legislation. An alert piece of reporting in the *Indian Express* made the plan public.[16] This time it was the NDA that was up in arms. The proposed ordinance was a gross abuse of power, some NDA delegates argued. Parliament was in session and the government sought to undermine it by creating a situation of 'legislative emergency' so as to make an ordinance nominally possible.[17] Interestingly, Dr Manmohan Singh's cabinet said little in its defence. The Congress Party, in particular, vacillated between denying and defending the proposed ordinance.[18] Because they, too, would have benefitted from it, the opposition's agitation, it claimed, was opportunistic. The implication was obvious: the ordinance route was justified so long as its spoils were equitably distributed. The public outcry over the leaked plan forced the Manmohan Singh cabinet to abandon its proposed ordinance. But in the five years between May 2004 and May 2009, the cabinet promulgated as many as thirty-six ordinances.[19]

[15] Anon, 'Sonia Resigns from Lok Sabha, NAC' *Business Line*, 24 March 2006. See Constitution of India, Article 102 (1)(a) ('A person shall be disqualified for being chosen as, and for being, a member of either House of Parliament if he holds any office of profit under the Government of India or the Government of any State, other than an office declared by Parliament by law not to disqualify its holder').

[16] R. Venkataraman, 'To Stop Office-of-Profit Axe, UPA Gets Ordinance' *Indian Express*, 21 March 2006. Anon, 'Uproar in Parliament over Ordinance "Shielding" Sonia' *Hindustan Times*, 22 March 2006.

[17] Anon, 'Govt. Ordinance: NDA Lodges Protest with Kalam' *Rediff News*, 23 March 2006, *available at*: http://www.rediff.com/news/2006/mar/22profit1.htm (accessed 23 April 2012).

[18] Anon, 'No Discussion on Ordinance in Cabinet' *Times of India*, 23 March 2006.

[19] Although plans for the ordinance were shelved, it was later enacted into law by parliament. The Parliament (Prevention of Disqualification) Amendment Act, 2006 (31 of 2006).

As these examples suggest, the story of ordinances in India's Constitution is, in effect, a story about how an extraordinary constitutional arrangement has come to be normalized into everyday governance and the ways in which it, to borrow Dr D. C. Wadhwa's phrase, 'endangers constitutionalism' in India.[20] Between 1952 and 2009, 615 ordinances have been promulgated at the national level. That comes to about 10.6 ordinances each year for nearly 60 years.[21] In other words, on ten or more occasions every year, presidents came to the conclusion that circumstances required them to take 'immediate action' that was in lieu of parliamentary legislation. These numbers are unacceptably high. They are equally disappointing in percentage terms; 615 ordinances amount to approximately 17.7 per cent of the 3,467 pieces of legislation parliament enacted into law during the same period. In other words, around one-sixth of all legislation at the national level originated as ordinances. Although there are variances in the numbers over the decades, the trend towards greater reliance on ordinances since the 1970s is unmistakable.

Two introductory observations can be made at this point. Attitudinally speaking, the distrust of ordinances when in opposition – and their convenient use when in power – enjoys support across the political spectrum. Parties of all hues have resorted to them. Further data would be required to make this point in detail. But the spread of ordinances over sixty years makes it safe to suggest that no political party is immune from ordinance-related excesses. By way of introduction, it may be sufficient to note the record of two coalition governments between June 1996 and March 1998, led by H. D. Deve Gowda and Inder K. Gujral, respectively. Both prime ministers belonged to the so-called United Front – a motley coalition of regional parties that claimed to represent the non-Congress, non-Bharatiya Janata Party (BJP) space in India's national politics. Between June 1996 and April 1997, the almost dysfunctional Deve Gowda cabinet promulgated as many as twenty-three ordinances. Not to be outdone, the Gujral cabinet promulgated another twenty-three ordinances between April 1997 and March 1998. These figures suggest that there is a hyper-consensus about the acceptability of ordinances as a

[20] D. C. Wadhwa, *Endangered Constitutionalism: Documents from a Supreme Court Case* (Gokhale Institute of Politics and Economics, Pune, 2008).

[21] Ordinance figures in this chapter and subsequently are based on a handbook published by the government of India. See *Statistical Handbook* (Ministry of Parliamentary Affairs, Govt. of India, New Delhi, 2010).

'parallel' legislative mechanism that cuts across party lines. It may be one of India's little noticed parliamentary features.

Substantively speaking, ordinances have been pressed in the service of both important and controversial policies on one hand and some mundane ones on the other hand. As I will later argue in detail, many of India's important national policies were 'legislated' through ordinances – matters that require careful deliberation rather than hasty enactment. But ordinances have also been used to legislate on routine issues – matters that cannot conceivably be said to require 'immediate action'. Attitudinally and substantively, therefore, the consequence of this expansive reliance on ordinances has been the same: The normalisation of a process that effectively outsources legislation to a small, 'select' group.

None of this should come as a surprise. Even before the Constitution was inaugurated in 1950, G. V. Mavalankar, later India's first speaker of the Lower House, warned about the perils of ordinances. At the Presiding Officers' Conference in 1947, he expressed concerns about their potential misuse. Ordinances were intended only for emergency circumstances, and relaxing that constraint, he predicted, may encourage governments to resort to them when faced with 'inconvenient legislation'.[22] In 1950, he wrote to Prime Minister Jawaharlal Nehru underlining the perils of relying on ordinances to carry out the government's legislative agenda. Apart from being 'inherently undemocratic', their effect on the legislative psyche worried Mavalankar.[23] 'The house', he regretfully noted, 'carries a sense of being ignored, and, the Central Secretariat perhaps gets into the habit of slackness', neither of which 'was conducive to the development of the best parliamentary traditions'.[24] He persisted against ordinances, once again reminding Nehru in 1954 that they should be limited to cases of 'extreme urgency or emergency'.[25] Acutely aware of the 'responsibility of laying down traditions' as the first parliament of the republic, the speaker added: 'It is not a question of present personnel in the Government, but [one] of precedents'. And if ordinances 'were not limited by convention only to extreme and very urgent cases', the result, Mavalankar warned, 'may be that, in future, the government may go on issuing ordinances giving the Lok Sabha no option, but to rubber-stamp'.[26] He was remarkably prescient. After more than sixty years, ordinances are neither

[22] *Presidential Ordinances 1950–1996* v (Lok Sabha Secretariat, New Delhi, 1996).
[23] *Ibid.*
[24] *Id.* at vi.
[25] *Ibid.*
[26] *Ibid.*

exceptional nor limited; they are a somewhat 'parallel' method in India's parliamentary system, and the numbers bear that out.

THE LARGER FRAME: NOTES FROM COMPARATIVE DESIGN

India is not the only jurisdiction where executive lawmaking of the kind described thus far is constitutionally provided for or otherwise practised. Jurisdictions in Eastern and Western Europe, Africa and Latin America frequently endow their presidents – and occasionally, the parliamentary head – with a range of legislative powers. And there is, unlike in India, a rather large body of sophisticated literature that both describes and analyses the exercise of such powers.[27] John Carey and Matthew Shugart's edited volume on decree authority is perhaps the most comprehensive comparative treatment of the subject.[28] Ten contributors assessed the evolution and exercise of such powers in eight jurisdictions, and in the process tested a set of hypotheses offered by the editors. Four of those jurisdictions were Latin American (Argentina, Brazil, Peru and Venezuela) and two were West European (Italy and France); Russia and the United States made up the remaining two. With the exception of Italy and France, the countries are thoroughly presidential systems, and that fact coloured the prism through which contributors presented and evaluated their arguments. Contesting the consensus in the literature at the time, Carey and Shugart argued that unilateral presidential actions do not necessarily imply an usurpation of legislative powers.[29] Parliamentary motives are complex, and legislators may tolerate – even encourage – such action if it is in their (political) interests.[30] Built into this argument

[27] For an introductory overview of decree powers as is it commonly referred to, see José Antonio Cheibub and Fernando Limongi, 'Legislative-executive relations', in Tom Ginsburg and Rosalind Dixon (eds.), *Comparative Constitution Law* 211, 226–229 (Edward Elgar Publishing, Cheltenhem, 2011); Matthew S. Shugart and John M. Carey, *Presidents and Assemblies: Constitutional Design and Electoral Dynamics* 131–147 (Cambridge University Press, New York, 1992). See also John M. Carey, 'Presidential versus Parliamentary Government', in C. M´enard and M. M. Shirley (eds.), *Handbook of New Institutional Economics* 91, 103–107 (Springer, Dordrecht, 2005).

[28] John M. Carey and Matthew S. Shugart (eds.), *Executive Decree Authority* (Cambridge University Press, Cambridge, 1998). For empirical notes on decree power, see José Antonio Cheibub, Zachary Elkins and Tom Ginsburg, 'Beyond Presidentialism and Parliamentarism' *British Journal of Political Science* (2013) (forthcoming).

[29] John M. Carey and Matthew Soberg Shugart, 'Calling Out the Tanks or Filling Out the Forms?' in John M. Carey and Matthew S. Shugart (eds.), *Executive Decree Authority* 1–29, 3 (Cambridge University Press, Cambridge, 1998).

[30] *Ibid.*

is the obvious assumption that a president's interests and those of the legislators are distinct, and unilateral action may amount to usurpation only if they clash. When interests align, such action may imply something else.[31]

Carey and Shugart offer a 2×2 matrix to explain how presidential decree authority can be constitutionally entrenched.[32] They focus on two aspects: permanence and timing. Are decrees permanent? Do they come into effect immediately? These two variables generate four possibilities. Russia, Peru, Colombia and Chile, they argue, are examples of the strongest possibility.[33] Presidential decrees in these jurisdictions are permanent, and they enjoy immediate effect – the prototypical decree authority. Because they are permanent, decrees can be undone only through contrary legislation in parliament. And immediate effect means that legislative chambers have no influence over them prior to their promulgation; parliamentary response, if any, is always ex post. But such powers often come with some additional limits. Article 90 in Russia's Constitution, for example, authorises the president to issue 'edicts and regulations' provided they do 'not conflict with the Constitution of the Russian Federation *and* federal laws'.[34] Similarly, in Peru, the president can exercise such power only 'on economic and financial matters, when so required by the national interest'.[35] Even though prototypical decree authority means that there are two distinct paths to primary legislation, parliament and president do not always enjoy similar legislative standing.

A second – and somewhat less strong – possibility is what Carey and Shugart refer to as provisional decree authority, whereby decrees take immediate effect but lapse after some designated period unless ratified by the legislature.[36] Article 62 in Brazil's Constitution, for example, provides that presidential decrees shall lapse after sixty days unless 'converted into

[31] The idea here is that legislators may delegate (formally through a piece of legislation, or simply by inaction) certain legislative decisions to a president for a variety of reasons. These may include partisan support for individual president, collective action problems within the legislature or electoral incentives of individual legislators.

[32] Carey and Shugart, *supra* n. 29, p. 10. [33] *Ibid.*

[34] Constitution of the Russian Federation Constitution 1993, Article 90 (3) ('Edicts and regulations of the President of the Russian Federation must not conflict with the Constitution of the Russian Federation and federal laws') (emphasis added).

[35] Constitution of Peru 1993, Article 118(9) ('It is the duty of the President... to promulgate special measures in economic and financial subject, through emergency decree with force of law, as required by national interest and reporting to Congress. Such emergency decrees may be modified or repealed by Congress').

[36] Carey and Shugart, *supra* n. 29, p. 11.

law' by Congress.[37] In neighbouring Argentina, the chief of the Ministerial Cabinet must personally submit – within ten days – promulgated decrees to the Joint Standing Committee of Congress for its consideration. The committee must make a report to both houses of Congress where it is 'immediately discussed'.[38] Whether a ratification requirement limits a president's ability to initiate long-term change depends in part on the legality of reissuing such decrees. If presidents are authorised to re-promulgate decrees, legislative opposition to such measures may not mean much. But the effectiveness of the ratification requirement also depends on 'cleanup costs'. If it is disproportionately costly to undo presidential initiatives, legislatures may ratify them despite their opposition to such measures.[39] Therefore, depending on how and why decrees are issued (and reissued), countries with provisional decree authority may in effect *function* like those with prototypical decree authority.

A third – and still less-strong possibility – is what Carey and Shugart refer to as delayed decree authority. As the name suggests, such decrees do not take immediate effect, but they become permanent law in the absence of legislative action.[40] This arrangement offers the legislative branch an opportunity to prohibit decrees from coming into effect – or to alter their content before authorising them. The scrutiny, if any, is ex ante. In Ecuador, the president can propose legislation declaring it 'urgent', and if the National Assembly fails to act within thirty days, the decree becomes law.[41] The Assembly, nonetheless, remains competent to amend or repeal such decrees at a later time.[42] Under Ecuadorian rules,

[37] Constitution of Brazil, Article 62(4) ('Provisional measures ... will lose efficacy, since back to the issuing date, if not converted into laws within sixty days, extendable, once ... for the same period of time, being up to the Congress to discipline, by means of a Legislative Decree, the juridic relations resulting of them').

[38] Constitution of the Argentine Nation, Article 99(3) ('Only when due to exceptional circumstances the ordinary procedures foreseen by this Constitution for the enactment of laws are impossible to be followed, and when rules are not referred to criminal issues, taxation, electoral matters, or the system of political parties, he shall issue decrees on grounds of necessity and urgency, which shall be decided by a general agreement of ministers who shall countersign them together with the Chief of the Ministerial Cabinet').

[39] Carey and Shugart, *supra* n. 29, p. 12.

[40] *Id.* at 11.

[41] Constitution of the Republic of Ecuador 2008, Article 140(1) ('The President of the Republic will be able to send to the National Assembly bills qualified as urgent on economic matters. The Assembly must adopt, amend or turn them down within thirty (30) days at the most as of their reception').

[42] Constitution of the Republic of Ecuador 2008, Article 140(3) ('When the Assembly does not adopt, amend or turn down the bill qualified as urgent in economic matters within the stipulated time-limits, the President of the Republic shall enact it as a decree-law or

the president may send only one 'urgent' decree to the Assembly at a time. Similarly, France's guillotine procedure may also be read as an example of delayed decree authority. There, if parliament rejects the executive's proposal, then the government is dismantled and a new government created, but if parliament takes no action, the decree becomes law.[43] Consistent with France's semi-presidential arrangement, the authority over the guillotine is vested in the French premier rather than the president. The effectiveness of delaying the implementation of decrees depends, in part, on legislators' willingness to challenge the president (or the parliamentary head). Because an affirmative vote is required to prevent an executive measure from becoming law, legislators can 'authorise' a decree simply by refusing to act on it. In such cases, too, delayed decree authority can effectively transform into prototypical decree authority.

Decree authorities of these kinds have been the source of unilateral presidential action – and occasionally, conflict – in many countries.[44] This is particularly true of those that have incorporated prototypical decree authority in their constitutions. In Russia, provisions for an independently elected president and decree authority were first introduced in 1991.[45] Almost immediately after taking office on 20 July 1991, President Boris Yeltsin invoked the provision, amongst other things, to ban 'political activity' within state institutions during office hours. He justified the decree as an attempt to ensure 'equal rights of political parties', but the Constitutional Court, under controversial circumstances, invalidated parts of it.[46] In 1994, a new Constitution gave the president even wider legislative powers. Decrees under Article 90, as previously mentioned, have the force of law, come into effect immediately upon publication and

shall order its publication in the Official Register. The National Assembly shall be able, at any time, to amend or repeal it, on the basis of the regular process provided for by the Constitution').

43 Constitution of France, Article 49(1) ('The Prime Minister, after deliberation by the Council of Ministers, may make the Government's programme or possibly a general policy statement an issue of a vote of confidence before the National Assembly').

44 There are other kinds of legislative powers, including delegated decree powers that executives in several jurisdictions exercise. These are outside the scope of this book. This book is principally – and exclusively – interested in decree powers that are directly provided for in constitutions, especially the Indian Constitution.

45 Scott Parrish, 'Presidential Decree Authority in Russia, 1991–1995' in John M. Carey and Matthew S. Shugart (eds.), *Executive Decree Authority* 62–103 (Cambridge University Press, Cambridge, 1998). See also Thomas F. Remington, S. S. Smith and M. Haspel, 'Decrees, Laws, and Inter-branch Relations in the Russian Federation', 14(4) *Post-Soviet Affairs* 287–322 (1998).

46 *Id.* at 69–71.

are obligatory on all levels of government. They do not require any confirmation by the legislative branches and are permanent in nature. Although presidential decrees may be overridden by parliamentary legislation, the president also has veto power. As a result, the president's decrees may be repealed or amended only with the support of a two-thirds majority in each house of the Federal Assembly in Russia.[47] President Yeltsin took advantage of this new arrangement to introduce decrees to, amongst other things, combat organized crime, partially privatize the airwaves and the state-owned television broadcasting corporation and introduce pension reforms.[48] These decrees often faced parliamentary opposition, with members at times enacting contrary legislation for Yeltsin to sign. But the divided body could not muster enough votes to overcome his veto.[49] Yeltsin's choices, therefore, remained in effect, except on rare occasions when he agreed to compromise with parliament.[50] It must be added that future Russian presidents may not have the same open field in which to play. Because presidential edicts under Article 90 'cannot contradict the Constitution of the Russian Federation *or Federal Law*', discretion to promulgate decrees will likely narrow as successive parliaments enact more codes and fill the legislative vacuum Yeltsin confronted in the early years of the new regime.[51]

The developments in Peru in the early years of the Fujimori administration are also a good example of how decree authority can precipitate a full-blown constitutional crisis. In 1990, Alberto Fujimori came to power with a landslide victory, but faced a thoroughly fragmented Congress. With the aid of delegated decree authority (that is, legislation passed by Congress authorizing presidential action), Fujimori enacted decrees in response to the economic crisis sweeping Peru during the period.[52] But it was his counterinsurgency decrees that faced stiff opposition in the

[47] Constitution of the Russian Federation Constitution 1993, Article 105(5) ('In the event that the State Duma disagrees with the decision of the Council of Federation a federal law shall be considered to have been adopted if in the second vote not less than two thirds of the total number of deputies of the State Duma has voted in favour of it').

[48] Parrish, *supra* n. 45, pp. 84–92.

[49] For an analysis of Russia's divided parliament in the 1990s, see Thomas F. Remington, *The Russian Parliament: Institutional Evolution in a Transitional Regime, 1989–1999* (Yale University Press, New Haven, 2001).

[50] Parrish, *supra* n. 45, pp. 90–91.

[51] There is some evidence to suggest that the reliance on decrees has decreased from the early 1990s–early 2000s. See Oleh Protsky, 'Ruling with Decrees: Presidential Decree Making in Russia and Ukraine', 56(5) *Europe Asia Studies* 637–660 (2004).

[52] For an overview of the period, see Philip Mauceri, 'An Authoritarian Presidency: How and Why Did Presidential Power Run Amok in Fujimori's Peru' in Julio Carrión (ed.),

legislative chambers; the provisions, many legislators alleged, threatened civil liberties and democratic governance. Of the 117 decrees on economic and counterinsurgency issues, Congress repealed 16, modified 14 and delayed action on 9 of them.[53] But it also enacted legislation, overriding a presidential veto, which asserted congressional authority over the president's legislative powers. Faced with the prospect of greater congressional scrutiny over his public – and some private – affairs, President Fujimori called out the tanks and closed – and later dissolved – Congress.

In line with Peru's earlier constitutions, a new one approved in a 1993 referendum endowed the president's office with a range of legislative powers. Particularly important is Article 118, which authorises the president to issue decrees on economic and financial matters, except for taxation purposes.[54] Even though such decrees have the force of law and come into effect immediately, Congress retains the authority to modify or annul them for any reason, and such modifications or annulments are not subject to presidential veto. These changes, it seems, have had an effect on the number of decrees. Initial assessments of the new arrangement suggested that President Fujimori's decrees had substantially declined in number.[55]

Prototypical decree authority, by design, offers the president an upper hand in translating his or her preferences into legislation permanently. However, both the provisional and delayed variants have at times functioned like the prototypical variant. Brazil and Argentina are perhaps the best examples of this. Article 62 in Brazil's Constitution (inaugurated in 1988) authorised the president, in important and urgent cases, to adopt provisional measures (*medidas provisórias*) with the force of law. But such measures required congressional approval through the ordinary legislative process within thirty days, failing which, the measures would lose their effectiveness. As Timothy Power describes in his assessment of decree authority in Brazil, three things helped make Article 62 a more potent source of presidential authority than it initially appeared. President José Sarney and his predecessors never took the requirement of urgency

The Fujimori Legacy: The Rise of Electoral Authoritarianism in Peru 39–60 (Pennsylvania State University Press, College Park, 2006).

53 Gregory Schmitt, 'Presidential Usurpation or Congressional Preference? The Evolution of Executive Decree Authority in Peru' in John M. Carey and Matthew S. Shugart (eds.), *Executive Decree Authority* 104–141, 112 (Cambridge University Press, Cambridge, 1998).

54 *Id.* at 127–129.

55 *Ibid.*

and relevance seriously.[56] Decree authority quickly became just another mechanism by which to 'enact' legislation. Second, he and his successors decided to reissue decrees unless Congress explicitly rejected any of them. As a result, provisional decrees ceased to be so; they were effectively permanent unless the legislative branch explicitly rejected them. Sarney's successor, Fernando Collor de Mello went to the extent of 'issuing explicit instructions to his aides to proceed automatically with the re-publication of any decree that Congress did not consider within thirty days'.[57] Third, the provision was interpreted to exclude any limits on the subject matter of decrees. And with more than three-quarters of all legislation coming through presidential initiatives, calls for reforming Article 62 only grew stronger.[58]

After several failed efforts to congressionally regulate the exercise of decree authority, the provision was amended in 2001 to include significant restraints on the reliance of this power. Under the revised arrangement, decrees in Brazil remain in force for a period of sixty days, but may be reissued only once. Also, subject-matter limits were imposed. Presidents are barred from promulgating decrees on matters including political rights, electoral law and budgetary matters.[59] Finally, the legislative chambers must take a view on any given decree before the expiry of sixty days. If Congress does not vote on it within forty-five days, it goes to the top of the legislative agenda and overrides any other item of business. In other words, legislative inaction is no longer an option under the new arrangement. And yet, despite these seemingly well-intentioned amendments, recent estimates suggest that presidential decrees in Brazil have *increased* since 2001.[60]

[56] Timothy Power, 'The Pen is Mightier than the Congress: Presidential Decree Power in Brazil' in John M. Carey and Matthew S. Shugart (eds.), *Executive Decree Authority* 197–233, 204 (Cambridge University Press, Cambridge, 1998). See also Gabriel L. Negretto, 'Government Capacities and Policy Making by Decree in Latin America: The Cases of Brazil and Argentina', 37(5) *Comparative Political Studies* 531–562 (2004).

[57] *Ibid.* at 209.

[58] See Carlos Pereira, Timothy J. Power and Lucio Rennó, 'Agenda Power, Executive Decree Authority, and the Mixed Results of Reform in the Brazilian Congress', 33(1) *Legislative Studies Quarterly* 5–33 (2008).

[59] Constitution of Brazil, Article 62(4) ('No provisional measures should treat about matters: (I) relative to: a) nationality, citizenship, political rights, political parties and electoral rights; b) criminal laws, criminal process and civil process; c) organization of Judiciary Power, Public Prosecution, the career and guarantees of their members').

[60] See Carlos Pereira, Timothy J. Power and Lucio Rennó, 'From Logrolling to Logjam: Agenda Power, Presidential Decrees, and the Unintended Consequences of Reform in

In neighbouring Argentina, the experience has had remarkable parallels. Until 1994, Argentina's Constitution did not explicitly recognise presidential decrees. They are nonetheless mostly associated with President Carlos Saul Menem; he issued as many as 336 of them between 1989 and 1994.[61] This sudden spurt was precipitated by a crippling hyperinflation on one hand, and the president's unwillingness to put up with 'the slowness of Congress' on the other hand.[62] Consequently, Menem's decrees largely, but not exclusively, dealt with economic matters. Those promulgated in 1989, for example, reformed public- and private-sector salaries whereas those issued in 1990 dealt with the nation's public debt.[63] Taxation-related decrees dominated the agenda for the next two years (1991–1993), whereas those that came in 1994 attempted to reform the public- and private-pension systems.[64]

As in Brazil, President Menem's decrees in Argentina had a dubious constitutional status; not all of them were urgently necessary.[65] Second, the president's legislative actions did not invite any serious congressional review. Of the 336 decrees promulgated, only 28 were completely or partially ratified by the legislative chambers, and 4 were completely or partially repealed.[66] But no action was forthcoming on the remaining 304 decrees; Congress never acted on them.[67] Third, the judiciary was inconsistent in reviewing the decrees under challenge, and importantly, was too forgiving about their nature and permissibility.[68] It was under

the Brazilian Congress' Working Paper CBS-71–06, Centre for Brazilian Studies, University of Oxford *available at* http://www.lac.ox.ac.uk/sites/sias/files/documents/Pereira%2C%2520Power%2C%2520Renno%2C71.pdf (accessed 28 March 2013). See also Carlos Pereira, Timothy J. Power and Lucio Rennó, 'Under What Conditions Do Presidents Resort to Decree Power? Theory and Evidence from the Brazilian Case' 67(1) *Journal of Politics* 178–200 (2005); Gary Reich, 'Executive Decree Authority in Brazil: How Reactive Legislators Influence Policy', 27 *Legislative Studies Quarterly* 5–31 (2002).

[61] Delia Ferreira Rubio and Matteo Goretti, 'When the President Governs Along: The Decretazo in Argentina 1989–93', in John M. Carey and Matthew S. Shugart (eds.), *Executive Decree Authority* 33–61, 33 (Cambridge University Press, Cambridge, 1998). There is some controversy about the numbers. President Menem issued more than 13,500 during the period in question, but the vast majority of these 'decrees' were, in effect, delegated legislation and, therefore, not the kind of legislation we are concerned about in this book. Rubio and Gorreti argue that of the more than 13,500 decrees, 336 of them may be classified as constitutional decrees, which is effectively primary legislation 'enacted' by the executive.

[62] *Ibid.* at 35.

[63] *Ibid.* at 45.

[64] *Ibid.*

[65] *Ibid.* at 50–51.

[66] *Ibid.* at 53.

[67] *Ibid.*

[68] *Ibid.* at 55.

these unsatisfactory circumstances that the Constitution was amended in 1994 to regulate the exercise of presidential decrees. Section 99(3) of the revised Constitution authorises the president to issue decrees on grounds of necessity and urgency, but only in 'exceptional circumstances [when] the ordinary procedures... for the enactment of laws [are] impossible to be followed'. Certain topics including criminal law issues, taxation, electoral matters, or the system of political parties are explicitly barred; president cannot promulgate decrees on these matters. Also, prior to their promulgation, decrees require 'a general agreement of ministers who shall countersign them' and must be sent to the Joint Standing Committee of the Congress within ten days. Within a period of further ten days, the Standing Committee shall submit its recommendation to both houses for immediate discussion.

Although the number of decrees declined in Menem's second term and De la Rúa's short tenure as president between 1999 and 2001, congressional inaction remains a major concern in Argentina. This is where the Brazilian experience has deviated from developments in Argentina. Brazil's 2002 reforms led to more decrees, but it also improved the 'conversion' rate; as Pereira, Power and Rennó argue, 'Amendment 32 has greatly speeded up the process by which presidential decrees become permanent'.[69] Argentina, however, has experienced no such change. Congress took no action on eighty-six of Menem's ninety-three decrees in his second term, and similarly took no action on forty-three of la Rúa's forty-nine decrees.[70] Although in different ways, decree authority remains central to the legislative experience in both Brazil and Argentina. They are, formally speaking, examples of provisional decree authority. In practice, however, they share significant commonalities with prototypical decree authority.

THE MISSING LITERATURE ON ORDINANCES IN INDIA

Unlike these Latin American and European studies, there are no comparable accounts of 'decree power' in India. Indeed, we have no systematic account of ordinances – their origins, incorporation or political use and abuse. Nor do we have a constitutional account of ordinances, including their law and interpretation. The two books on ordinances – although important in their own ways – are not a comprehensive treatment of the

[69] Pereira, Power and Rennó, *supra* n. 58, p. 19.
[70] Negretto, *supra* n. 56, pp. 553–554.

subject.[71] Authored by Dr D. C. Wadhwa, both books have an interesting history. Dr Wadhwa, an agrarian economist by training, stumbled upon a peculiar fact while researching agrarian structure and land reforms under the Chota Nagpur Tenancy Act, 1908.[72] He noticed that an amendment to that piece of legislation was being repeatedly promulgated through an ordinance, and 'kept alive' for varying periods of time. As he delved into the matter, he realised that the ordinance relating to land reforms was one of the many ordinances that had been repeatedly promulgated in the state of Bihar between 1967 and 1981 to retain their force of law. During that period, about 256 ordinances were re-promulgated by the governor (on the advice of the cabinet), and they remained in effect for periods varying from one to fourteen years. The Bihar State Assembly had all but ceased to function, and the state cabinet had taken over the task of legislating through ordinances provided for in Article 213. His first book – *Re-promulgation of Ordinances: A Fraud on the Constitution of India* – was a tabular study of ordinances in Bihar between 1967 and 1981, which included tables designed to provide a contextual understanding of the executive's intrusion into the legislative role. The book received enthusiastic acclaim, with nearly 200 reviews appearing in both newspapers and academic journals.

Partly inspired by that support, he approached the Supreme Court under Article 32, arguing that the practice of re-promulgating ordinances was a 'fraud' on the Constitution: Legislation is the province of the state assembly and the cabinet cannot undo that arrangement simply by repeatedly reissuing the same ordinance. The court agreed. In *Dr D. C. Wadhwa v. The State of Bihar*,[73] the Supreme Court invalidated a number of ordinances, holding that the practice amounted to a clear 'subverting [of] the democratic process'.[74] 'It is contrary to all democratic norms that the executive should have the power to make law . . . [and the] exercise of this power must, therefore, of necessity be limited in point of time', the court said.[75] Readers will find a critical analysis of the decision in Chapter 3, but I mention it here to point out the extent to which Dr Wadhwa's research has helped shape the law of ordinances in India. As Upendra Baxi put it, his research 'is a remarkable archive of the betrayal of public

[71] D. C. Wadhwa, *Re-promulgation of Ordinances: A Fraud on the Constitution of India* (Gokhale Institute of Politics and Economics, Pune, 1983).

[72] Act 6 of 1908 (Bengal).

[73] AIR 1987 SC 579.

[74] *Id.* at para 4.

[75] *Id.* at para 6.

trust in the forms and functioning of representative democracy'.[76] And it distinguishes itself by bringing to light not merely cases of '*episodic* violations', but a systematic abuse of state power.[77] In 2008, Dr Wadhwa published his second book – *Endangered Constitutionalism: Documents from a Supreme Court Case* – which as the subtitle suggests, includes a collection of documents submitted to the Supreme Court by parties to the litigation and a select reproduction of reviews and editorials of his earlier book.

Both books are eminently important to the understanding of ordinances in India. But Dr Wadhwa's works are limited in many respects. I shall mention three here. The first relates to scope. His research was limited to the constitutionality of re-promulgation: Can an ordinance be reissued after the state assembly is no longer in session? However, re-promulgation, as I will demonstrate, is only *one* of the several questions that must be wrestled with for a comprehensive account of ordinances in India. Ordinances raise a large number of constitutional issues with implications for parliament's (ordinary) legislative power, cabinet's executive power, the president's independent discretion and the very basis of India's parliamentary system. The second limitation relates to geography. Dr Wadhwa's tabular account of ordinances was overwhelmingly about re-promulgation in the eastern state of Bihar. There is yet no account of ordinances at the national level and the ways in which they have been used to obstruct – or further – parliament's ordinary legislative process. Although some of the tables appended to his *Re-promulgation of Ordinances* shed light on the use of ordinances at the national level, they do not tell us anything beyond the practice of re-promulgation. The third limitation relates to period. Dr Wadhwa's research is mostly limited to the period from 1967 to 1981. We do not yet have a fully worked-out analysis of ordinances from the founding of the republic until now. Nonetheless, despite these shortcomings, Dr Wadhwa's works are the only ones to directly deal with ordinances in India and, therefore, important in their own ways.

Interestingly, the large body of literature on the politics and performance of India's parliament has almost nothing to say about ordinances – this despite the fact that ordinances seriously compromise

[76] Upendra Baxi, 'Introduction' in D. C. Wadhwa, *Endangered Constitutionalism: Documents from a Supreme Court Case* lxxix – xc, lxxxix (Gokhale Institute of Politics and Economics, Pune, 2009).

[77] *Ibid* (emphasis in the original).

parliament's legislative exclusivity and to a limited extent, its legislative supremacy. Morris-Jones's *Parliament of India* was one of the earliest post-independent assessments of India's parliament, its law, politics and performance.[78] The author discusses some of the key offices in India's parliamentary set-up and lists several of its achievements.[79] Even though he notes some of the shortcomings, especially with regards to the role of the opposition and parliament's ability to control the use of executive power, he makes no reference to ordinances – the principal mechanism through which the executive may bypass the legislative branch. Arun Shourie in his book *The Parliamentary System*, is critical of India's parliamentary arrangement. It is, he argues, not representative, efficient or accountable. He writes: 'Under the parliamentary system, the argument goes, the Executive is accountable to Parliament'.[80] But this presumption is a myth in the Indian context because 'far from the Council of Ministers being accountable to and controlled by Parliament, it is the Council of Ministers precisely because *it* controls Parliament'.[81] Even though he gives several examples to make his point, Shourie has nothing to say about ordinances. Despite being classic examples of his larger point about the lack of executive accountability and parliament's inability to control the legislative process, ordinances do not feature in his analysis. The omission is equally apparent in Shankar and Rodrigues's *The Indian Parliament: A Democracy at Work*.[82] In their otherwise exhaustive study of India's parliament, the authors almost entirely leave out even basic references to ordinances. This is surprising because parliament's evolving attitude towards legislation – why it enacts certain laws or refuses to debate others – cannot be understood in isolation; some background understanding of ordinances is essential. Whereas Morris-Jones's omission is understandable given its year of publication, the same cannot be said of Shourie or Shankar and Rodrigues. A rare exception to this rule of omission is Vernon Hewitt and Shirin Rai's recent article-length assessment of India's parliament.[83] They acknowledge the arbitrary and at times high-handed use of ordinances, arguing that ordinances have been used both to avoid debating legislation and as an interim measure by minority governments otherwise

[78] *Supra* n. 3 *ibid.*

[79] *Id.* at 316–333.

[80] *Supra* n. 4 at 25.

[81] *Ibid.* (emphasis in original). See also Prakash, *supra* n. 6, pp. 116–125, 177–187. He discusses various aspects of executive power, including the ways in which the executive exercises control over parliament, but makes no mention of ordinances.

[82] *Supra* n.9 *ibid.*

[83] Hewitt and Rai, *supra* n. 6 *ibid.*

unable to get legislation through parliament.[84] Although these peripheral references to ordinances are good starting points, both empirically and analytically, key questions remain.[85]

THE STRUCTURE OF THE BOOK

This book is intended to fill that void. It carefully explores the law and practice of ordinances, its history, rationale and interpretation starting with the historical origins of ordinances both in England and India, the debates in the Constituent Assembly, its inclusion in the Constitution, and the ways in which ordinances have become a perennial feature in India. In particular, it lays bare the mosaic of political practices and judicial interpretations that have turned ordinances into a somewhat 'parallel' source of legislation in India's legal system. It is structured around three themes: the historical, the empirical and the interpretative. As a practice, ordinances historically originated in England; the Stuarts were amongst its most egregious supporters. The practice eventually faded from English public law, but its introduction in India gave it a new lease on life. Chapter 1 opens with a discussion of this history, and an account of how an English practice, although lost in England, came to be 'found' in India. Later, the chapter picks up this thread in the deliberations of the Constituent Assembly. It investigates the reasons that led the original authors to incorporate ordinances into the Indian Constitution. In particular, it places special emphasis on the defence of ordinances by Dr B. R. Ambedkar and later by H. M. Seervai in his *Constitutional Law of India*.[86] The chapter points out both the philosophical and practical

[84] *Id.* at 38–41.

[85] This lack of interest – in the academic literature and in public conversations – about ordinances is an interesting phenomenon. It seems to me that the idea of parliament as a *legislative* body – as opposed to parliament as a representative body – is yet to be fully internalized in India (from a governance point of view). This is evident in the way political parties conduct themselves in parliament. Whereas such parties are often concerned about the membership profile of parliament (especially with reference to caste and religion), they do not appear particularly concerned about its legislative achievements. This, I think, has two implications for ordinances. First, because parliament no longer takes its legislative task seriously, ordinances do not appear egregious. Second, it is also possible that the cabinet is seen as a compressed version of parliament, and, therefore, when the cabinet makes law, it is not necessarily seen as stepping out of its limits. I am grateful to the referee for pointing me in this direction.

[86] See H. M. Seervai, *Constitutional Law of India* 19 (N.M. Tripathi, Bombay, 1968).

inadequacies of these arguments, while explaining why legal systems can function perfectly well without ordinances.

Chapter 2 is an empirical study of federal ordinances in India. It explains how, when and for what purposes ordinances have been put to use in the sixty years between 1950 and 2009. In particular, the chapter points out two things: 1) the ways in which important legislative proposals were turned into law using ordinances and the politico-legal implications of resorting to this and 2) it proposes an argument for explaining why ordinances became relatively commonplace in India. That is to say, why have ordinances – originally designed for emergencies – become a 'normal' legislative alternative? Beyond that, the chapter points out, once again – now with empirical evidence – why Dr Ambedkar and Seervai's defence of ordinances was inadequate, and why their arguments do not account for the manner in which they have been used in India.

With this background of where the provision for ordinances came from, why it was included in India's Constitution and the ways in which it has been used in the last sixty years, Chapters 3– 5 provide what I hope is an original interpretative account of ordinances. The focus here is on Article 123 (and its state counterpart, Article 213) – the provisions that introduce ordinances to the Constitution, and their legal interpretation. Chapter 3 focuses on analytical questions – how and when do ordinances come into effect, the possibility of retrospective and prospective ordinances, the legality of re-promulgating ordinances and the effect of 'failed' or lapsed ordinances. In developing this analysis, I will critically engage with judicial decisions of the Supreme Court and the High Courts, explaining why much of the interpretation placed on Article 123 is potentially incorrect. In addition, I will present an analysis of issues that have not yet become judicial controversies in India, anticipating the ways in which they may be interpretatively resolved.

Chapter 4 discusses the important question of judicial review. Ordinances under Article 123 may be promulgated only if the president 'is satisfied that circumstances exist' that make it necessary to take immediate action. Are courts authorised to review the president's satisfaction that an ordinance is necessary? That is the question I shall deal with in this chapter. In developing an analysis, I will draw on materials on judicial review of legislative proceedings in the United Kingdom and the United States, arguing that some of the judicial practices in these jurisdictions are relevant to understanding the question of review in India. Specifically, I will propose three legal strategies for dealing with the matter. And relying on empirical evidence from Chapter 2, I will explain why the

Supreme Court's interpretative strategy is incorrect, and what should take its place.

Chapter 5 explores issues of presidential power with respect to assent of ordinances. Ordinances present a set of competing challenges. On one hand, they do not enjoy ordinary parliamentary scrutiny prior to becoming law. On the other hand, they are meant to redress legislative emergencies. Considering these competing interests, should presidents and governors deal with ordinances and Acts differently? If so, should they scrutinise ordinances to a greater or lesser degree? These issues have not been addressed previously – judicially or otherwise. I will attempt to provide an original argument in this regard. Relying on my argument in Chapter 4, I will argue that additional presidential scrutiny of ordinances is constitutionally defensible; they stem from the very fact that ordinances – contrary to the words of Article 123 – do *not* have 'the same force and effect' as Acts.

I shall defend three broad claims. Let me briefly preview them here. First, there were no good reasons to provide for ordinances in the Constitution. Included principally on grounds of institutional inertia, most rationalisations about the need for ordinances, including those offered by Dr Ambedkar and H. M. Seervai, fail. Second, ordinances – abetted by the falling standards of legislative performance, the rise of coalition governments and the inability or unwillingness of political actors to develop working majorities, and uncharacteristically lax interpretations by the Supreme Court – are no longer tied to legislative immediacy; they have become the preferred legislative route. Third, ordinances, in their current legislative scheme, are best understood as products of an *intermediate* legislative power – a novel category that is neither wholly legislative nor executive, but with important ingredients of both. When interpreted through this intermediate lens, it should become readily obvious that, despite words to the contrary, ordinances are not like Acts and that the Supreme Court's hermeneutic methods require a radical overhaul.

Albeit comprehensive in several respects, two shortcomings of the book must be mentioned here. I have made an effort to discuss several analytical questions regarding ordinances, including some that are yet to become judicial controversies. However, they are not exhaustive in nature. I do not claim to have discussed all possible questions with respect to ordinances. Secondly, the empirical part of this book is mostly limited to ordinances at the national level. With the exception of Dr Wadhwa's studies in relation to Bihar, ordinances at the state level remain woefully understudied. This book makes no contribution in that regard, either.

An analysis of ordinances in the various states is eminently required, but its scope is wide enough to be the subject matter of a separate book, or perhaps, several books.

Finally, a caveat must also be added. One way to misread the arguments in the book is to raise the following objection. By my own admission, India's ordinary legislative process is a compromised one; today it is mostly, if not entirely, about expediency. Cabinets pursue legislation not because they are necessary or beneficial, but because some interest group or the other demand them. Nor do parliamentarians any longer take their task of debating legislation seriously. And legislative votes do not matter because back-room deals decide the fate of most legislation. Do ordinances not raise similar concerns? If so, what makes them distinct? This objection confuses two separate issues and makes a misleading comparison. At its best, the legislative process still is – or can be – public, deliberative and relevant. That the process has degenerated into something else is true. But that can be reversed, and the legislative process can still be salvaged with appropriate reforms. Ordinances, however, are entirely different. Even at their very best, they are closed, hidden and, by definition, insulated from any ex ante parliamentary scrutiny. Indeed, ordinances of the Indian variety must have these qualities, and unlike legislation, they cannot be 'improved'. To do so would undermine the very rationale for ordinances. This is why parliamentary legislation and ordinances are still distinct in theory. In practice, the legislative process increasingly resembles the manner in which ordinances are made. But that does not make ordinances any less problematic. It only means that in India today, *both* legislation and ordinances are problematic.

Part I

Origins and Practice

1

The Transplant Effect: Early Origins of Ordinances in England and India

The executive power in the state must have certain powers to act in cases for which legislation has not provided, and modern legislation has not got beyond the expedient of investing the executive with the authority to meet such critical occasions. The crown is able on several matters to legislate by orders in council at the present day, but by a deputed not a prerogative power; but there are conceivable occasions on which, during an interval of parliament, the ministers of the crown might be called upon to act provisionally with such authority as would require an act of indemnity to justify it.

William Stubbs, *The Constitutional History of England* Vol. II, 615 (Clarendon Press, Oxford, 1896).

A. 'ORDINANCE': MAKING SENSE OF SEMANTICS

An ordinance, the *Oxford Dictionary* says, is a 'by-law'.[1] The *Cambridge Advanced Learner's Dictionary* defines it similarly as 'a law or rule made by a government or authority'.[2] *Macmillan's*, however, defines it as 'an official *order* by a government, king [or] queen'.[3] These disparate meanings are brought together in *Longman's*, which says that an ordinance may be both 'a law, usually of a city or town, that forbids or restricts an activity' and 'an order given by a ruler or governing organisation'.[4] Although subtly different, these meanings share an 'inferior' quality.

[1] *New Oxford Dictionary of English* 1306 (Oxford University Press, New York, 2001).

[2] *Cambridge Advanced Learner's Dictionary* 1003 (3rd ed., Cambridge University Press, Cambridge, 2008).

[3] *Macmillan English Dictionary* 1055 (2nd ed., A and C Black Publishers, Oxford, 2007). (emphasis added)

[4] *Longman Dictionary of Contemporary English* 1160 (4th ed., Pearson Education, Essex, 2003).

An ordinance, in these versions, is something *less* than an Act: Whereas an Act originates in parliament, an ordinance comes from a government department or municipal body. In that sense, an ordinance does not have 'vertical' equivalence. But it is also less than an Act in another sense; in these meanings, an ordinance does not have 'horizontal' equivalence. Unlike an Act, an ordinance cannot abridge rights, create major offences or impose substantial taxes or penalties; it can only do limited things. *Longman's* example of 'a city ordinance that says parks must be closed at 11 p.m.' is a good illustration of its limited scope.[5] Therefore, lexically speaking, an ordinance is law of an inferior kind; it lacks both vertical and horizontal equivalence.

Now consider some *legal* definitions. The *Oxford Dictionary of Law*, for example, explains an ordinance as 'one of the forms taken by legislation under the royal prerogative'.[6] *Osborne's Concise Law Dictionary* elaborates on this by stating that an ordinance used to be an Act of parliament that 'lacked the consent of one of the three elements: crown, lords, and commons'.[7] Two U.S. law dictionaries, however, define the term differently. *Black's Law Dictionary* defines it 'as an authoritative law or decree; esp., a municipal regulation'.[8] The scope of such regulations, it adds, is limited to whatever 'the state government allows to be regulated at the local level'.[9] *West's Encyclopedia* reiterates this view. According to it, an ordinance is 'a law, statute, or regulation enacted by a municipal corporation . . . [for] maintaining public safety, health, morals, and general welfare . . . [including] housing ordinances . . . [and] fire and safety regulations'.[10] Clearly, the legal meanings differ as well. In some versions, an ordinance is almost like an Act and, therefore, has vertical – and possibly horizontal – equivalence. In other versions, it has neither. Like the lexical meanings earlier, an ordinance, in the American reading of the term, is a 'lesser' law.

Both lexically and legally, an ordinance, it seems, means different things. Depending on the source, it may be something like a parliamentary Act or a more limited regulation of the governmental or municipal variety. But this inconsistency is not inadvertent. As I will argue in the

5 *Ibid.*
6 *Oxford Dictionary of Law* 346 (5th ed., Oxford University Press, Oxford, 2002).
7 *Osborn's Concise Law Dictionary* 294 (11th ed., Sweet and Maxwell/Thomson Reuters, London, 2009).
8 *Black's Law Dictionary* 1208 (9th ed., West, St. Paul, MN, 2009).
9 *Ibid.*
10 *West's Encyclopedia of American Law* 324 (2nd ed., Thomson/Gale, Detroit, 2005).

next section, the term and its origins, in the common-law context, is rooted in English legal history. Therefore, making sense of it – and the attendant inconsistencies – requires an introductory account of English parliamentary supremacy and the competing conceptions of legislative power that challenged its emergence.

The rest of the chapter will unfold as follows: I shall describe the rise and fall of ordinances in English legal history – including the origin of the term, its influence and the controversies that came along with it. Thereafter, I will turn to ordinances in British India and offer an account of their formal introduction in 1861 and their use (and abuse) until 1947. Lastly, I shall revisit the debates in the Constituent Assembly: Why did the founding authors provide for ordinances in the Constitution? In the lead-up to independence, India's leaders were critical of the administration's repeated use of ordinances. Yet they abandoned those objections when it mattered most and bought into British rationalisations for extraordinary legislation. The question, however, remains: Do we really need ordinances? I shall close with a discussion about the necessity for a provision on ordinances in India.

B. THE EMPERORS' CLOTHES: RISE AND FALL OF ORDINANCES IN MEDIEVAL ENGLAND

The idea of parliamentary sovereignty stands tall in England. It is, as A. V. Dicey famously put it, the idea that parliament 'under the English constitution, [has] the right to make or unmake any law whatever . . . [and] . . . no person or body is recognised . . . as having a right to override or set aside [any such] legislation'.[11] Historically, it was not always this way. As with other fundamental concepts in English public law, parliamentary supremacy 'grew' – out of wars and words. Rivalling this idea, up until the seventeenth century, was the monarch's power – at times wide, at other times more qualified – to legislate *independent* of his parliamentary constituents. In this section, I shall provide a brief account of this independent legislative power and how ordinances fit into the scheme of things.

Medieval British kings were always known to consult their advisors in important affairs of the state. But events between 1254 and 1290 set in motion a series of incremental changes that, in hindsight, dramatically

[11] A. V. Dicey, *An Introduction to the Study of the Law of the Constitution* 40 (Universal Law Publishing, New Delhi, 2003).

altered the course of the British monarchy.[12] They mostly had to do with wars and revenues. With his treasury depleted by incessant wars, Henry III met with the clergy and knights in 1254 to have them 'approve' a general tax on the people.[13] By 1295, that ad hoc meeting turned into a national assembly with audiences from all three estates of the realm – clergy, barons and commons[14] – referred to as *parliamenta*. The assembly met frequently and habitually at the king's behest, but made it clear that he no longer had the right to tax his people without common consent.

During the fourteenth century, this new body evolved in several ways. First, it distinguished itself from the already existing council that was made up of the king's professional counsel, prelates and magnates. At some point, the knights and burgesses in the new body began to deliberate together and separate from their social betters – the archbishops, bishops, abbots and nobles who would later constitute the House of Lords. Second, despite sitting separately, both bodies – together known as the 'High Court of Parliament' – deliberated on the same 'petitions' that aggrieved individuals brought before the king. Some of these were considered by the king's council in its judicial setting. Of those that came before parliament, most petitions required statutes to be drawn up, and in 1322, the commons insisted that *their* consent was necessary in the making of new laws.[15] That insistence was not always honoured in practice, but they were aided by the fact that nearly all legislation in the fourteenth century were based on petitions of parliament – something that allowed the commons to have a say in the process.[16] As a result, it helped settle the view that statutes, to be properly made, required the consent of the king, lords and commons. Third, the High Court of Parliament developed a distinct corporate identity with special rights and privileges. Redressing people's grievances was no longer the only task; over time, it turned into a forum where representatives parleyed about 'national

[12] For a quick description of some of the important moments of this period, see George Burton Adams, *The Constitutional History of England* 169–190 (H. Holt, New York, 1921).

[13] *Id.* at 174–176.

[14] For description of the three estates, see F. W. Maitland, *The Constitutional History of England* 74–77 (Cambridge University Press, Cambridge, 1908).

[15] Theodore Plucknett, *A Concise History of Common Law* 31–32 (Little, Brown and Co., Boston, 1956).

[16] For the evolution of the form and substance of these 'petitions', see William Stubbs, *The Constitutional History of England* Vol. II, 598–610 (Clarendon Press, Oxford, 1896).

affairs'.[17] More importantly, it gained undisputed control over revenue matters and increasingly grew assertive – and at times antagonistic – to the king and his council. Even though parliamentary supremacy was still a long way away, parliament was no longer to be trifled with. It was a national forum of 'the people' and, therefore, had pronounced say at least on legislative matters.[18]

Although parliament grew in stature and legislation became more 'participative', monarchs always claimed – and the law often recognised – 'an uncertain amount' of legislative exception.[19] The precise boundaries of this tableau of legislative exception has never been fully clear, but it is safe to say that it included, amongst others, the *claim* that the king had authority to (1) legislate independently of parliament on occasions, (2) nullify legislation by dispensing with the operation of statutes in individual cases (the 'dispensing power'), (3) suspend their operation altogether (the 'suspending power') and (4) raise money without parliamentary grant.[20] Rich and complicated accounts of these independent or 'discretionary' powers may be found elsewhere, but for our discussion, the first one – the king's power to legislate independently – is the most relevant.

That *some* laws did not require the estates' counsel or consent was never in doubt; monarchs made them on their own.[21] Up until the seventeenth century, Edward I and everyone after him claimed – and many exercised – a measure of independent legislative power. Kings, in exercise of this power, could at least make 'ordinances', if not statutes.[22] But how are we to differentiate one from the other? Unfortunately, there are no easy answers; the nature, scope and extent of ordinances has been mired in controversy. As Professor F. W. Maitland, an English historian who taught at Cambridge University from 1885 to 1906, put it, distinguishing the province of statutes from the province of ordinances has been a 'fruitful source of difficulty'.[23]

An Oxford University professor William Stubbs thought of a statute as something permanent and of great importance: 'The statute is a law

[17] Sir William Holdsworth, *A History of English Law* Vol. II, 429 (Methuen and Co., London, 1936).

[18] It may be noted that in A. F. Pollard's account, the commons' evolution into a separate House with distinct rights and privileges occurred much later. See A. F. Pollard, *The Evolution of Parliament* 258–277 (Longmans Green and Co., London, 1929).

[19] *Supra* n. 14 at 187.

[20] Sir William Anson, *The Law and Custom of the Constitution* Vol. I, 340 (Clarendon Press, Oxford, 1886).

[21] *Supra* n. 18 at 262.

[22] *Supra* n. 16 at 92.

[23] *Ibid.*

or an amendment of law, enacted by the king in parliament, and enrolled in the statute roll, not to be altered, repealed, or suspected with the authority of parliament, and valid in all particulars until it has been so revoked'.[24] But an ordinance, he felt, was a 'rather tentative act which, if it be insufficient to achieve its objective or if it operates mischievously may be easily recalled, and, if it be successful, may be a subsequent act made by statute'.[25] Maitland agreed. He thought of a statute as a 'solemn affair' – one that altered the law of the land in an important and a permanent way and, therefore, needed the consent of prelates and barons.[26] An ordinance, on the other hand, was like a piece of 'temporary legislation' and mostly used to introduce regulations that did not affect the nation at large.[27] Professor William Holdsworth (who taught at Oxford from 1922 to 1944) held a similar view. According to him, an enactment that made 'a permanent and deliberate change in the law' was a statute, but anything that 'was intended to be somewhat in the nature of a temporary provision of a more or less experimental nature' was more like an ordinance.[28] Whether temporary or not, all of them agreed that ordinances added to the law of the land.

The emphasis on 'permanence', however, does not settle the matter. As Stubbs and Maitland readily conceded, their distinctions were inadequate because statutes and ordinances came much closer in practice. Stubbs knew that his distinction could not accurately account for laws that were *regarded* as statutes, but were enacted as ordinances. The Magna Carta, for example, was an ordinance, but became 'one of the fundamental laws of the realm almost immediately after its promulgation'.[29] Similarly, the two pillars of real property law – the *Quia Emptores* and the *De Donis Conditionalities* – were made without the assent of any representatives, but are still regarded as statutes.[30] And then there are several examples from the fourteenth century that altogether undercut the idea that ordinances were temporary, limited in scope and not of national relevance.[31]

As Maitland predicted, properly distinguishing statutes from ordinances is a challenging endeavour. Several factors are at play, but three interrelated ones are especially worth mentioning. First, consider their common origins. Both statutes and ordinances were based on petitions submitted to the king for redress. The official response to such grievances often came from similar people working in different capacities. The king,

[24] *Supra* n. 16 at 611.
[25] *Ibid.*
[26] *Supra* n. 14 at 92.
[27] *Ibid.*
[28] *Supra* n. 17 at 438.
[29] *Supra* n. 16 at 612.
[30] *Supra* n. 14 at 187.
[31] *Supra* n. 16 at 428, 613–614.

in the fourteenth century, still 'regarded himself as the sovereign lawgiver as well as the sovereign administrator'.[32] He, therefore, performed a dual function. His magnates, or a large proportion of them, also had dual capacities; they were simultaneously members of the royal council and parliament. As a result, 'although the form of statute differed from that of ordinance, the two were now and then issued by the same powers and occupied the same ground'.[33] Second, consider their chaotic history. At certain times, the law and practice of the king's ordaining power widely diverged. By 1295, as mentioned previously, it was a law of the land that the monarch could no longer tax his people without common consent. Nevertheless, 'in 1359 the king and council obtained from the merchants... a grant of *6d.* on the pound on exports and imports'.[34] Again, 'in 1360, before a parliament was held, the king ordered a fifteenth and tenth which had been granted by the commons in five provincial assemblies, to be collected'.[35] These actions called into question the commons' ability to enforce its legislative will and highlighted the king's ability to make laws by other means. Finally, there is the problem of blurred boundaries. The line between what the king could do without a parliament and what he could do only with the aid of parliament was only drawn gradually, and it fluctuated from time to time.[36] Ordinances, generally speaking, were (legislative) products of the king's executive power – a nuance that sharpened over time. Until then, the king's ordaining power was put to varied use, including in ways intended to defeat the operation of laws that limited the monarch's power.[37] The charter granted by Edward I to the foreign merchants, for example, was an ordinance meant to evade the intention of the *Confirmatio Cartarum*.[38] However, these circumventions declined as parliament grew more assertive and its hold over statutes improved. In 1389, for example, commons made a direct plea that the chancellor and council should not make ordinances contrary to common law, statute or the ancient law of the land, especially after the close of parliament.[39] When Richard II resisted the demands, in a sign of the times to come, he was promptly deposed.

These tussles between the king and his council on one hand and the parliament on the other hand meant that statutes and ordinances grew side by side, but often in conflict with one another. It was only with the gradual separation of the 'crown in council' from the 'crown in

[32] *Id.* at 613.
[33] *Ibid.*
[34] *Id.* at 424.
[35] *Ibid.*
[36] *Supra* n. 14 at 196.
[37] *Supra* n. 16 at 614.
[38] *Id.* at 614.
[39] *Supra* n. 14 at 188.

parliament' that some of the disagreements surrounding the nature and scope of ordinances were resolved.[40] It became clear over time that the king, for example, could not revoke or alter statutes through ordinances, and when he did so, it was generally regarded as an abuse. Similarly, he could not tax his people or impose other pecuniary responsibilities through those instruments.[41] Also, there were growing doubts about the legality of nullifying the effect of statutes through ordinances. But short of these, there was still an uncertain reservoir of legislative power that the king could tap into – the limits of which, even at the close of the Middle Ages, were rather unclear.[42]

After a period of relative quiet, ordinances made a return in the sixteenth century under the Tudors.[43] Now called proclamations – not ordinances, the Tudor kings put them to vigorous use, thereby exploiting the earlier lack of clarity.[44] It culminated in Henry VIII's Statute of Proclamations in 1539[45] which, curiously enough, only remained in force for approximately eight years before being repealed in 1547.[46] Despite its limited tenure, the purpose of the statute has since been intensely disputed.[47] Amongst other things, it provided that:

> [T]he King . . . with the advice of his council, . . . *or with the advice of the more part of them*, may set forth at all times by *authority of this act his* proclamations, under such penalties and pains and of such sort as . . . shall seem necessary and requisite; and that those same shall be obeyed, observed, and kept as though they were made by act of parliament [emphasis in original].

However, it also added that

> the King's people . . . should not have any of their inheritances, lawful possessions, offices, liberties, privileges, franchises, goods or chattels taken from them or any of them, nor by virtue of the same act suffer any pains of death other than shall be hereafter in this act declared, nor that by any proclamation to be made by virtue of this act, any acts, common laws . . . nor any lawful customs . . . shall be infringed, broken or subverted.

40 *Supra* n. 17 at 307–310.

41 *Supra* n. 14 at 187.

42 *Supra* n. 17 at 220.

43 See Robert Heinz, *The Proclamations of the Tudor Kings* (Cambridge University Press, Cambridge, 1976).

44 *Id.* at 65–84.

45 Ch. 8, 31 Henry VIII. The official title of the Statute of Proclamations was, 'An Acte That Proclamations Made By The King Shall Be Obeyed'.

46 § 5, Ch. 12, 1 Edward VI.

47 *Supra* n. 43 at 153–165.

What all this meant has never been fully settled. By and large, three views have battled for acceptance. Bishop Stubbs, William Blackstone, A. V. Dicey, William Anson and Frederic Maitland advanced what is now the 'older' view. They saw in the machinations of Henry VIII an effort to supplant statutes with royal fiats, thereby undermining parliament's authoritative say in the legislative process. Stubbs, for instance, thought of the 1539 statute as the *Lex Regia* of English history. To him, 'it amounted to a virtual resignation of the essential character of parliament as a legislative body'.[48] Similarly, Blackstone noticed in the statute a calculated attempt 'to introduce the most despotic tyranny', which, if not for its early repeal, would have 'proved fatal' to English liberties.[49] Dicey, too, offered a similar reading; the moment marked, for him, the 'highest point of legal authority ever reached by the Crown' and with a capacity to produce 'revolutionary' results.[50] Maitland later affirmed this view, adding that the statute's repeal in 1547 confirmed inter alia 'the doctrine that the king is not supreme, king and parliament are supreme [and that] statute is distinctly above ordinance or proclamation ... [which is a kind of] subordinate legislative power'.[51]

Then there is the 'revised' view – one that prefers a less alarmist reading of the statute and its intent. Edward Adair, Theodore Plucknett, Albert Pollard, Geoffrey Elton and Rudolph Heinz were its main proponents. Their positions are subtly different from one another, but they share the basic theme that the older view had misread the statute's importance. Of them, Adair took the most sceptical position. 'Neither the enactment of the statute of proclamations nor its repeal altered the nature or force of royal proclamations in the slightest degree [and] the sovereign before 1539 or after 1547 considered himself just as much at liberty to issue proclamations and punish offenders against them as he did between those two dates'.[52] This, he added, was 'the only possibly conclusion'.[53] Although largely sympathetic to this line of thinking, others were more restrained. Plucknett, for example, conceded that the statute had some importance, but argued against the claim 'that the King hoped ... to establish an absolutism or to supersede legitimate activities of Parliament'.[54]

[48] *Supra* n. 16 at 614.

[49] Sir William Blackstone and Thomas Cooley, *Commentaries on the Law of England* Bk. 1, Ch. 7, 271 (Callahan and Cockcroft, Chicago, 1871).

[50] *Supra* n. 11 at 51.

[51] *Supra* n. 12 at 253.

[52] E. R. Adair, 'The Statute of Proclamations', 32(125) *English Historical Review* 34–46, 45 (1917).

[53] *Ibid.*

[54] *Supra* n. 15 at 45–46.

Similarly, based on contemporary accounts, Pollard claimed that Henry VIII 'did not regard the statute as enabling him to dispense with the assistance of parliament in legislation'.[55] It was, according to him, simply meant to re-emphasise the idea that 'within their proper and recognised sphere proclamations were to have the binding force of law'.[56] And Heinz, in an important study in 1976, took the view that 'although [the statute] did not have a major impact on the role, authority or respect for proclamations, it did change the method of enforcement both by setting up a special court and by making available the system of enforcement used in penal statutes'.[57] The statute, in other words, sharpened the enforcement of proclamations, rather than their standing.

Finally, there is what we might refer to as the 'agnostic' view – one that is hesitant to take sides in this debate, especially because much of the contemporary accounts necessary for an accurate assessment have been lost to history. We do not know what Henry VIII thought of his statute. Neither do we know how far the lords and commons amended its language. And we do not fully understand why it was repealed. Conrad Russell put it best:

> The 1539 Act is an attempt at definition: it recounts that some people have not been obeying proclamations to the dishonour of the King, 'who may ill bear it' and gives the government statutory authority to punish breaches of proclamations. We know that the act was substantially amended during its passage, but we do not know how. Whether this act is simply designed to clear up ambiguities, or whether it embodies the same principles of delegated legislation, giving statutory authority to council regulations . . . whether it is concerned with enforcement, or whether it is a serious attempt to give the King a legislative power without Parliament, we cannot say. The act only remained in force till 1547 and its effects are obscure.[58]

Whatever the salience of the 1539 statute – and we need not pass judgment on this controversy – its repeal did not mark the end of proclamations. On the contrary, they were freely enacted; the Tudor queens persisted with them.[59] The matter eventually came to a judicial head, and in 1610, Chief

[55] *Supra* n. 18 at 266.
[56] *Supra* n. 18 at 267.
[57] R. W. Heinz, *The Proclamations of the Tudor Kings* 199 (Cambridge University Press, Cambridge, 1976). See also G. R. Elton, *England under the Tudors* 168–175 (Methuen and Co., London, 1955).
[58] Conrad Russell, *The Crisis of Parliament: English History 1509–1660* 119–120 (Oxford University Press, Oxford, 1971).
[59] *Supra* n. 14 at 256–257.

Justice Edward Coke of the Common Pleas was summoned to render this opinion on the legality and scope of proclamations.[60] In a decision of far-reaching importance, Sir Edward Coke laid down the following:

1. The King cannot change any part of the common law, nor create any offence by his proclamation, which was not an offence before, without Parliament.
2. The King hath no prerogative, but that which the law of the land allows him.
3. But the King for prevention of offences may by proclamation admonish his subjects that they keep the laws, and do not offend them; upon punishment to be inflicted by the law, etc.
4. If the offence be not punishable in the Star-Chamber (i.e. the court of law that sat at the royal Palace of Westminster), the prohibition of it by proclamation cannot make it so.

In theory, although not necessarily in practice, the opinion settled issues of jurisdictional inconsistencies. The decision limited the monarch's independent legislative power. He or she could not make new laws or create new offences; these matters were left exclusively to parliament. Proclamations or ordinances, it became clear, were not equivalent to Acts. They could not do everything Acts could. Ordinances, in other words, did not have horizontal equivalence. In their standing, too, ordinances were less than Acts of parliament. They became more akin to by-laws than ordinary legislation, and in that sense did not have vertical equivalence, too. Although the decision brought conceptual clarity, regal practice varied.[61] Monarchs continued making ordinances (of the unlawful kind) and enforced them, too. Only with the establishment of parliamentary supremacy towards the end of the seventeenth century did the law and practice of ordinances finally become consistent; from then on, it would always be a subordinate legislative power.

Because of this meandering history, ordinances, it is safe it say, *never* had one generally agreed meaning. They meant different things at different times. When concepts of 'counsel' and 'consent' were in their early stages, ordinances and statutes were analytically indistinguishable from one another. But as 'popular' participation strengthened and later became essential, statutes surged in their effectiveness and legitimacy. And despite notable initiatives to revive their force, ordinances eventually receded.

[60] (1611) 12 Co Rep 74.

[61] *Supra* n. 20 at 343–346.

By the close of the seventeenth century, statutes represented parliament's ultimate authority to enact legislation whereas ordinances, generally speaking, came to represent the executive's more limited authority to make narrow and specific regulations.

Now that we have an introductory account of the rise and fall of ordinances as a distinct legislative category in the United Kingdom, I shall turn to its history in British India. In particular, I will pursue two lines of enquiry. First, what were the principal legislative moments that naturalised ordinances into India? Second, what does the practice of ordinances in British India tell us about its later incorporation in the Constitution?

C. THE GOVERNOR-GENERAL'S LEGISLATIVE POWER IN BRITISH INDIA

The very first English Royal Charter granted to the 'Governor and Company of Merchants of London trading with the East Indies' in 1600 introduced the 'ordinance' vocabulary to India. The charter conferred on the company, amongst others, the power 'to make, ordain, and constitute such and so many reasonable laws, constitutions, orders, and *ordinances* ... [that] shall seem necessary and convenient for the good of the said Company'.[62] Although the term was repeated in succeeding charters and Acts of parliament, the fusion of executive and legislative powers made their references relatively unproblematic.[63] That changed with the introduction of the Indian Councils Act, 1861 (1861 Act) – and the subsequent rudimentary separation of powers brought about by the colonial administration.

Under the new arrangement, the power of making laws and regulations was vested in the 'Governor-General in Council' – a body consisting of six to twelve non-official members, apart from the ordinary and extraordinary members belonging to the Governor General's Executive Council.[64] The council's legislative powers were greatly limited; in some respects, the governor-general's prior sanction was required.[65] Then there were

[62] C. L. Anand, *Constitutional Law and History of Government of India* 117 (Universal, New Delhi, 2008). (emphasis added)

[63] For a quick overview of the evolution of legislative powers, see *id.* at 117–139; A. B. Keith, *A Constitutional History of India 1600–1935* 171–180 (Barnes and Noble, New York, 1969).

[64] § 10, 1861 Act.

[65] § 19, 1861 Act.

matters on which the council was entirely prohibited from legislating.[66] Subject to these limitations, the council became British India's primary legislative body.[67]

Even this limited primacy was further compromised. The 1861 Act, in certain circumstances, vested original legislative power on the governor-general, independent of the council:

> Notwithstanding anything in this Act contained, it shall be lawful for the Governor-General, in cases of emergency, to make and promulgate, from time to time, ordinances for the peace and good government of the said territories or of any part thereof, . . . and every such ordinance shall have like force of law or regulation made by the Governor-General in Council, as by this Act provided, for the space of not more than six months from its promulgation, unless the disallowance of such ordinance by Her Majesty . . . or unless such ordinance shall be controlled or superseded by some law or regulation made by the Governor-General in Council.[68]

Note that this power was limited to situations of emergency only – especially of the kind relating to 'peace and good government'. Ordinances enjoyed the 'force of law' – a status equivalent to legislation enacted by the Governor-General in Council. But they were limited in time and subject to control or supersession by the Council. In other words, the provision, on its face, had both vertical and horizontal equivalence. While introducing the bill in the House of Commons, Sir Charles Woods spelt out his impatience with deliberative niceties and explained the need for such a law: 'Questions might arise', he said, 'about the Arms Act, or the press, as to which it would be very injudicious that delay should occur; and we, therefore, propose to empower the Governor-General on his own authority to pass an ordinance having the force of law'.[69] If Woods was correct, the provision was principally motivated by concerns about maintaining control over *British* interests in India. Nonetheless, almost ninety years later, aided by linguistic mutations and self-serving justifications, it would become Article 123 in India's Constitution.

[66] § 22, 1861 Act.
[67] *Supra* n. 20 *ibid.*
[68] § 23, 1861 Act.
[69] Sir Charles Woods's speech on the Indian Councils Bill, 1861 H.C. (6 June 1861) extracted in Anil Chandra Banerjee, *Indian Constitutional Documents 1757–1939* Vol. II, 52–64 (A. Mukherjea and Co., Calcutta, 1948).

1. Early Practices: From Exception to Rule

The 1861 Act remained in effect until 1915. In those fifty-five years, the governor-general's power to promulgate ordinances was sparsely used – no more than nineteen ordinances were promulgated in all.[70] Of these, seven were promulgated between 1861 and 1912. The remaining twelve were brought into effect in 1914–1915. True to Woods's intention, the nineteen ordinances were promulgated mostly to protect British colonial interests rather than undermine the council.

The very first ordinance is a classic example. The American Civil War had begun. Queen Victoria, on the advice of Prime Minister Lord Palmerston, declared a policy of British neutrality in May 1861. It served as a kind of recognition of Southern belligerency, and gave their ships the same rights and privileges afforded to U.S. ships in foreign ports. The Confederate States of America, however, wanted complete diplomatic recognition. Accordingly, two of its envoys, James Mason and John Slidell, set sail for Europe on a British mail packet – the *Trent* – to press the case for the Confederates. But days into their journey, Charles Wilkes, a Union captain commanding the *San Jacinto*, intercepted the ship and arrested the envoys. The arrests of the Confederate 'contrabands', as Wilkes referred to them, set off a diplomatic row. In the United Kingdom, it was widely reported as a hostile act. Removing subjects from a vessel in the service of Her Majesty, it was claimed, was in violation of maritime law. The British retaliated. Foreign Secretary Lord Russell ordered a ban on saltpetre exports, including from India – the principle source of Union gunpowder at the time.[71]

On 27 December 1861, Viscount Canning, India's then governor-general, memorialised the foreign secretary's order into statute, promulgating the Export of Saltpetre Ordinance, 1861.[72] The ordinance

[70] A. P. Pandey, 'Hundred Years of Ordinances in India: 1861–1961', 10 *Journal of Indian Law Institute* 259, 263–264 (1968).

[71] On the 'Trent Affair', as it is commonly known, see David Donald, Jean Baker *et al*., *The Civil War and Reconstruction* 314–316 (W. W. Norton and Co., New York, 2001). The incident brought the United States and Britain to the brink of war. Eventually, however, calmer heads prevailed after U.S. diplomats conceded that Wilkes had erred in arresting the prisoners. See also Gordon H. Warren, *Fountain of Discontent: The Trent Affair and Freedom of the Seas* (Northeastern University Press, Boston, 1981).

[72] The four ordinances promulgated between 1861 and 1876 were not separately numbered; nor did they have the 'feel' of Acts. The early ordinances read more like executive orders than proper legislation. The practice of numbering ordinances in a manner similar to Acts began only in the twentieth century. Starting with the Regulation of Meetings

TABLE 1.1. *Year-wise breakdown of ordinances for the 1861–1915 period*

Year	Ordinances
1861	01
1862	01
1869	02
1876	01
1907	01
1912	01
1914	09
1915	03

prohibited the export of saltpetre from any port of Her Majesty's territories in India 'except in a British vessel bound either to the port of London or to the port of Liverpool'.[73] The ban did not apply to exports for which permits had already been granted, but the ordinance made it unlawful for officers of the customs to grant new passes or permits.[74] No expiration period was mentioned; the ban was to remain in place until the council decided otherwise. A week later, the ordinance was replaced with a new one – the Export of Saltpetre Ordinance, 1862. It retained the earlier ban, but authorised saltpetre exports to all ports in the UK, not just London and Liverpool.[75] The restriction was eventually revoked on 28 February 1862.[76]

Thus began the legacy of ordinances in India. It took an international incident on the high seas to precipitate the first one, and in the early years, they were few and far between. Until 1914, there were only six more ordinances, including those regarding 'dramatic performances',[77]

Ordinance, 1907 (1 of 1907), they were formally recorded as Acts, and their language was modified to make them sound more like ordinary legislation.

73 § 1, Export of Saltpetre Ordinance, 1861. ('Until the Governor-General, in Council, shall otherwise order, it shall not be lawful for any person to export saltpetre from any port of Her Majesty's territories in India, except in a British vessel bound either to the port of London or to the port of Liverpool'.)

74 *Id.* at § 3.

75 § 1, Export of Saltpetre Ordinance, 1862. ('Until the Governor-General, in Council, shall otherwise order, it shall not be lawful to export saltpetre from any part of Her Majesty's territories, except in a British vessel bound to a port of the United Kingdom'.)

76 Notification No. 1098, dated 28 February 1862.

77 The Dramatic Performances Ordinance, 1876.

'regulation of meetings'[78] and 'cotton gambling'.[79] But as many as twelve were brought into effect in 1914–1915 in the context of World War I. Partly inspired by fears that 'enemies within' may collude with foreign benefactors to plot against the British government, several ordinances imposed restrictions on activities of foreigners in India. Examples include the Foreigners Ordinance, 1914;[80] the Ingress into India Ordinance, 1914;[81] the Commercial Intercourse with Enemies Ordinance, 1914[82] and the Foreigners (Amendment) Ordinance, 1914.[83] Even though the 1861 Act limited ordinances to six months, the tenures for these new ordinances were extended for the entire duration of World War I through the Emergency Legislation Continuance Act, 1915; they were deemed to 'have been enacted by the Governor-General in Council'.[84] Because of this, all nine ordinances promulgated in 1914 lasted more than seven years. Of the remaining ten promulgated between 1861 and 1915, none lasted more than six months – the maximum tenure prescribed under the 1861 Act.

In 1915, the 1861 Act was repealed and replaced with the Government of India Act, 1915 (the 1915 Act).[85] This latter Act marked the beginning of a more heightened use of ordinances. As a law designed to consolidate enactments relating to the Government of India, the 1915 Act, in its amended version, established for the first time an 'Indian Legislature' – comprised of the governor-general and the two chambers: the Council of State and the Legislative Assembly.[86] And yet the Act, in s. 72, retained almost in its entirety the governor-general's legislative power under the 1861 Act:

> The Governor-General may, in cases of emergency, make and promulgate ordinances, for that peace and good government of British India or any part thereof, and any ordinance so made shall, for the space of not more than six months from its promulgation, have the like force of law as an Act passed by the Governor-General in Legislative Council, but the power of

[78] The Regulation of Meetings Ordinance, 1907.
[79] The Bengal Cotton Gambling Ordinance, 1912.
[80] Ordinance III of 1914.
[81] Ordinance V of 1914.
[82] Ordinance VI of 1914.
[83] Ordinance VII of 1914.
[84] I of 1915.
[85] Ch. 61, 5 and 6 Geo. 5.
[86] § 63, Government of India Act, 1919. (9 and 10 Geo. 5, Ch 101) ('Subject to the provisions of this Act, the Indian legislature shall consist of the Governor and the two chambers, the Council of State and the Legislative Assembly. Except as otherwise provided by or under this Act, a Bill shall not be deemed to have been passed by the Indian legislature unless it has been agreed to by both chambers, either without amendment or with such amendments only as may be agreed to by both chambers').

TABLE 1.2. *Year-wise breakdown of ordinances for the 1916–1935 period*

Year	Ordinances
1916	08
1917	04
1918	03
1919	97
1920	04
1921	05
1922	03
1924	01
1925	01
1929	01
1930	11
1931	15
1932	12
1935	03

making ordinances under this section is subject to the like restrictions as the power of the Governor-General in Legislative Council to make laws; and any ordinance made under this section is subject to the like disallowance as an Act passed by the Governor-General in Legislative Council and may be controlled and superseded by any such Act.

The 1915 Act remained in effect for about twenty-one years. In all, seventy-eight ordinances were promulgated between 1916 and 1935 – four times more than the nineteen ordinances promulgated under the 1861 Act. Of these seventy-eight ordinances, thirty-five were promulgated in the ten years between 1916 and 1925; there were no ordinances in 1923. The remaining forty-three were promulgated between 1926 and 1935. But there were no ordinances in 1926, 1927, 1928, 1933 and 1934. Effectively, the forty-three ordinances during the latter period were promulgated over a period of five years. With the exception of one – the Registration Ordinance, 1917, all ordinances were repealed or replaced by another act or ordinance, or expired at the end of six months.

Almost all seventy-eight ordinances had one of two origins. Some had to do with wartime regulations or the conclusion of the war. Obvious examples include controls on currency, gold and silver;[87] restrictions on

[87] The Indian Paper Currency (Amendment) Ordinance, 1916 (I of 1916); the Gold (Import) Ordinance, 1917 (III of 1917); the Silver (Import) Ordinance, 1917 (IV of

export and import;[88] ban on trade with 'enemies'[89] and the recognition of treaties concluding the war.[90] The remaining ordinances had to do with suppressing – what was to the British – 'revolutionary activities' and the maintenance of law and order. When Mohandas Gandhi emerged on the nationalist stage in the late 1910s, his style of civil disobedience inspired millions to join the anti-colonial struggle. A large number of ordinances were promulgated to contain the resulting civil unrest, especially in the context of the Non-Cooperation Movement and the Civil Disobedience Movement. They included the imposition of martial law for prolonged periods,[91] restrictions on press activity[92] and limits on freedom of association.[93] There were also ordinances designed to try alleged revolutionary activists in special courts, especially from Bengal and Punjab. Amongst the most prominent were the Bengal Criminal Law (Amendment) Ordinance, 1924[94] and the Lahore Conspiracy Case Ordinance, 1930 – under which Bhagat Singh, Shivaram Rajguru and Sukhdev Thapar, along with twenty-one others, were infamously tried and sentenced to death.[95]

By the time the Government of India Act, 1935[96] (1935 Act) replaced the 1915 Act, ordinances had a prominent presence in British India's regulatory landscape. Their prominence presaged several trends in the later years, and four in particular are worth pointing out. First, ordinances were not exceptions anymore. They became, in many respects, the primary mechanism through which to enact legislation.

1917); the Gold Coinage Ordinance, 1918 (II of 1918); the Gold Ordinance, 1920 (III of 1920).

88 The Import and Export of Goods Ordinance, 1916 (IV of 1916).

89 The Enemy Trading Ordinance, 1916 (V of 1916).

90 The Treaty of Peace Ordinance, 1920 (I of 1920); the Treaty of Peace (Austria) Ordinance, 1920 (IV of 1920); the Treaty of Peace (Hungary) Ordinance, 1921 (1 of 1921).

91 The Martial Law Ordinance, 1919 (I–IV of 1919); the Martial Law Ordinance, 1921 (II of 1921); the Public Safety Ordinance, 1929 (I of 1929); the Martial Law Ordinance, 1930 (VIII of 1930). For commentary, see Ujjwal Kumar Singh, 'Penal Strategies and Political Resistance in Colonial and Independent India' in Kalpana Kannabiran and Ranbir Singh (eds.), *Challenging the Rule(s) of Law: Colonialism, Criminology and Human Rights in India* 227, 233–237 (Sage, New Delhi, 2008).

92 The Indian Press Ordinance, 1930 (II of 1930); the Unauthorised News Sheets and Newspapers Ordinance, 1930 (VII of 1930); the Indian Press and Unauthorised News Sheets and Newspapers Ordinance, 1930 (X of 1930).

93 The Unlawful Association Ordinance, 1930 (IX of 1930).

94 Ordinance I of 1930. See also the Bengal Criminal Law (Amendment) Ordinance, 1930 (I of 1930).

95 Ordinance III of 1930. For an account of the trial, see A. G. Noorani, *The Trial of Bhagat Singh: Politics of Justice* (Oxford University Press, New Delhi, 2004).

96 Ch. 2, 26 Geo. 5 and 1 Edw. 8.

Second, the practice of promulgating a 'series' began during this period. Take, for example, the raising of currency reserves through the repeated use of ordinances. On 16 January 1915, the Indian Paper Currency (Amendment) Ordinance, 1915 was promulgated into law as a wartime measure to increase currency reserves. Another amended version came into effect in January 1916 with the stated objective of granting power 'to increase the sterling investment of paper currency reserve... [from a] legal maximum of Rs. 4 crores to a maximum of Rs. 10 crores'.[97] The ordinance was amended and brought into effect in November of that year, and later again in December.[98] There was another ordinance in 1917,[99] and two more in 1918.[100] This was one of the earliest efforts to regulate a particular matter through a series of ordinances over a limited period of time. The practice quickly took hold, and was repeated on numerous occasions.[101]

Third, for the first time, the power to promulgate ordinances was invoked as a *parallel* legislative arrangement. The Public Safety Ordinance, 1929 is a classic example.[102] In September 1928, a Public Safety Bill authorising 'the removal from British India... of certain persons engaged in subversive propaganda' was introduced in the Legislative Assembly.[103] After long consideration, the assembly rejected it. In January 1929, Lord Irwin's government introduced a new version in the assembly and when the bill came up for consideration, Vithabhai Patel, president of the Legislative Assembly, objected to it. He suggested alternatives that were not acceptable to the administration.[104] Nevertheless convinced that a similar legislation was necessary to ensure 'good government', Lord Irwin promulgated the ordinance that incorporated the provisions earlier

[97] Anon, 'Paper Currency Act: Proposed Amendment' *Times of India*, 11 January 1916. A crore is the equivalent of 10 million rupees.

[98] Anon, 'Paper Currency Reserves Increased by 12 Crores' *Times of India*, 15 November 1916; Anon, 'India and the War: Paper Currency Reserve' *Times of India*, 15 December 1916.

[99] The Indian Paper Currency (Amendment) Ordinance, 1917 (II of 1917).

[100] The Indian Paper Currency Ordinance, 1918 (1 of 1918); the Indian Paper Currency (Amendment) Ordinance, 1918 (III of 1918).

[101] For the series of martial law ordinances, see *supra* n. 91 *ibid.*

[102] Ordinance 1 of 1929.

[103] Anon, 'Public Safety Ordinance: Preventive Purpose' *The Straits Times*, 1 May 1929.

[104] The president's ruling refusing to proceed with the bill almost created a constitutional crisis. Lord Irwin decided to address both chambers of the legislature to express his outrage against an attack on the Central Assembly and to explain his promulgation of an ordinance. See Anon, 'Viceroy to Issue Ordinance: Address to Legislature' *Times of India*, 13 April 1929.

rejected by the assembly. The law set a new precedent, making ordinances an executive alternative to parliamentary legislation. Clearly aware of his extraordinary innovation, the governor-general invoked the support of the 'vast majority of India's people' in promulgating it. In a statement attached to the ordinance, he explained the 'serious character of [his] personal decision', claiming that he had no doubt that his action would command 'the approval of that vast majority of India's people who have faith in India's future and whose first desire is to see their country prosperous, contented and secure'.[105]

Fourth, stricter understandings of 'emergency' gave way to more convenient meanings. Administrative inconvenience, for example, now counted as an 'emergency'. The circumstances leading to the promulgation of the Lahore Ordinance mentioned earlier is a good example. The trial of the assistant superintendent of police, John Saunders, and head constable, Chanan Singh, began in Lahore on 11 July 1929. It proceeded slowly; Bhagat Singh and several of his colleagues resorted to a hunger strike and that led to repeated adjournments. 'Disorderly conduct' in the courtroom and demonstrations by the public outside led to some more adjournments. By March 1930, only 234 of the 600 potential witnesses had been produced in the court. With the trial likely to drag on indefinitely, Lord Irwin exercised his legislative powers to promulgate the Lahore Ordinance, arguing that 'disorderly conduct and revolutionary demonstrations, [had] tended to bring the administration of justice into contempt, [making] it impossible to count upon obtaining a conclusion by the normal methods of procedure within any calculable period'.[106] And because public policy, as he understood it, required that the grave charges be 'thoroughly scrutinised and finally adjudicated upon with the least possible delay', he set up a tribunal of three judges, investing them 'with powers to deal with wilful obstruction'.[107]

Notice the administrative character of the events mentioned here; they involved nothing more than challenges in enforcing ordinary law and

[105] Anon, 'Viceroy's Action: Public Safety Ordinance' *Times of India*, 15 April 1929.

[106] Statement of Lord Irwin appended to the Lahore Conspiracy Case Ordinance, 1 May 1930, Shimla.

[107] *Ibid.* Amongst the most egregious in the ordinance were the special powers of the tribunal and the special rules of evidence. The tribunal was vested with powers to take measures necessary 'to secure the orderly conduct of the trial', including the power to dispense with the attendance of accused persons and proceed with the trial in their absence. In addition, contrary to the provisions in the Indian Evidence Act, 1872, statements recorded by a magistrate were made admissible in evidence, and judgment of the tribunal in pursuance of such evidence was declared 'final and conclusive'.

procedure. But in describing them as an 'emergency' requiring special legislation, Lord Irwin brought the power to promulgate ordinances ever closer to the legislature's power to enact primary legislation. When contested, the Privy Council returned a verdict inscribing the governor-general's view into law. In *Bhagat Singh and Others v. The King-Emperor*,[108] Viscount Dunedin concluded that a state of emergency 'is something that [did] not permit of any exact definition'. As a state of matter calling for drastic action, 'emergency' had to be judged by someone. That someone, he wrote, could be 'the Governor-General, and he alone'.[109] In other words, emergency was whatever the Governor-General felt it was; nothing else mattered.

Taken together, these developments made ordinances the new normal in India, both in numbers and status. Numerically, they were vastly common – much more than in the earlier period. It was 'normal' in its status, too. By 1935, there were effectively two legislative authorities. The Imperial Legislature obviously had legislative powers. But seventy-five years after it was first introduced to protect British interests in emergency times, the governor-general's power to promulgate ordinances incrementally morphed into a parallel legislative power. All this was contrary to the historical developments in the UK; as we saw earlier, the monarch's personal power to legislate waned and eventually ceased to exist. But things unfolded differently in India. When the 1935 Act was enacted into law, it greatly expanded the governor-general's *independent* legislative powers. The new normal was now also official. The next section will review the developments under the 1935 Act, assessing how ordinances – now catholic and convenient – became irrevocably 'Indian'.

2. *Past Its Autocratic Origins: The Making of 'Indian' Ordinances*

Under the 1935 Act, the governor-general was authorised to 'enact' three kinds of ordinances. The Act in s. 42 introduced what may be regarded as 'substitutive' legislative powers: 'If at any time when the Federal Legislature is not in session the Governor-General is satisfied that circumstances exist which render it necessary for him to take immediate action, he may promulgate such ordinances as the circumstances appear to him to

[108] (1931) 55 Ind. App. 169.

[109] *Id.* at 172. This exclusionary rule quickly became standard reasoning. See, e.g., *King-Emperor v. Benoari Lal Sharma And Others* (1945) 72 Ind. App. 57; *Hubli Electricity Co. Ltd. v. Province of Bombay L.R.* (1948) 76 Ind. App. 57; *Lakhi Narayan Das v. The Province of Bihar* [1949] F.C.R. 693.

require'.[110] The governor-general, in such cases, was required to act in accordance with the advice of his Council of Ministers only if the legislature was not in session. Ordinances so promulgated, as before, were limited to a period of six months.[111]

In contrast, s. 43 provided for ordinances in their classic sense; that is, in situations where 'immediate action' was needed for the purpose of satisfactorily discharging *his* functions under the Act. Despite introducing a largely cabinet form of government, the governor-general, under the 1935 Act, retained independent responsibility on certain matters including defence, ecclesiastical affairs, external affairs and in relation to matters concerning tribal areas.[112] Additionally, he also had special responsibility, amongst others, of preventing 'any grave menace to the peace or tranquillity of India', of safeguarding 'the financial stability and credit of the Federal Government; ... [and] the legitimate interests of minorities', and protecting 'the rights and dignity of the Ruler'.[113] Initially valid for six months, such ordinances could be extended for a further period not exceeding six months.[114] Importantly, neither the cabinet nor the federal legislature had control over such ordinances: the only requirement was to have the law laid before both houses in Westminster.[115]

Finally, s. 44 introduced a new type of legislation called the 'Governor-General's Act' – a truly independent and parallel source of legislative power. As with s. 43, the power in s. 44 concerned the satisfactory discharge of his discretionary functions. But unlike s. 43, s. 44 was not conditioned on the necessity for any 'immediate action'. The governor-general could 'legislate' his Act anytime he wanted, but after explaining 'to both Chambers of the Legislature ... the circumstances which in his opinion [rendered] legislation essential'.[116] Also, unlike s. 43, such an Act

110 § 42, the Government of India Act, 1935.

111 *Id.* at § 42(2)(a).

112 *Id.* at § 11(1).

113 *Id.* at § 12(1).

114 *Id.* at § 43(2) ('An ordinance promulgated under this section shall continue in operation for such period not exceeding six months as may be specified therein, but may be a subsequent ordinance be extended for a further period not exceeding six months').

115 *Id.* at § 43(3) ('An ordinance promulgated under this section shall have the same force and effect as an Act of the Federal Legislature assented to by the Governor-General, but every such ordinance – (a) shall be subject to the provisions of this Act relating to the power of His Majesty to disallow Acts as if it were an Act of the Federal Legislature assented to by the Governor-General; (b) may be withdrawn at any time by the Governor-General; and (c) if it is an ordinance extending a previous ordinance for a further period, shall be communicated forthwith to the Secretary of State and shall be laid by him before each House of Parliament').

116 *Id.* at § 43(1).

was *permanent*; it was in no way different from ordinary Acts. Clearly, the Governor-General's Act was the most egregious of the three. In true authoritarian style, it vested original legislative authority in a single (and unrepresentative) office. Whereas ordinances under s. 42 depended on the council of ministers' collective satisfaction and were subject to some legislative control post-enactment, those under s. 43 were limited in point of time. None of these applied to Governor-General's Acts; they were neither dependent on ministerial satisfaction nor limited in point of time.

This three-tiered categorisation of ordinances under the 1935 Act was a direct result of the experiences under the 1915 Act. The provisions formalised into law several trends mentioned earlier, especially the practice of treating ordinances as a parallel legislative power. Also, by conferring permanence on the Governor-General's Acts, concerns about the limited tenure of emergency legislation were taken care of. But these expanded powers never came into effect: the Congress Party rejected the 1935 reforms. Accordingly, the power to promulgate ordinances even after 1935 continued as provided in the 1915 Act, s. 72. That provision was incorporated into the Ninth Schedule of the 1935 Act and remained in force as a 'transitional provision'.[117]

Between August 1939 and January 1950, 394 ordinances were promulgated. Of these, 295 were promulgated in the eight years between 1939 and 1947. The remaining ninety-nine came into effect after independence, but prior to the inauguration of the Constitution in 1950. Overall, the circumstances leading to a majority of these ordinances were much as before. World War II had just begun and Gandhi was making plans for his Quit India Movement, one he officially launched in 1942. The normal legislative process had almost ceased to function, and ordinances, not surprisingly, took over. With one key change, the earlier trends continued in this period – and with greater vigour.

The change had to do with the tenure of ordinances. In 1940, with World War II as the background, the British parliament enacted the India and Burma (Emergency Provisions) Act, 1940 entirely removing the six-month limit on ordinances promulgated during the period of

[117] *Id.* at § 317(1) ('The provisions of the Government of India Act set out, with amendments consequential on the provisions of this Act, in the Ninth Schedule to this Act [being certain of the provisions of that Act relating to the Governor-General, the Commander-in-Chief, the Governor-General's Executive Council and the Indian. Legislature and provisions supplemental to those provisions] shall, subject to those amendments, continue to have effect notwithstanding the repeal of that Act by this Act').

TABLE 1.3. *Year-wise breakdown of ordinances for the 1939–1950 period**

Year	Ordinances
1939	09
1940	14
1941	13
1942	68
1943	45
1944	56
1945	48
1946	28
1947†	32
1948	38
1949	33
1950*	11

* Until 25 January 1950.
† From 15 August 1947, ordinances were promulgated under the India (Provisional Constitution) Order, 1947.

emergency.[118] The Act was passed on 27 June 1940 and the state of emergency remained in effect until 1 April 1946. As a result, ordinances promulgated during this period became *indefinitely* valid, unless amended or repealed. About 248 ordinances, including some repeal ordinances, were promulgated during this period of emergency.[119] These ordinances were overwhelmingly – although not exclusively – about the Indian defence forces,[120] regulation of war activities,[121] controls on currency[122] and

118 Ch. 33, 3 and 4 Geo. 6.

119 For a summary of these ordinances, see Hans Raj, *Executive Legislation in Colonial India 1939–1947* (Anamika Prakashan, New Delhi, 1989).

120 See, e.g., the Indian Air Force Volunteer Reserve (Discipline) Ordinance, 1939 (VII of 1939); the Civic Guards Ordinance, 1940 (VIII of 1940); the Women's Auxiliary Corps Ordinance, 1942 (XIII of 1942); the Indian Royal Navy (Powers of Command) Ordinance, 1943 (XVII of 1943); the Military Safety (Power of Detention) Ordinance, 1944 (IV of 1944).

121 See, e.g., the War Risks (Goods) Insurance Ordinance, 1940 (IX of 1940); the War Injuries Ordinance, 1941 (VII of 1941); Essential Service (Maintenance) Ordinance, 1941 (XI of 1941).

122 See, e.g., the Currency Ordinance, 1940 (IV of 1940); the Burma Notes Ordinance, 1942 (XXVIII of 1942); the Banking Notes (Declaration of Holdings) Ordinance, 1946 (II of 1946); the High Denomination Bank Notes (Demonitisation) Ordinance, 1946 (III of 1946).

tax measures.[123] Because the six-month limit was done away with, their tenure varied widely. A large number of ordinances only remained in force for a maximum of three years, but at least twenty-nine lasted up to five years, fifteen lasted up to six years, two lasted up to seven years and another five lasted up to eight years. In 1946, a major repeal ordinance did away with as many as 113 ordinances, while another twelve were repealed in 1947.[124] The remaining 123 ordinances promulgated during the emergency continued in the law books despite the conclusion of the war.

A new era began with the enactment of the Indian Independence Act, 1947 (1947 Act) and the creation of two Dominions – India and Pakistan.[125] There was, however, nothing new about the provision on ordinances; it continued just as before. The 1947 Act authorised the governor-general to modify and adapt parts of the 1935 Act, and accordingly the India (Provisional Constitution) Order, 1947 was promulgated. As part of this adaptation, the power to promulgate ordinance was retained, but made conditional on the advice of the cabinet. The governor-general, in other words, was not to promulgate them on his own.[126] This retention was not an imposition; the national leadership opted for it. Accordingly, all ordinances promulgated during the proclamation of emergency and not repealed – some 123 of them – were naturalised into the new legal system.

This was a stunning reversal. Throughout the 1930s, Jawaharlal Nehru – as a free citizen and also while in prison – had scorned the British for their use of ordinances. For him, ordinances and the suppression of civil liberties went together and, therefore, were incompatible with democratic ideals.[127] In a letter to an Englishman in 1936, Nehru objected to the idea of a 'constitutional road' in India's struggle against the British. 'I can understand constitutional activities where there is a democratic constitution', he wrote, 'but where there is no such thing, constitutional methods have no meaning'.[128] The term, Nehru felt, meant lawful, and

[123] See, e.g., the Excess Profit Tax Ordinance, 1943 (XVI of 1943); the Indian Income Tax (Amendment) Ordinance, 1945 (X of 1945).

[124] The Repealing Ordinance, 1946 (1 of 1946).

[125] Ch. 30, 10 and 11 Geo. 6.

[126] § 9(1), the Government of India Act, 1935 (as adapted in 1947) ('There shall be a council of ministers, not exceeding ten in number, to aid and advise the Governor-General in the exercise of his functions, except in so far as he is by or under this Act required to exercise his functions or any of them in his discretion').

[127] Jawaharlal Nehru, *Towards Freedom* 157 (Jones Day, New York, 1940).

[128] Jawaharlal Nehru, *India and the World* 180 (George, Allen and Unwin, London, 1936).

that simply meant 'in accordance with the wishes of an autocratic executive which [could] make laws and issue decrees and ordinances regardless of public opinion'.[129] Later that year, in his Presidential Address to the Congress Party he spoke of the 'humiliation of ordinances' and the peoples' 'enforced submission' to them. 'A charter of slavery is no law for the slave', he told his audience, 'and though we may perforce submit for a while to it and to the humiliation of ordinances and the like, inherent in that enforced submission is the right and the desire to rebel against it and to end it'.[130] Clearly, Nehru had no liking for ordinances. Their use, to him, was despotism by a different name.

But that was then. In 1947, he was the prime minister and ordinances flourished under him. Ninety-nine of them were promulgated into law between August 1947 and January 1950. A large number of these ninety-nine ordinances were partition measures. Amongst them were ordinances concerning property-related matters,[131] refugees,[132] prisoners,[133] public order[134] and the defence forces.[135]

Then there were ordinances designed to coagulate – and secure – the new state, or resolve administrative rising from accession or otherwise.[136] The Securities (Hyderabad) Ordinance, 1948 (1948 Ordinance) is a good example.[137] It was June 1948. Hyderabad's Nizam was resisting accession talks with India. Lord Mountbatten proposed the 'Heads of Agreements' – one that guaranteed Nizam his executive powers while giving New Delhi control over military and foreign affairs of the state. New Delhi, obviously, was on board, but Hyderabad spurned the offer. At this point, wary of Nizam's plans, Nehru promulgated the 1948 Ordinance, prohibiting the transfer of government securities 'which may be detrimental to the interests of India'. Under the ordinance, government securities held

[129] *Id.* at 181.

[130] *Id.* at 86–87.

[131] See, e.g., the Delhi Evacuee Property (Supplementary) Ordinance, 1947 (XXIII of 1947).

[132] See, e.g., the Delhi Refugees Registration Ordinance, 1947 (XXIV of 1947); the Influx from West Pakistan (Control) Ordinance, 1948 (XVII of 1948); the Displaced Person (Institution of Suits) Ordinance, 1948 (XVIII of 1948).

[133] See, e.g., the Exchange of Prisoners Ordinance, 1948 (VI of 1948); the Transfer of Detained Persons Ordinance, 1949 (XVI of 1949).

[134] See, e.g., the Bombay Public Security Measures Act (Delhi Amendment) Ordinance, 1948 (XIV of 1948); the Public Safety Ordinance, 1948 (XXIV of 1948).

[135] See, e.g., the Pakistan Military Personnel Amnesty Ordinance, 1948 (I of 1948); the Indian Army (Amendment) Ordinance, 1948 (XIX of 1948); the Armed Forces (Miscellaneous Provisions) Ordinance, 1950 (VIII of 1950).

[136] See, e.g., the Mangrol and Manavader (Administration of Property) Ordinance (22 of 1948); the Merchant Shipping (Acceding States) Ordinance (28 of 1948).

[137] Ordinance XVI of 1948.

by or on behalf of the Hyderabad government and the Hyderabad State Bank could not be transferred without the approval of the central government. In a communiqué attached to the ordinance, the cabinet explained that 'the Hyderabad Government had decided to transfer Government of India securities worth Rs. 20 crores to the Pakistan Government'.[138] This was in violation of the earlier 'Standstill Agreement' that prohibited initiating contacts with foreign states. Additionally, there was evidence, the government claimed, that 'all available resources of the Hyderabad Government [were] being utilized for the purchase of warlike materials, which must inevitably lead to conflict'.[139] The conflict eventually came, but at India's behest. By September that year, Nizam's forces surrendered and Hyderabad was integrated into India. Incidentally, the ordinance never became law; it expired on 1 January 1949.

Of the ninety-nine ordinances, fifty-two were enacted into legislation and made permanent, forty-five – including Nizam's ordinance – expired and the remaining two were repealed by ordinances. At least twenty-one of these were still in effect as of 26 January 1950. These were in addition to the scores of 'permanent' ordinances under the 1935 Act that continued in effect despite the cessation of emergency. And both sets of ordinances entered India's new constitutional order when Article 372 retained 'all the laws in force in the territory of India immediately before the commencement of this Constitution' until altered or repealed or amended. As a result, the Coinage Ordinance, 1940, for example, promulgated nearly seventy years ago, still remains in force – a fact that was only recently brought to light.[140] In 2009, the Parliamentary Standing Committee on Finance stumbled upon the ordinance while examining the Coinage Bill, 2009, aimed at replacing four existing laws on metal coins and tokens. When the committee, headed by former Finance Minister of India, Yashwant Sinha, queried about its strange longevity, it was informed by the Ministry of Law and Justice that the ordinance has not yet been repealed and, therefore, remains in effect.[141]

[138] Anon, 'Transfer of India Securities held by the Nizam banned' *Times of India*, 2 July 1948.

[139] *Ibid.* For an account of the circumstances leading to the accession, see Lucien Benichou, *From Autocracy to Integration: Political Developments in Hyderabad State 1938–1948* 176–196 (Orient Longman, Chennai, 2000).

[140] IV of 1940.

[141] Anon, 'Ordinance on Near-Extinct Rs.1 Note Survives Seven Decades' *Deccan Herald*, 12 September 2010, *available at*: http://www.deccanherald.com/content/95919/ordinance-near-extinct-rs1-note.html (accessed 31 August 2011).

This act of constitutional importation was an important break. Ninety years after they were first introduced to protect imperial interests, ordinances became quintessentially 'Indian' in 1950. The founding authors gave British India ordinances that continued authority in the new republican order. But they went further, writing Article 123 into the Constitution – one that authorised new ordinances when the president felt necessary. With that, the parallel histories of ordinances in the UK and India were nearly complete. By 1950, Britain had all but ridden herself of the monarch's medieval powers, particularly the independent power to legislate.[142] India, on the other hand, chose to memorialise them into its body politic. India's new cabinet was both modern and medieval; their powers rivalled the most autocratic of British monarchs. In another sixty years (between 1950 and 2009), this independent power to legislate would be put to vigorous use so as to nearly supplant the ordinary legislative process.

But before we turn to the post-independent years, one other question remains: Why did the Constituent Assembly provide for ordinances in the new Constitution? The founding authors wrote on a relatively clean slate. And yet, they chose a borrowed script. In the next section, I will reconstruct the debates in the Constituent Assembly, assessing the extent to which their inclusion in the Constitution was opposed, if at all.

D. LIMITED OPPOSITION: ORDINANCES IN THE CONSTITUENT ASSEMBLY

On 30 April 1947, the Constituent Assembly appointed the Union Constitution Committee to report on the 'main principles' of the Union Constitution. Constitutional Adviser B. N. Rau was tasked with collecting the members' views on the matter. Based on replies to a questionnaire he circulated to all members, Rau prepared an independent memorandum – one that became the basis for all further discussions regarding the Union Constitution. It was in this document that he raised the possibility that India's Constitution may contain a provision for ordinances. 'If at any time, when the Union Parliament is not in session, the President is satisfied that circumstances exist which render it necessary for him to take

[142] Maurice Amos, *The English Constitution* 122 (Longmans, Green and Co., London, 1930). Writing in 1930, he said, 'The Crown has, of course, lost for almost all purposes what was formerly an important prerogative, namely, that of legislation by means of proclamation or ordinance issued by the King in Council'.

immediate action, he may promulgate such Ordinances as the circumstances appear him to require'.[143] Keeping in line with previous versions, his proposal granted ordinances the 'same force and effect' as Acts of parliament. But in a departure from earlier versions, he suggested that they remain in force for a 'period not more than six weeks from the reassembly of Parliament'.[144]

Clearly aware that his suggestions could raise a storm, Rau appended a pre-emptive note, explaining – or rather justifying – its inclusion. Although ordinances are 'the subject of great criticism under the present Constitution', he pointed out that circumstances may exist 'where the immediate promulgation of a law is absolutely necessary and there is no time in which to summon the Union Parliament'.[145] Ironically, he resorted to an imperial example to make his point. 'Lord Reading found it necessary to make an Ordinance abolishing the cotton excise duty when such action was immediately and imperatively required in the interests of the country'.[146] This was a good example of selective emphasis. For every Cotton Excise Ordinance Rau could point to, there were dozens that Indians had bitterly agitated against. But as if to allay suspicions of similar misuse, he boldly declared that Indians had nothing to fear from future presidents: 'The President who is elected by the two Houses of Parliament and who has normally to act on the advice of Ministers responsible to Parliament is not likely at all to abuse any Ordinance-making power with which he may be vested. Hence the proposed provision'.[147] A few members echoed similar views; to them, an extraordinary legislative arrangement was necessary.[148] And apparently without discussion or dissent, Rau's proposal on ordinances and his note was included in the Committee's official report. On 4 July 1947, Nehru in his capacity as the chairman of the Union Constitution Committee submitted the report to the Constituent Assembly – the body with the ultimate authority to accept or reject the ordinance proposal.

On 23 May 1949, the provision came up for debate in the assembly. The discussion, it must be pointed out, was limited to the nature and scope of ordinances; members hardly spoke against the very *idea* of ordinances.

[143] B. N. Rau, 'Memorandum on the Union Constitution' in B. Shiva Rao (ed.), *The Framing of India's Constitution* Vol. II, 485 (Universal Law Publishing, New Delhi, 2006).

[144] *Id.* at 485–486.

[145] *Id.* at 486.

[146] *Ibid.* See Cotton Excise Duty (Suspension) Ordinance, 1925 (I of 1925).

[147] *Ibid.*

[148] N. Gopalswami Ayyangar and Alladi Krishnaswami Ayyar, 'Memorandum on the Principles of the Union Constitution' in B. Shiva Rao (ed.), *The Framing of India's Constitution* Vol. II, 540–551, 546 (Universal Law Publishing, New Delhi, 2006).

Professor K. T. Shah, a representative from Bihar, was the most articulate voice against ordinances. 'However, we may clothe it, however it may be necessary, however much it may be justified', an ordinance, he said, was 'a negation of the rule of law'.[149] And yet, he acknowledged that it might be unavoidable under certain circumstances. Therefore, all he wanted was to make clear that an ordinance could not 'last a minute longer than such extraordinary circumstances would require'.[150] This grudging, if limited, approval of ordinances, it should be mentioned, was a world away from Nehru's rhetoric about the 'humiliation' and 'illegalities' in the name of ordinances. Their old views jettisoned, the national leadership, at the moment of founding, warmed up to them. Apparently, ordinances were not that humiliating after all.

Much of the focus, as I mentioned earlier, was not on if, but the *extent* to which ordinances were needed. Some members pressed for substantive limits on ordinances; they were opposed to the idea of ordinances restricting people's fundamental freedoms. B. Pocker Sahib, a representative from Madras, wanted a proviso to the draft article stating that 'such ordinance shall not deprive any citizen of his right to personal liberty except on conviction after trial by a competent court of law'.[151] The growing trend of enforcing Public Safety Acts through ordinances, he thought, was a troubling precedent. And because it was important to him that 'the fundamental right of the citizen to be tried by a court of law' was not lost, he advocated for a provision that would make it illegal to deprive citizens of their liberty through ordinances.[152]

P. S. Deskmukh and Dr B. R. Ambedkar spoke against the proposal. In their view, the draft article, as it stood, accounted for Sahib's concerns. The article included the following clause: 'If and so far as an Ordinance under this article makes any provision which Parliament would not under this Constitution be competent to enact, it shall be void'.[153] Acts and ordinances, in other words, had identical legislative width; ordinances could not achieve anything that was prohibited for Acts. This provision, both Deshmukh and Ambedkar thought, resolved the matter. I will argue that they were mistaken: The provision they pointed to could not have accounted for Sahib's objection.

Consider, for a moment, his proposed amendment: 'Provided that such ordinance shall not deprive any citizen of his right to personal liberty except on conviction after trial by a competent court of law'.[154]

[149] Constituent Assembly Debates (CAD), Bk. 3. No. VIII, 208 (23 May 1949).
[150] *Id.* at 208.
[151] *Id.* at 203.
[152] *Ibid.*
[153] *Id.* at 211.
[154] *Id.* at 203.

Note that persons in India may be deprived of their right to personal liberty either upon conviction by a court of law, or under a law on preventive detention without trial or conviction.[155] Viewed in this light, did the draft article account for Sahib's concerns? The simple answer is that it did not. Laws on preventive detention are constitutional. Parliament has authority to enact such legislation and presidents, therefore, are permitted to promulgate ordinances authorizing preventive detention. If promulgated, an ordinance may deprive a person of his or her personal liberty without trial by a court of law. Sahib was opposed to this possibility. Therefore, in rejecting the amendment, the Constituent Assembly really rejected the idea of *substantive* limits on ordinances – a rejection, as we shall see later, matters for interpretative purposes.

Also, there were concerns about the duration of ordinances. H. V. Kamath, for example, felt that 'six weeks from the date of reassembly of Parliament' was too long.[156] Worried that a president inclined to dictatorship might take undue advantage of the tenure, he proposed that every ordinance be 'laid before both Houses of Parliament within four weeks of its promulgation'.[157] H. N. Kunzru wanted something similar – a tenure not exceeding four weeks.[158] But K. T. Shah would not tolerate even that. According to him, ordinances had to end *immediately* on reassembly of parliament: 'Every such Ordinance shall be laid before both Houses of Parliament immediately after each House assembles, unless approved by either House of Parliament by specific Resolution, shall cease to operate forthwith'.[159]

Dr Ambedkar, once again, rejected the proposals. The extended tenure, he thought, was justified. He defended it by comparing the draft article with the provisions for ordinances in the 1935 Act. According to him, the draft provision, unlike s. 43 and s. 44 in the 1935 Act, did not provide the executive with any parallel or independent power of legislation.[160] The extraordinary power was limited only to cases of legislative

[155] Constitution of India, Article 22(4) ('No law providing for preventive detention shall authorize the detention of a person for a longer period than three months unless – (a) an Advisory Board consisting of persons who are, or have been, or are qualified to be appointed as, Judges of a High Court has reported before the expiration of the said period of three months that there is in its opinion sufficient cause for such detention: Provided that nothing in this sub-clause shall authorize the detention of any person beyond the maximum period prescribed by any law made by Parliament under sub-clause (b) of clause (7); or (b) such person is detained in accordance with the provisions of any law made by Parliament under sub-clauses (a) and (b) of clause (7)').

[156] *Supra* n. 149 at 205.

[157] *Id.* at 204.

[158] *Id.* at 206.

[159] *Id.* at 208.

[160] *Id.* at 213.

emergency, and that, too, when either house of parliament was not in session. On this, he was correct. But Dr Ambedkar avoided mention of the fact that the draft also expanded on the existing provision on ordinances in some respects. First, the provision on ordinances in the 1935 Act was limited only to matters concerning 'peace and good government'. However, the draft provision was substantively agnostic; the president could promulgate 'any' ordinance. Second, the 1935 provision was categorically limited to six months. The draft provision, however, avoided direct mention of tenure; it simply provided that ordinances would remain in effect until the expiry of six weeks from the reassembly of parliament. This choice of drafting strategy, I will later argue in Chapter 3, has profound implications for the tenure of ordinances – under certain circumstances, they may last for periods *far* beyond six months. Kamath clearly understood the consequences and he vented his frustrations at Ambedkar, saying that 'in framing this article, we have gone one better than the British regime, and it is a most atrocious position'.[161] Despite these complaints, the provision, as originally drafted, was voted into the Constitution.[162]

The draft article, initially conceptualised by Rau and later supported by Dr Ambedkar, became Article 123 in the new Constitution, thereby authorising the president to promulgate ordinances if he is 'satisfied that circumstances exist which render it necessary for him to take immediate action', provided both houses are not in session.[163] Importantly, in writing the provision, the founding authors gave ordinances both vertical and horizontal equivalence – or so it seems.[164] Vertical equivalence was granted in Article 123(2): 'An Ordinance promulgated under this article shall have the same force and effect as an Act of Parliament'. It is because of this provision that presidential ordinances in India are not by-laws, decrees, orders or regulations; they are the equivalent of Acts. Article 123(3) granted horizontal equivalence: 'If and so far as an Ordinance under this article makes any provision which Parliament would not under this Constitution be competent to enact, it shall be void'. In other words, ordinances and Acts have similar legislative width; the former can do everything that the latter has jurisdiction to do.

[161] *Id.* at 216. [162] *Id.* at 217.

[163] On 14 June 1949, the assembly voted to give governors similar powers to promulgate ordinances at the state level. It became Article 213 in the Constitution of India. Except for issues relating to overlapping legislative competence, Article 213 is identical to Article 123.

[164] I say 'so it seems' because in Chapters 3–5, I argue that despite words to the contrary, ordinances and acts do not have the same scope and effect.

The Constituent Assembly's debate on ordinances – or lack of it – was strikingly at odds with the leadership's earlier attitude. That should not come as a surprise. Although important, the Assembly's vote on the provision for ordinances, in many ways, was little more than a formal act – the outcome was never in doubt. By 23 May 1949 – the date on which ordinances were debated and voted upon – Nehru's cabinet had already promulgated as many as sixty-three ordinances in independent India. The allure of extraordinary powers was too strong, and once put into practice, there was clearly no going back. In less than two years, Nehru and his colleagues folded their practical and philosophical objections. What was earlier authoritarian, undemocratic and humiliating, they now believed, was necessary. And the Constituent Assembly agreed.

But does India *really* need ordinances? That is the one remaining question I turn to in the final section of this chapter.

E. THE CASE AGAINST ORDINANCES: WHY DR AMBEDKAR AND H. M. SEERVAI ARE WRONG

Similar to Rau in his earlier memorandum, Dr Ambedkar thought of ordinances as 'necessary'. 'It is not difficult to imagine cases', he told the Constituent Assembly, 'where the powers conferred by the ordinary law existing at any particular moment may be deficient to deal with a situation which may suddenly and immediately arise'.[165] And in such situations, there could be no fundamental objection to the idea of arming the president with powers to make a new law.

But empirically speaking, Ambedkar's claim does not hold up. While some neighbouring jurisdictions have adopted the concept of legislative emergency in non-emergency times, others have functioned (rather well) without such powers. Influenced by the British Indian experience, Pakistan,[166] Bangladesh[167] and Nepal,[168] for example, have incorporated

[165] *Supra* n. 149 at 214.

[166] Constitution of The Islamic Republic of Pakistan, Article 89(1) ('The President, may, except when the National Assembly is in session, if satisfied that circumstances exist which render it necessary to take immediate action, make and promulgate an Ordinance as the circumstances may require').

[167] Constitution of The People's Republic of Bangladesh, Article 93(1) ('At any time when [Parliament stands dissolved or is not in session], if the President is satisfied that circumstances exist which render immediate action necessary, he may make and promulgate such Ordinances as the circumstances appear to him to require, and any Ordinance so made shall, as from its promulgation have the like force of law as an Act of Parliament').

[168] Interim Constitution of Nepal, Article 88(1) ('If at any time, except when the Legislative – Parliament is in session, the Government of Nepal is satisfied that circumstances

similar ordinance-related provisions in their respective constitutions. But other jurisdictions including Sri Lanka,[169] Malaysia[170] and Singapore,[171] for example, provide for ordinances only during 'emergencies' and are, therefore, conceptually closer to the 'Emergency Provisions' in India's Constitution.[172] This is also true of commonwealth jurisdictions outside of Asia. Australia, Canada and the United Kingdom, for example, confer varying degrees of legislative authority on the executive.[173] The powers, however, are predicated on *specific* cases of emergency. In the United Kingdom, a senior Minister may make regulations[174] under the Civil Contingencies Act, 2005, if it is urgently 'necessary to make provision for the purpose of preventing, controlling or mitigating an aspect or effect of the emergency'.[175] Emergency under the Act means 'an event or situation which threatens serious damage to human welfare... [or]... threatens serious damage to the environment... or (c) war, or terrorism, which threatens serious damage to the security of the United Kingdom'.[176] And unlike ordinances in India, such regulations have a maximum tenure of thirty days.[177]

exist which render it necessary to take immediate action, without prejudicing the provisions set forth in this Constitution, the government of Nepal may promulgate any Ordinance as deemed necessary').

169 Constitution of The Democratic Socialist Republic of Sri Lanka, Article 155(1) (The Public Security Ordinance as amended and in force immediately prior to the commencement of the Constitution shall be deemed to be a law enacted by Parliament'). Public Security Ordinance (XXV of 1947) ('An Ordinance to provide for the enactment of emergency Regulations or the adoption of other measures in the interests of the public security and the preservation of public order and for the maintenance of supplies and services essential to the life of the community').

170 Federal Constitution of Malaysia, Article 151(2B) ('If at any time while a Proclamation of Emergency is in operation, except when both Houses of Parliament are sitting concurrently, the Yang di-Pertuan Agong is satisfied that certain circumstances exist which render it necessary for him to take immediate action, he may promulgate such ordinances as circumstances appear to him to require').

171 Constitution of Singapore, Article 150 (2) ('If a Proclamation of Emergency is issued when Parliament is not sitting, the President shall summon Parliament as soon as practicable, and may, until Parliament is sitting, promulgate ordinances having the force of law, if satisfied that immediate action is required').

172 Constitution of India, Part XVIII ('Emergency Provisions').

173 See Ch. 36, Civil Contingencies Act, 2004 (UK); Ch. 22, Emergencies Act, 1985 (4th Supp.) (Canada). For commentary on the Civil Contingencies Act, see Clive Walker and James Broderick, *The Civil Contingencies Act 2004: Risk, Resilience and the Law in the United Kingdom* (Oxford University Press, Oxford, 2006). Emergency legislation in Australia varies in the provinces. See, e.g., Victoria State Emergency Act, 2005 (Act 51 of 2005).

174 § 20(2), Civil Contingencies Act, 2004.

175 *Id.* at § 21.

176 *Id.* at § 19.

177 *Id.* at § 21.

What these examples show is that a general provision for ordinances – especially of the Indian type meant to address issues of regular governance – is by no means necessary. To be sure, emergency provisions, including provisions for legislation, are necessary and India, like other jurisdictions, specifically provides for them. But the power to promulgate ordinances, such as the one in Article 123, is something else – it is the executive's power to enact legislation in *non*-emergency times. And contrary to Ambedkar's claim of necessity, a large number of legal systems have done without it.

Presumably, H. M. Seervai anticipated this sort of an objection. Therefore, he defended ordinances through the lens of judicial review, arguing that the provision has 'secured considerable flexibility both to the Union and to the State to enact laws to meet emergent situations as also to meet circumstances created by laws being declared void by courts of law'.[178] The Bombay High Court's decision in *United Motors India Ltd. v. State of Bombay*, he thought, was a good example.[179] In that case, the court voided the Bombay Sales Tax Act, 1952 on the ground that the definition of 'sale' was beyond the state legislature's competence.[180] Because the definition permeated the whole Act, it was 'impossible to sever any specific provision of the Act so as to save the rest'.[181] As a result, the entire Act was voided. In such circumstances, without a provision for ordinances, Seervai thought that 'gravest public inconvenience would be caused if . . . no machinery existed whereby a valid law could be promptly promulgated to take the place of the law declared void'.[182] Seervai seems to think that judicial review and ordinances go together; if one exists, the other is necessary. That is to say that the internal working of the Constitution (through the application of judicial review) might itself generate moments of legislative urgency. This claim is clearly distinct from Ambedkar's insistence on administrative – or 'external' – necessity as the basis for ordinances. But on closer look, several difficulties emerge.

First, empirically speaking, the argument is over-inclusive: judicial review and ordinances need not go together. The United States is the best example of this. Whereas the U.S. Supreme Court has the power to invalidate legislation, and often does so, the president does not have a corresponding power to independently 'enact' a law. American

[178] H. M. Seervai, *Constitutional Law of India* 19 (N.M. Tripathi, Bombay, 1968).

[179] (1953) 55 Bom LR 246.

[180] *Id.* at para 25.

[181] *Id.* at para 25.

[182] *Ibid.* (references omitted).

presidents do have the power to issue 'signing statements', but they are not the equivalent of congressional legislation.[183] Appended to legislation, such statements perform a limited task; they may be used to comment on the law generally, describe the bill, explain its purpose, guide executive-branch officials in implementing the law, guide the judiciary in interpreting the law's provisions, or on occasions, raise constitutional objections to the provisions of the law. None of this, however, is the equivalent of enacting a piece of legislation.

Second, his argument is under-inclusive. Legislative emergencies of the kind Seervai anticipates may arise even in situations that do *not* involve matters relating to judicial review of legislation. Take, for example, a recent controversy regarding bail and pretrial detention in the UK. Ordinarily, the police could detain a person of interest for up to twenty-four hours for questioning. This period may be extended up to ninety-six hours if a judge so agrees. For nearly twenty-five years, the Police and Criminal Evidence Act, 1984[184] (1984 Act) was interpreted to allow for a convenient use of the ninety-six hours. It was common practice for the police to interrogate people, release them on bail, and weeks or months later bring them back for questioning, subject to a maximum total of ninety-six hours in police custody. But all that changed after *Q v. Salford Magistrates' Court and Paul Hookway* when the Salford District Judge refused to issue a warrant authorising the police to detain him for a second round of questioning.[185] Hookway was suspected of murder, and first arrested on 5 November 2010. He was released on bail after twenty-eight hours. In April 2011, the police applied for a warrant seeking to extend his period of detention to ninety-six hours. It was refused. Contrary to police practice of more than twenty-five years, the Salford District Judge broke new ground in suggesting that the ninety-six-hour window was not a standalone period, but ran continuously from the moment a person is first arrested. Because that period had run out in Hookway's case months before, the warrant was refused.

[183] On signing statements, see Curtis A. Bradley and Eric A. Posner, 'Presidential Signing Statements and Executive Power', 23(3) *Constitutional Commentary* 307 (Winter 2006); T. J. Halstead, Congressional Research Service Report for Congress, Presidential Signing Statements: Constitutional and Institutional Implications (2007), *available at*: http://www.fas.org/sgp/crs/natsec/RL33667.pdf (accessed 31 August 2011). For a contrary view see generally William Howell, *Power without Persuasion: The Politics of Direct Presidential Action* (Princeton University Press, Princeton, 2003).

[184] Ch. 60, 1984 Act.

[185] [2011] EWHC 1578 (Admin).

To the law enforcement authorities, the decision was 'close to a disaster'.[186] It brought into question the fate of nearly 80,000 suspects in England and Wales who were then on police bail.[187] Reacting to the decision, West Yorkshire Chief Constable, Sir Norman Bettison, warned about the prospect of having to release thousands of serious criminals without charge. 'We are running around like headless chickens wondering what this means to the nature of justice', he complained. 'It's a mess'.[188] Essex Chief Constable Jim Barker-McCardle expressed similar concerns saying that the ruling would have a 'profound impact' on the way police investigate crime.[189] By any measure, this was a crisis of a kind that required a new piece of legislation or amendments to an existing one.[190] But the origins of the controversy lay in the court's power to *interpret* – not invalidate – legislation. What this shows is that even without the application of judicial review of legislation, situations may arise where new laws are urgently needed.

When put together, these examples demonstrate that judicial review and ordinances have nothing to do with one another. Legal systems that have judicial review function perfectly well without any provision for ordinances. Conversely, legislative emergencies of the kind Seervai is concerned about may arise even in situations that have nothing to do with judicial review of legislation. But there is a third problem, too – one that is more of the syllogistic kind. If judicial review and the possibility of voiding legislation underpin the case for ordinances, syllogistically speaking, a similar arrangement is also required for constitutional amendments. The Supreme Court in *Kesavananda Bharati v. State of Kerala*[191] introduced the 'basic structure' doctrine, thereby claiming authority to invalidate constitutional amendments.[192] As a result, concerns Seervai

[186] Alan Travis, 'Court Ruling 'A Disaster', Say Police' *The Guardian*, 29 June 2011, *available at*: http://www.guardian.co.uk/politics/2011/jun/29/bail-ruling-theresa-may-considers-emergency-legislation (accessed August 31, 2011).

[187] Alan Travis, 'Court Ruling Leaves Police Powerless To Enforce Bail Conditions' *The Guardian*, 1 July 2011, *available at*: http://www.guardian.co.uk/uk/2011/jul/01/police-powerless-enforce-bail-conditions?intcmp=239 (accessed 31 August 2011).

[188] *Supra* n. 186 *ibid.*

[189] Anon, 'Bail Suspects Could be Released after Court Ruling' *BBC News*, 29 June 2011, *available at*: http://www.bbc.co.uk/news/uk-13957873 (accessed August 31, 2011).

[190] Alan Travis, 'Emergency Law to Overturn Court Ruling on Police Bail' *The Guardian*, 30 June 2011, *available at*: http://www.guardian.co.uk/uk/2011/jun/30/emergency-law-bail-ruling?intcmp=239 (accessed 31 August 2011).

[191] (1973) 4 SCC 225.

[192] On Basic Structure Doctrine, see Sudhir Krishnaswamy, *Democracy and Constitutionalism in India* (Oxford University Press, New Delhi, 2010).

earlier identified with legislation could be made to apply to constitutional amendments as well. But as far as I can tell, neither he nor has anybody else ever argued, and rightly so, that it is necessary or desirable that presidents be provided with the 'flexibility' to promulgate constitutional amendments in cases of emergency. And if ordinances are not needed with respect to constitutional amendments, then there is no reason to believe that they are any more important with respect to legislation.

Neither claims about necessity nor arguments from judicial review, it seems, is adequate to account for ordinances in the Constitution. What then explains the Constituent Assembly's less-than-probing attitude towards them? Earlier, I argued that the vote was a mere formality – by the time the matter came up for debate in May 1949, Nehru's cabinet was far too invested in the use of extraordinary legislative powers. But that analysis must be supplemented by an additional observation.

Debates in the Constituent Assembly make it fairly clear that the leading voices against ordinances, or at least against extended tenure for ordinances, tended to view future political leadership with suspicion. Once again, H. V. Kamath is instructive: 'Suppose the President summons Parliament say, after one year – Dr Ambedkar says 'no' by a gesture – perhaps he is constitutionally minded and he does not aspire to dictatorial powers if he be elected President – certainly a man different from him take unfair advantage of this article and refrain from summoning parliament within a reasonable period'.[193] K. T. Shah echoed similar worries. 'It is true that though the nominal authority which makes the Ordinance, is that of the President, he would be acting only on the advice of the Prime Minister'.[194] Therefore, rather than 'leave it to the exigencies or to the possibilities of party politics', he wanted a specific duration beyond which ordinances could not remain in effect.[195] But Dr Ambedkar would have none of this. With his charitable view of future political leadership and parliamentary functioning, there was no cause for alarm. 'I do not know what exactly may happen, but my point is this that the fear', he said in reply, 'is really unfounded'.[196] Especially, 'having regard to the necessity of the Government of the day to maintain the confidence of Parliament I do not think that any ... dilatory process will be permitted by the Executive of the day as to permit an ordinance promulgated ... to remain in operation for a period unduly long', he

[193] *Supra* n. 149 at 205.
[194] *Id.* at 209.
[195] *Id.* at 209.
[196] *Id.* at 215.

added.[197] His charity prevailed, and Article 123 was voted into the Constitution.

That was in 1949. More than sixty years have elapsed. We now have sufficient evidence on which to assess the executive's ordinance-related record in independent India. Were Kamath, Kunzru and Shah blinded by their distrust of future cabinets? Or was Dr Ambedkar unduly taken in by the promise of accountable and responsible cabinets in new India? In Chapter 2, I shall turn to the federal cabinet's record on ordinances – assessing how, when and why they have been put to use between 1952 and 2009.

197 *Ibid.* (emphasis added). See also Amal Ray, 'From a Constitutional to an Authoritarian System of Government: Interactions Between Politics and the Constitution in India', 25(3) *Journal of Commonwealth and Comparative Politics* 275–291 (1987).

2

Legislative Surrogacy: Cabinets and Ordinances, 1952–2009

No Ordinance is being issued for the nationalisation of banks nor any has been drafted by the Law Ministry for the take-over of five or six top banks, according to an official release issued here today.

Anon, 'Tighter Control of Banks: Bill in Parliament Likely' *Times of India*, 18 July 1969.

Indira Gandhi called in I. G. Patel, the Union economic affairs secretary [and] told him without any preamble or pretence. 'For political reasons, it has been decided to nationalise the banks. You have to prepare within 24 hours the bill, a note for the cabinet and a speech for me to make to the nation tomorrow evening. Can you do it and make sure that there is no leak?'... The prime minister had all the papers she needed the next morning. Twenty-four hours later, on [July 19], a Saturday, the ordinance to nationalise 14 major banks was issued and instantly became a sensation.

Inder Malhotra, 'Run Over the Banks' *Indian Express*, 10 July 2009.

By a mere stroke of the pen the Government has taken control of the deposits of 14 banks, totalling about Rs. 2,741 crores or nearly 70 per cent of the aggregate amount of deposits under the banking system.

Anon, 'Fourteen Top Banks are Nationalised' *Times of India*, 20 July 1969.

Thus far, India's presidents have promulgated 615 ordinances between 1952 and 2009.[1] That makes it an average of 10.6 ordinances *every* legislative year. Put another way, more than ten times every year,

[1] Unless otherwise mentioned, data in this chapter are based on the figures provided by the Ministry of Parliamentary Affairs in two of its publications. See *Presidential Ordinances, 1950–2009* (Lok Sabha Secretariat, New Delhi, 2011); *Statistical Handbook of Ministry of Parliamentary Affairs* (Ministry of Parliamentary Affairs, New Delhi, 2009).

presidents – perhaps implausibly – claimed that circumstances made it necessary for them to promulgate ordinances. In this chapter, I have two principal objectives. My first objective is to provide an analysis of the numbers, and through that an explanation of the use of ordinances – the 'what', 'when', and 'who' questions. My second objective is to develop an account of their prodigious use. This latter objective attends to the following question: Why are ordinances so prevalent in India?

Before that, a short explanation of the dates is in order. The tables in this chapter are limited to the period between 1952 and 2009. Even though the Constitution came into force on 26 January 1950, a new parliament did not convene until May 1952. Until then, the Constituent Assembly functioned as a provisional parliament, supplemented by an amended version of the Government of India Act, 1935. Because this study of ordinances is structured as an analysis of a legislative process that is, in effect, a parliamentary surrogate, including the interregnum would not provide for meaningful comparisons.

To briefly mention the numbers here, between 26 January 1950 and 13 May 1952, Jawaharlal Nehru's cabinet promulgated thirty-six ordinances. Of these, twenty-one were promulgated in 1950, ten in 1951 and the remaining five prior to the commencement of the first Lok Sabha (or Lower House) in 1952. In fact, three ordinances were promulgated on the very day the Constitution came into effect: one pertaining to 'offices of profit' and parliamentary disqualification, another regarding the 'use of seals of common form and design by the High Courts' and the third 'to declare the Judicial Commissioner's Courts in Part C States to be High Court for certain purposes'.[2] These ordinances were in addition to the large numbers of British India ordinances that were naturalised into the new legal system – measures originally enacted during World War II but, nonetheless, retained after the Constitution came into force.

Chapter 1 described Nehru's about-face on ordinances. That earlier policy continued between 1950 and 1952. Nonetheless, some allowance should also be made for the fact that those were extraordinary times, and the compulsions of change and continuity may have necessitated some of them. A quick survey of the thirty-six ordinances suggests that a large number of them involved issues of migration, transfer, rehabilitation,

[2] See the Parliament (Prevention of Disqualification) Ordinance, 1950 (12 of 1950); the High Court (Seals) Ordinance, 1950 (13 of 1950); the Judicial Commissioner's Courts Ordinances, 1950 (14 of 1950).

compensation and related matters. Obvious examples in this category include the Influx from Pakistan (Control) Amendment Ordinance, 1950;[3] the Administration of Evacuee Property (Amendment) Ordinance, 1950;[4] the Abducted Persons (Recovery and Restoration) Amendment Ordinance, 1951[5] and the Displaced Persons (Claims) Continuance Ordinance, 1952.[6] Then there were ordinances that dealt with issues of national security and state control in the aftermath of partition. Possible examples include the Preventive Detention (Amendment) Ordinance, 1950;[7] the Naval Force (Miscellaneous) Provisions Ordinance, 1950;[8] the East Punjab Public Safety (Amendment) Ordinance, 1951[9] and the Foreign Exchange Regulation (Amendment) Ordinance, 1951.[10] Finally, there were those that dealt with issues concerning national governance including income tax, tariffs, price control, essential services and industrial disputes.[11] Also, of the thirty-six ordinances, twenty were amendments to or extensions of existing legislation, fifteen were pieces of new legislation, and one involved the repeal of an existing piece of legislation. Whether defensible or otherwise, this early resort to ordinances, for diverse purposes, may have set the justificatory tone for the future. As we shall see, ordinances grew dramatically, and with time, became a cynical – and an incorrigible – feature of India's parliamentary democracy. So much so that by the republic's fifth decade, with parliament almost non-functional, ordinances surpassed acts as the preferred legislative choice. This chapter lays out the empirical data and explains the evolution of this parliamentary surrogacy.

A. ORDINANCES AND THE WRITING OF NATIONAL POLICY

Ordinances have been promulgated almost every year between 1952 and 2009. Of the fifty-eight years, 1963 is the only year without an ordinance and 1960 and 1982 have the second-best records: both years saw no more than one ordinance each. Conversely, 1993 has the worst record (as many as thirty-four ordinances were promulgated that year) and

[3] 22 of 1950.
[4] 27 of 1950.
[5] 7 of 1951.
[6] 5 of 1952.
[7] 20 of 1950.
[8] 21 of 1950.
[9] 5 of 1951.
[10] 10 of 1951.
[11] See the Indian Income-Tax (Amendment) Ordinance, 1950 (28 of 1950); the Indian Tariff (Amendment) Ordinance, 1950 (30 of 1950); the Supply and Prices of Goods Ordinance, 1950 (26 of 1950); the Essential Service (Prevention of Strikes) Ordinance, 1951 (1 of 1951); the Industrial Disputes (Amendment) Ordinance, 1951 (9 of 1951).

TABLE 2.1. *Decade-wise breakdown of ordinances*

Decade	Ordinances
1952–1959	52
1960–1969	67
1970–1979	135
1980–1989	93
1990–1999	196
2000–2009	72

1996 and 1997 were close behind with thirty-two and thirty-one ordinances, respectively.

Measured in absolute numbers, the 1970s and 1990s were the worst decades. They account for substantially more ordinances (331) than the remaining four decades combined (283). Interestingly, compared to the fifty-two ordinances promulgated during 1950s, every decade since then has produced more. This is counterintuitive. If the point of ordinances was to provide an alternative arrangement by which legislation could be immediately 'enacted' in moments of legislative crisis, the 1950s, given the challenges of putting a nation and its legal system in order, should have thrown up many more ordinances. In practice, the reverse happened. Ordinances increased as the nation matured, peaking in the 1990s at 196 – the most ever promulgated during any decade.

These numbers are unacceptably high. To put them into perspective, consider how ordinances compare with parliament's performance, measured by its success in legislating acts. Year-wise, apart from 1963, 1981 fares best: the only ordinance promulgated that year amounted to 1.36 per cent of the seventy-three Acts in the same period. Conversely, 1996 and 1997 are the worst. The thirty-two and thirty-one ordinances amounted to 88.88 per cent and 88.58 per cent, respectively, of all legislation enacted in those two years. Also, decade-wise, the 1950s fare best. As a fraction of all legislation enacted in parliament, fifty-two ordinances amount to 9.45 per cent of the 550 Acts enacted in that decade. Conversely, the 1970s and 1990s, once again, fare worst. The 132 ordinances in the 1970s amounted to 20.3 per cent of acts legislated in that decade, while the 196 ordinances in the 1990s amounted to as much as 41.88 per cent of the 468 acts enacted during that decade.

Incidentally, 468 Acts is parliament's worst legislative record for any given decade; it is even lower than the 665 Acts enacted in the 1970s,

TABLE 2.2. *Decade-wise breakdown of ordinances and Acts*

Decade	Ordinance	Acts	Ordinances over Acts (%)
1952–1959	52	550	9.45
1960–1969	67	583	11.49
1970–1979	135	665	20.3
1980–1989	93	662	14.04
1990–1999	196	468	41.88
2000–2009	72	539	13.35

notwithstanding Mrs Indira Gandhi's proclamation of 'Emergency' and its effect of parliamentary functioning. Put together, 331 ordinances in the 1970s and 1990s amount to 29.21 per cent of the 1,133 Acts legislated in that period. This is in contrast to the 283 ordinances in the remaining four decades which amount to 12.12 per cent of the 2,334 Acts that came to life during that period. Clearly, *both* in absolute numbers and as a fraction of parliamentary legislation, the 1970s and the 1990s hold the worst record for ordinances.

However, throughout the fifty-eight year period, there is no statistical correlation between parliament's legislative performance and the likelihood of ordinances. Contrary to intuitive expectations, ordinances in any given year do not necessarily rise with a fall in the number of Acts enacted that year. To make this assessment clear, Table 2.3 lists the ten

TABLE 2.3. *Top ten years with the largest number of Acts and corresponding ordinances*

Year	Acts	Ordinances
1976	118	16
1956	106	9
1985	92	8
1971	87	23
2002	86	7
1972	82	9
1952	82	4
1993	75	34
1982	73	1
1984	73	15

TABLE 2.4. *Top ten years with the smallest number of Acts and corresponding ordinances*

Year	Acts	Ordinances
2004	18	8
1990	30	10
1979	32	12
1997	35	31
1996	36	32
1967	38	9
1989	38	2
1999	39	10
1998	40	20
2009	41	9

years with the most number of Acts and the corresponding number of ordinances. In those ten years, on average, 87.4 Acts were enacted every year in comparison to the 12.6 ordinances every year during that period. Similarly, Table 2.4 lists the ten years with the least number of Acts and the corresponding number of ordinances. In those ten years, 34.7 Acts were enacted. However, the corresponding number of ordinances rose only marginally to 14.3 every year on average. In other words, a substantial drop in the number of Acts passed by parliament does not necessarily correspond to a substantial increase in ordinances promulgated by the president.[12]

With this preliminary breakdown of ordinances by decades and their comparison to Acts, we may now turn to the 'what' question. The question has two components. The first relates to the substantive content of ordinances: What *areas* of law figure prominently in the overall list of ordinances? Are ordinances concentrated in particular areas of law? The second question relates to parliament's response: How has parliament responded to the promulgation of ordinances? I shall deal with both questions in the following section.

1. Ordinances and Subject-Matter Concentrations

To make generalised comments about their substantive use, the 615 ordinances must be put in order. Accordingly, I have divided them into seven

[12] For a regression analysis of the number of parliamentary acts, their correlation with ordinances, and the corresponding *p* value, see Annex 2A.

categories: (1) administrative law (including local self-government), (2) criminal law (including criminal procedure and national security), (3) finance law (including direct and indirect taxation, banking and company affairs), (4) labour laws (including employment and service-related matters), (5) property laws (including intellectual property), (6) regulatory laws (including statutory bodies and educational institutions) and (7) ordinances relating to religious affairs (including personal law and minority rights). Needless to say, I make no claims regarding the scientificity of this categorisation, assuming that so-called scientific categories are even possible. The primary purpose, as I mentioned, is to impose some order so as to assess the systemic concentration of ordinances in the particular areas of law, if any, and to make comparisons across decades. The categorisation is useful to the extent that it covers most areas of law in largely, although not entirely, self-contained boxes.

Nonetheless, a word of clarification must be placed here, especially regarding the administrative and regulatory categories. I have used the administrative category mostly as a 'left-over' box and it is, therefore, best understood in the context of what is excluded from the regulatory category. For this latter category, I have in mind statutory bodies, professional groups, municipal bodies and educational institutions (particularly universities) established by statutes. They exist in large numbers, and are governed by statutes that often provide for their incorporation, membership, jurisdiction and related matters. Therefore, an ordinance amending the University Grants Commission Act, 1956[13] or the Indian Railways Act, 1890[14] would be classified as regulatory. The administrative category, in contrast, includes the remaining disparate areas of law that do not pertain to statutory bodies, and cannot be meaningfully included within any of the remaining four categories. Examples include laws ranging from political reforms to citizenship on one hand, and those relating to court fees or the regulation of advertisements on the other hand.

This categorisation has several weaknesses. Let me mention two obvious ones. First, there will be cases where an ordinance comfortably falls into two or more categories. An ordinance amending the Hindu Succession Act, 1956[15] – and altering the share of property to which married women are entitled – is both about property and religious-personal law. There is no formula by which to allocate such an ordinance to one category rather than another. Secondly, there will be cases where an ordinance

[13] 3 of 1956.
[14] 9 of 1890.
[15] 30 of 1956.

TABLE 2.5. *Subject-matter breakdown of ordinances*

Decade	Administrative	Criminal	Finance	Labour	Property	Regulatory	Religion
1952–1959	17	03	13	06	05	08	–
1960–1969	23	05	16	02	09	12	–
1970–1979	34	13	21	14	30	22	01
1980–1989	30	17	07	05	18	12	04
1990–1999	72	11	34	20	09	47	03
2000–2009	20	05	16	02	01	28	–
Total	196	54	107	49	72	129	08

is relevant to a number of categories, but does not easily fit into any of them. An ordinance regulating foreign exchange has some connection with finance, property and administration, but does not fit easily into any of them. In all such cases of both 'equal treatment' and 'under treatment', some degree of authorial discretion is inevitable. Bearing these limits in mind, we may turn to an overview of the substantive use of ordinances.

Table 2.5 makes it clear that with the exception of 'religious affairs', ordinances are present across the broad range of topics. Not surprisingly, the 'administrative' (198) and 'regulatory' (129) categories dominate the table, followed by 'finance' (107) and 'property' (72), with 'criminal' (54) and 'labour' (49) coming in last. Whereas these numbers reveal the broad distribution of ordinances, the decade-wise breakdown suggests some interesting trends. The 1990s account for the most number of ordinances in the 'administrative', 'finance', 'labour' and 'regulatory' categories in any given decade, but criminal law-related ordinances are the highest in the 1980s, and the same is true of property law-related ordinances in the 1970s. The 'administrative' category dominates in all decades, with the exception of the 2000s, which threw up more 'regulatory' ordinances (28) than 'administrative' ones (20). However, compared to the distribution of ordinances in the 1950s, the 'regulatory' category registered the highest growth in the subsequent decades. There were eight of those in the 1950s; by the 1990s, the number had swollen to forty-seven. And although it declined to twenty-eight in the 2000s, as mentioned earlier, it was still higher than the number of ordinances in the 'administrative' category.

A closer look at these ordinances reveals three noteworthy concentrations. First, in the area of nationalisation, ordinances were systematically used to implement policies dear to relevant cabinets. Nehru was the architect of the tradition. Consider this: On 19 January 1956, Nehru's cabinet brought in the Life Insurance (Emergency Provisions) Ordinance, 1956, effectively nationalising the life insurance business in India.[16] It took over the management of 109 Indian and 3 foreign companies exclusively dedicated to life insurance. In addition, of the forty Indian and thirteen foreign companies that offered both life and other insurance products, the ordinance vested the life insurance management of these businesses in the government.[17] In an extensive broadcast to the nation, Finance Minister C. D. Deshmukh defended the law. The nationalisation, he said, 'was a step in the direction of more effective mobilisation of the people's savings', especially because 'with a second plan in the offing... deepening of all possible channels of public savings had become more than ever necessary'.[18] But he also railed against, what was to him, the inefficiency of the market players. 'During the last decade, as many as twenty-five life insurance companies went into liquidation and another twenty-five had so frittered away their resources that their business had to be transferred to other companies at a loss to the policy-holders'.[19] This 'misuse of power, position and privilege', he claimed, was 'one of the most compelling reasons that [had] influenced [them] in deciding to nationalise life insurance'.[20]

Whatever the merits of the argument, Deshmukh never explained why an *ordinance* was necessary. Recall that Article 123 is limited to circumstances when it is necessary to take 'immediate action'. The previous session of parliament had ended three weeks earlier on 23 December 1955, and the next session was another three weeks away. Given the circumstances, was immediate action necessary? If anything, Deshmukh's claim that the decision was taken after 'a full examination of the views expressed by the interests involved' and 'public debate and discussion for several months' suggests otherwise.[21] It was a meticulous policy choice – one that had been in the works for a long period of time.[22] The ordinance, in that sense, was neither immediately made, nor immediately required.

[16] 1 of 1956.

[17] Anon, '165 Firms Will Be Affected' *Times of India*, 20 January 1956.

[18] Anon, 'Insurance Firms "Misused" Power and Privilege' *Times of India*, 20 January 1956. See also, 'Insurance Nationalisation Helps Plan' *Times of India*, 21 January 1956.

[19] *Ibid.* See also, Anon, 'Life Insurance to Be Nationalised with Immediate Effect' *Times of India*, 20 January 1956.

[20] *Ibid.* See also, Kamal Kabra, 'Nationalisation of Life Insurance in India', 21 (47) *Economic and Political Weekly* 2045–2053 (22 November 1986).

[21] *Ibid.*

[22] See Anon, 'Loss to Foreign Markets' *Times of India*, 20 January 1956.

The *Times of India*, in a perceptive editorial, pointed this out: 'What prompted the Government to resort to an ordinance which is only meant for meeting an emergency is puzzling'.[23] It was an 'unprecedented step' and 'democratic traditions', the editorial argued, 'at least demanded that the Lok Sabha should have been called upon to give its verdict on the Government's intention'.[24] In taking recourse to an ordinance, Nehru's cabinet showed its reluctance to treat the limits in Article 123 seriously. And it set a precedent regarding nationalisation and ordinances, the full force of which would only come to life during Mrs Indira Gandhi's long tenure as India's prime minister.

With the exception of about three years from early 1977 to early 1980, Mrs Indira Gandhi held India's reigns from 1966 to 1984. During that period, she led India through a socialist phase – one that has been extensively studied and commented on. As Austin describes in some detail, Mrs Gandhi's socialist beliefs initially – and her actions later on – were egged on by factionalism in the Congress Party, her personal quest for complete authority and electoral dividends.[25] But less well known about the program is its prodigious reliance on ordinances. At the core of this socialist program was the call for nationalisation – of banks in particular, but also of other 'productive forces in the economy'. Although bank nationalisation had been part of the Congress platform since 1956, it was only in 1963 that the idea took centre stage in parliamentary debates. By 1967, the drum beats grew deafening and eventually found its way into the Congress manifesto as the party's official position.[26] But Mrs Gandhi's tryst with ordinances, although mostly associated with bank nationalisation, did not begin there. Nor did it take up most of her ordinance-related 'space'. In fact, of the at least thirty ordinances promulgated between 1966 and 1984 nationalising various industries, firms or parts thereof, only three pertained to banks. The rest fell into a miscellaneous category that ranged from metals and coal to shipping, textiles and cars.

[23] Anon, 'Hasty Decision' *Times of India*, 21 January 1956.

[24] *Ibid.* Similarly, Cowasji Jehangir, the chairman of the Board of Directors of the Oriental Government Security and Life Insurance Company, claimed that the ordinance was 'undemocratic' and 'there was no reason for doing so unless Government feared opposition and criticism'. Anon, 'Cowasji Jehangir: Ordinance Is Undemocratic' *Times of India*, 21 January 1956.

[25] Glanville Austin, *Working a Democratic Constitution* 173–195 (Oxford University Press, New Delhi, 1999).

[26] See Michelguglielmo Torri, 'Factional Politics and Economic Policy: The Case of India's Bank Nationalisation', 15(12) *Asian Survey* 1077–1096 (December 1975).

The spate of ordinances began with the managerial takeover of the Jayanti Shipping Company in 1966.[27] The company's liabilities abroad had grown significantly and that, the cabinet said, was 'likely to [damage] the prestige of Indian flag ships as a whole'.[28] In classic interventionist style, a bureaucrat took office as the chairman, and later handed over the management to the state-owned Shipping Corporation of India.[29] The 1966 Ordinance was only for five years, and limited to the management of the firm. But in 1971, by another ordinance, the company's shares also transferred to the state, thereby becoming a full-fledged government company.[30] Although the reasons were never fully explained, the template was then set: 'market failure' and 'national productivity' were the reasons, ordinances were the means and nationalisation was the end result. As the decade progressed, the template was applied to at least nineteen other firms – including Asian Refractories, Indian Copper Corporation, Indian Coal & Steel Company, Caltex, British India Corporation and most spectacularly, Maruti Limited – whose management and shares were taken over in similar manner. This pronounced reliance on ordinances primarily accounts for the fact that compared to the other decades, the 1970s had the most number of 'property' ordinances.

Industries were also nationalised, including general insurance,[31] coke,[32] textiles[33] and coal.[34] But bank nationalisation is the most compelling story of them all. Although plans for nationalising banks had been floating around for some time, Mrs Gandhi considered it to be the principal vehicle by which to cement herself as the leader of the government *and* the party. On the evening of 18 July 1969, a senior draftsman from the Law Ministry, S. K. Maitra, was ordered by the Prime Minister's Secretariat to draft an ordinance. He did so in the company of top bureaucrats – including I. G. Patel, L. K. Jha and D. N. Ghose – who

27 The Jayanti Shipping Company (Taking over of Management) Ordinance, 1966 (1 of 1966).

28 Anon, 'Shipping Corporation to Manage Jayanti' *Times of India*, 11 June 1966.

29 *Ibid.*

30 The Jayanti Shipping Company (Acquisition of Shares) Ordinance, 1971 (14 of 1971).

31 The General Insurance (Emergency Provisions) Ordinance, 1971 (6 of 1971). Anon, 'Govt. to Control General Insurance' *Times of India*, 14 May 1971; Anon, 'Mixed Reaction to Step' *Times of India*, 14 May 1971.

32 The Coking Coal Mines (Emergency Provisions) Ordinance, 1971 (12 of 1971). Anon, 'Govt. to Manage Coking Coal Mines' *Times of India*, 17 October 1971.

33 The Sick Textile Undertakings (Nationalisation) Ordinance, 1974 (12 of 1974). Anon, 'Centre Takes Over Forty Six "Sick" Mills' *Times of India*, 1 November 1972.

34 The Coal Mines (Taking over of Management) Ordinance, 1973 (1 of 1973). Anon, 'Ordinance Issued on Non-Coking Coal Mines' *Times of India*, 31 January 1973.

TABLE 2.6. *List of Mrs Gandhi's acquisitions through ordinances*

Ordinance	No.	Date
1. The Jayanti Shipping Company (Taking over of Management) Ordinance, 1966	4 of 1966	10.06.66
2. The Metal Corporation of India (Acquisition of Undertaking) Ordinance, 1966	10 of 1966	13.09.66
3. The Banking Companies (Acquisition and Transfer of Undertaking) Ordinance, 1969	8 of 1969	19.07.69
4. The Banking Companies (Acquisition and Transfer of Undertaking) Ordinance, 1970	3 of 1970	14.02.70
5. The General Insurance (Emergency Provisions) Ordinance, 1971	6 of 1971	13.05.71
6. The Coking Coal Mines (Emergency Provisions) Ordinance, 1971	12 of 1971	16.10.71
7. The Asian Refractories Limited (Acquisition of Undertaking) Ordinance, 1971	13 of 1971	17.10.71
8. The Jayanti Shipping Company (Acquisition of Shares) Ordinance, 1971	14 of 1971	17.10.71
9. The Indian Copper Corporation (Taking over of Management) Ordinance, 1972	4 of 1972	10.03.72
10. The Indian Iron and Steel Company (Taking over of Management) Ordinance, 1972	6 of 1972	14.07.72
11. The Sick Textile Undertaking (Taking over of Management) Ordinance, 1972	9 of 1972	31.10.72
12. The Coal Mines (Taking over of Management) Ordinance, 1973	1 of 1973	30.01.73
13. The Konkan Passenger Ships (Acquisition) Ordinance, 1973	4 of 1973	07.11.73
14. The Sick Textile Undertakings (Nationalisation) Ordinance, 1974	12 of 1974	21.09.74
15. The Coal Mines (Nationalisation) Ordinance, 1976	3 of 1976	29.04.76
16. The Burn Company and Indian Standard Wagon Company (Nationalisation) Ordinance, 1976	8 of 1976	23.06.76
17. The Indian Iron and Steel Company (Acquisition of Shares) Ordinance, 1976	10 of 1976	17.07.76
18. The Laxmirattan and Atherton West Cotton Mills (Taking over of Management) Ordinance, 1976	11of 1976	19.07.76
19. The Metal Corporation of India (Nationalisation and Miscellaneous Provisions) Ordinance, 1976	12 of 1976	02.08.76
20. The Caltex (Acquisition of Shares of Caltex Oil Refining) Limited Ordinance, 1976	15 of 1976	30.12.76

(*continued*)

TABLE 2.6 *(continued)*

Ordinance	No.	Date
21. The Banking Companies (Acquisition and Transfer of Undertaking) Ordinance, 1980	3 of 1980	15.04.80
22. The National Company Limited (Acquisition and Transfer of Undertaking) Ordinance, 1980	4 of 1980	27.04.80
23. The Maruti Limited (Acquisition and Transfer of Undertaking) Ordinance, 1980	13 of 1980	13.10.80
24. The Bird and Company Limited (Acquisition and Transfer of Undertakings and other Properties) Ordinance, 1980	18 of 1980	25.10.80
25. The British India Corporation (Acquisition of Shares) Ordinance, 1981	5 of 1981	11.06.81
26. The Dalmia Dadri Cement Limited (Acquisition and Transfer of Undertakings) Ordinance, 1981	6 of 1981	23.06.81
27. The Textile Undertakings (Taking over of Management) Ordinance, 1983	10 of 1983	08.10.83
28. The Transformer and Switchgear Limited (Acquisition and Transfer of Undertakings) Ordinance, 1983	11 of 1983	08.11.83
29. The Ganesh Flour Mills Company Limited (Acquisition and Transfer of Undertakings) Ordinance, 1984	2 of 1984	28.01.84
30. The Incheck Types Limited and National Rubber Manufactures (Nationalisation) Ordinance, 1984	4 of 1984	14.02.84
31. The Hooghly Docking and Engineering Company Limited (Acquisition and Transfer of Undertakings) Ordinance, 1984	7 of 1984	28.06.84

provided both philosophical and provisional inputs. Early the next morning, Mrs Gandhi looked through the draft and made minor modifications.[35] Later, approved unopposed by a cabinet that had neither seen nor heard about it earlier, the draft was sent to President V. V. Giri, who signed it into law.[36] A day later, parliament came back to session.

Although egregious, Mrs Gandhi's recourse to the bank nationalisation ordinance was not novel: after all, in Nehru, she had an august

[35] *Supra* n. 25 at 214–215.

[36] The Banking Companies (Acquisition and Transfer of Undertaking) Ordinance, 1969 (3 of 1970). Anon, 'Top Fourteen Banks Are Nationalised' *Times of India*, 20 July 1969.

precedent. But as before, the criticisms were sharp. M. R. Masani and C. Rajagopalachari, leaders of the free-market Swatantra Party (SP), criticized the takeover, and not just for policy reasons. An ordinance, a day before parliament was to convene, they said, 'was immoral'.[37] A. B. Vajpayee, then president of the Jan Sangh (JS), made a similar point. Imposing a far-reaching decision on the nation 'through the backdoor of an ordinance and that too just on the eve of the Parliament session is in itself proof', he said, 'that the Government is afraid of facing Parliament in a straightforward manner'.[38] Nani Palkiwala would later present that as a 'legal argument' in *R. C. Cooper v. Union of India*.[39] But in the immediate context, none of that mattered anymore. As a *Times of India* editorial put it, 'the die [was] cast'.[40] Whereas ordinances in Article 123 were established as temporary measures that eventually required formal parliamentary approval, by 1969 – in practice – there was clearly no going back after promulgation.[41] Ordinances by then had acquired a firm quality, such that, once promulgated, it only had the effect of tying parliament's hand.

Second, there is also a systematic concentration of ordinances in the area of 'national security' legislation. With the sole exception of the Terrorist and Disruptive Activities Act, 1985,[42] *every* major security-related Act in independent India has been introduced through an ordinance. As with nationalisation, here, too, Nehru set the trend. On 17 May 1958, his cabinet promulgated the Armed Forces (Assam and Manipur) Special Powers Ordinance, 1958[43] – the parliamentary version of which remains in effect even after six decades. Nehru visited the Nagaland region in 1953 for the first – and only – time, and felt slighted by an entire audience that walked out on him, slapping their bottoms.[44] He never went

[37] Anon, 'C. R. Doubts Validity of Ordinance' *Times of India*, 19 July 1969.

[38] Anon, 'UF Circles Hail Bank Nationalisation' *Times of India*, 20 July 1969.

[39] 1970 (3) SCR 550. Anon, 'Banking Ordinance is Challenged' *Times of India*, 22 July 1969.

[40] Anon, 'The Die Is Cast' *Times of India*, 21 July 1969.

[41] This practice, as I shall explain in Chapter 3, eventually earned a legal status when the Supreme Court ruled that even ordinances that fail to secure parliamentary approval can create permanent effects.

[42] 31 of 1985.

[43] 1 of 1958.

[44] Charles Chasie and Sanjoy Hazarika, 'The State Strikes Back: India and the Naga Insurgency', Policy Studies 52, East West Center, Washington D.C., 2009, p. 15 *available at*: http://www.eastwestcenter.org/fileadmin/stored/pdfs/ps052.pdf (accessed 13 January 2012). See also, Ramchandra Guha, *India After Gandhi: The History of the World's Largest Democracy* 276 (Harper Collins, New York, 2007).

back. We do not know if the humiliation hardened his attitude towards the region, but the ordinance that came into force was irredeemably harsh and sweeping. Under the law, Assam and Manipur, if declared to be in 'disturbed or dangerous condition', could rely on the armed forces to maintain 'public order'.[45] Subject to certain (rather arbitrary) conditions, officers were authorised to 'fire upon' or cause the death of any person, destroy 'any shelter', 'arrest, without warrant, any person' or 'enter and search without warrant any premises'.[46] Importantly, for all such actions, the law gave the armed forces near complete immunity.[47] Two weeks after the ordinance came into effect, Chief Commissioner of Manipur, J. N. Raina, citing 'depredation by Naga rebels', confirmed his interest to call 'in the army in the aid of civil authorities'.[48] Since then, there has been no looking back. The ordinance later became an Act, and future cabinets gradually introduced it to new areas including Punjab[49] and Jammu and Kashmir.[50]

The ordinance came under withering criticism from the very moment it was promulgated. In parliament, Surendra Mahanty of the little-known Gantantra Parishad Party described it as a 'martial law' – one that turned free India into a 'free India with barbed wires and concentration camps'.[51] More recently, several human rights organizations have sternly criticized the law[52] and its implementation.[53] In 2005, even the government-appointed Jeevan Reddy Committee[54] recommended that it be repealed, finding that the law was 'too sketchy, too bald and quite

[45] § 3, Armed Forces (Assam and Manipur) Special Powers Ordinance, 1958.

[46] *Id.* at § 4.

[47] *Id.* at § 6.

[48] Anon, 'Army's Help to Be Sought if Necessary' *Times of India*, 4 June 1958; Anon, 'Fighting Naga Rebels: Aid of Armed Forces' *Times of India*, 7 June 1958.

[49] The Armed Forces (Punjab and Chandigarh) Special Powers Act, 1983 (34 of 1983).

[50] The Armed Forces (Jammu and Kashmir) Special Powers Act, 1990 (21 of 1990).

[51] Samantha Subramaniam, 'The Long View: AFSPA's Bitter Roots' *New York Times*, 21 November 2011 *available at*: http://india.blogs.nytimes.com/2011/11/21/the-long-view-afspas-bitter-roots/#more-8705 (accessed 13 January 2012).

[52] See, e.g., South Asia Human Rights Documentation Centre, 'Armed Forces Special Powers Act: A Study in National Security Tyranny', *available at*: http://www.hrdc.net/sahrdc/resources/armed_forces.htm (accessed 13 January 2012).

[53] See Amnesty International, 'Briefing on the Armed Forces (Special Powers) Act, 1958, Asa 20/025/2005' *available at*: http://web.amnesty.org/library/pdf/ASA200252005ENGLISH/$File/ASA2002505.pdf (accessed 13 January 2012). See also, Anon, 'Getting Away with Murder: 50 Years of the Armed Forces Special Powers Act' *Human Rights Watch*, August 2008, *available at*: http://www.hrw.org/legacy/backgrounder/2008/india0808/india0808webwcover.pdf (accessed 13 January 2012).

[54] Ministry of Home Affairs Office Order No. 11011/97/2004-NE-III (19 November 2004).

inadequate in several particulars'.[55] It has become, the committee concluded, 'a symbol of oppression, an object of hate and an instrument of discrimination and highhandedness' and, therefore, was best done away with'.[56] Even though these criticisms are important and fair, they are not novel. Nehru, for example, was fully cognizant of the law's 'invasive' potential and its effect on human rights. And yet, in parliamentary debates, he upheld the security – and unity – of the Indian state as paramount. Fearing the 'fascist methods' of private groups, he insisted that government had 'to deal with violence whatever the reason for it', or risk turning 'infirm'.[57] That, unfortunately, is a lesson future prime ministers and their cabinets conveniently took to heart. In keeping with Nehru's precedent, nearly all national security-related laws were promulgated as ordinances and only later enacted as Acts.

Table 2.7 lists the national security-related ordinances that have been promulgated in the last five decades. In particular, note the manner in which they have come from cabinets across the political spectrum. Mrs Indira Gandhi and her cabinets from 1966 to 1984 promulgated, amongst others, the Unlawful Activities (Prevention) Ordinance, 1964;[58] the Maintenance of Internal Security Ordinance, 1971[59] and several amendments to it; the National Security Ordinance, 1980[60] and the Terrorist Affected Areas (Special Courts) Ordinance, 1984.[61] The Rajiv Gandhi cabinet promulgated, amongst others, the all-too-important Terrorist and Disruptive Activities (Prevention) Amendment Ordinance, 1987[62] and several amendments to the National Security Ordinance, 1980.[63] The Vishwanath Singh cabinet representing the National Front (NF) Government promulgated the Armed Forces Special Powers (Jammu and Kashmir) Ordinance, 1990,[64] whereas its successor, the Chandra Shekhar

[55] Justice B. P. Jeevan Reddy Committee Report on the Armed Forces (Special Powers) Act 1958, 74 *available at*: http://www.hindu.com/nic/afa/afa-part-iv.pdf (accessed 15 January 2012).

[56] *Id.* at 75. Parenthetically, it should be noted that the Supreme Court had upheld the constitutionality of the law in *Naga People's Movement for Human Rights v. Union of India* AIR1998 SC 431.

[57] *Supra* n. 51 *ibid.*

[58] 6 of 1966. See R. Subrahmanyam, 'The Unlawful Activities (Prevention) Act, 1967: A Legislative Case Study', 2 *Journal of Constitutional and Parliamentary Studies* 111 (1968).

[59] 5 of 1971.

[60] 11 of 1980.

[61] 9 of 1984.

[62] 2 of 1987.

[63] See, e.g., The National Security (Amendment) Ordinances, 1987 (3 of 1987).

[64] 3 of 1990.

TABLE 2.7. *List of 'national security'–related legislation introduced through ordinances*

1. The Armed Forces (Assam and Manipur) Special Powers Ordinance, 1958	1 of 1958	22.05.58
2. The Defence of India Ordinance, 1962	4 of 1962	26.10.62
3. The Armed Forces (Special Powers) Continuance Ordinance, 1964	1 of 1964	02.04.64
4. The Unlawful Activities (Prevention) Ordinance, 1966	6 of 1966	17.06.66
5. The Maintenance of Internal Security Ordinance, 1971	5 of 1971	07.05.71
6. The Maintenance of Internal Security (Amendment) Ordinance, 1974	11 of 1974	17.09.74
7. The Maintenance of Internal Security (Amendment) Ordinance, 1975	4 of 1975	29.06.75
8. The Maintenance of Internal Security (Second Amendment) Ordinance, 1975	7 of 1975	15.07.75
9. The Maintenance of Internal Security (Fourth Amendment) Ordinance, 1975	22 of 1975	16.11.75
10. The Maintenance of Internal Security (Amendment) Ordinance, 1976	5 of 1976	16.06.76
11. The National Security Ordinance, 1980	11 of 1980	22.09.80
12. The Punjab Disturbed Areas Ordinance, 1983	5 of 1983	07.10.83
13. The Chandigarh Disturbed Areas Ordinance, 1983	6 of 1983	07.10.83
14. The Armed Forces (Punjab and Chandigarh) Special Powers Ordinance, 1983	9 of 1983	15.10.83
15. The National Security (Amendment) Ordinance, 1984	5 of 1984	05.04.84
16. The National Security (Second Amendment) Ordinance, 1984	6 of 1984	21.06.84
17. The Terrorist Affected Areas (Special Courts) Ordinance, 1984	9 of 1984	14.07.84
18. The Terrorist and Disruptive Activities (Prevention) Amendment Ordinance, 1985	4 of 1985	05.06.85
19. The Terrorist and Disruptive Activities (Prevention) Amendment Ordinance, 1987	2 of 1987	23.05.87
20. The National Security (Amendment) Ordinances, 1987	3 of 1987	09.06.87
21. The National Security (Amendment) Ordinances, 1988	4 of 1988	26.05.88
22. The Armed Forces (Jammu and Kashmir) Special Powers Ordinance, 1990	3 of 1990	05.07.90
23. The Terrorist and Disruptive Activities (Prevention) Amendment Ordinance, 1991	5 of 1991	02.05.91
24. The Prevention of Terrorism Ordinance, 2001	9 of 2001	24.10.01
25. The Prevention of Terrorism (Amendment) Second Ordinance, 2001	12 of 2001	30.12.01
26. The Unlawful Activities (Prevention) Amendment Ordinance, 2004	2 of 2004	21.09.04

cabinet, brought in the Terrorist and Disruptive Activities (Prevention) Amendment Ordinance, 1991.[65] In 2001, the Vajpayee cabinet representing the NDA Government promulgated the Prevention of Terrorism Ordinance, 2001 and later re-promulgated it.[66] Most recently, in 2004, the Manmohan Singh cabinet representing the UPA Government brought in the Unlawful Activities (Prevention) Amendment Ordinance,[67] one that repealed the existing law against terrorism, but retained several of its important provisions as part of another piece of legislation.[68] As the list of twenty-six ordinances shows, unlike nationalisation, Nehruvian legacy on national-security ordinances endures. The template ('ordinances') and rationale ('state monopoly on violence') have stayed the same; only the 'enemy' has changed with time. This repeated – and multipartisan – reliance on ordinances to enact anti-terror measures can only be described as, what Rajeev Dhawan once called, creating legislation 'by cheating democracy'.[69]

Third, nationalisation and national security apart, the 1990s and 2000s also threw up a curious concentration of ordinances establishing national bodies including the Securities and Exchange Board of India (SEBI),[70] the National Human Rights Commission (NHRC)[71] and the Central Vigilance Commission (CVC).[72] As Table 2.8 shows, these are – or were intended to be – important national regulatory agencies whose establishment required thorough understanding and careful consideration. But the reliance on ordinances in creating them raises both principled and pragmatic concerns. On one hand, this is incontrovertible evidence that cabinets have effectively written off the 'immediate' requirement in Article 123. That a mechanism meant for immediate action should be used to establish national bodies is a telling indictment of how far ordinances have intruded into India's parliamentary space. On the other

[65] 5 of 1991.

[66] 9 of 2001.

[67] 12 of 2001.

[68] 2 of 2004. For analysis on many of these anti-terror legislation, see Anil Kalhan, Gerald P. Conroy, Mamta Kaushal and Sam Scott Miller, 'Colonial Continuities: Human Rights, Terrorism, and Security Laws in India', 20 *Columbia Journal of Asian Law* 93 (2006–2007). See also Derek P. Jinks, 'The Anatomy of an Institutionalized Emergency: Preventive Detention and Personal Liberty in India', 22 *Michigan Journal of International Law* 311 (2001).

[69] Rajeev Dhavan, 'Op-Ed, Terrorism by Ordinance' *The Hindu*, 1 October 2004, available at: http://www.hindu.com/2004/10/01/stories/2004100104781000.htm (accessed 13 January 2012).

[70] 5 of 1992.

[71] 30 of 1993.

[72] 4 of 1999.

TABLE 2.8. *List of national institutions established through ordinances*

1. The Securities and Exchange Board of India Ordinance, 1992	5 of 1992	31.01.1992
2. The National Commission for Backward Classes Ordinance, 1993	23 of 1993	01.02.1993
3. The Protection of Human Rights Ordinance, 1993	30 of 1993	28.09.1993
4. The National Institute of Pharmaceutical Education and Research (Second) Ordinance, 1998	9 of 1998	23.04.1998
5. The Central Vigilance Commission Ordinance, 1998	15 of 1998	25.08.1999
6. The National Tax Tribunal Ordinance, 2003	3 of 2003	16.10.2003
7. The National Commission for Minority Educational Institutions Ordinance, 2004	6 of 2004	11.11.2004
8. The Pension Fund Regulatory and Development Authority Ordinance, 2004	8 of 2004	29.12.2004

hand, pragmatically speaking, because of their often hasty promulgation, implementation under ordinances, especially on complex matters, is rarely optimal. Often, they leave much to be desired.

Two examples should easily drive home these points. First, take the establishment of the NHRC. The 1993 ordinance created a national body and similar agencies at the state level with the authority to inquire into allegations of human rights abuses, review legislative and constitutional safeguards, study international treaties and conventions and promote human rights literacy in India.[73] As part of its inquiring or investigative functions, the body was vested with the powers of a civil court including the power to summon and enforce attendance of witnesses, receive evidence, requisition public records and issue commissions.[74] When created, it was a national milestone, and partly in furtherance of international obligations.[75] Benign as it may have been, the question still remains: Was an *ordinance* needed? While explaining its salient features at a news conference, senior government officials boasted of the law's 'deliberated' status. It was 'an entirely new kind of legislation', they claimed, 'drafted

[73] § 12, the Protection of Human Rights Act, 1993.

[74] *Id.* at § 13.

[75] See Principles relating to the Status of National Institutions (The Paris Principles) (48/134 of 20 December 1993) *available at*: http://www2.ohchr.org/english/law/parisprinciples.htm (accessed 13 January 2012). In its early days, the commission was viewed with grave suspicion. See, e.g., Anon, 'Human Rights Panel a "Fraud on People"' *Times of India*, 8 December 1993; Anon, 'Parliament Okays Rights Bill' *Times of India*, 23 December 1993. For a more optimistic early assessment, see Anon, 'To Right Wrongs' *Times of India*, 4 October 1993.

after sixteen months of intense discussions'.[76] 'All shades of public opinion' were heard, including consultations with federal ministries and state governments.[77] If true, these expansive briefings take away the very justification for the ordinance: something written, reviewed and revised during a period of sixteen months cannot plausibly claim the mantle of urgency. After all, ordinances are precisely meant for occasions when such deliberations are not possible. It is in this sense that successive cabinets have written off the 'immediate' requirement in Article 123: The provision has morphed into a parallel legislative mechanism that may be invoked at will.

Second, consider the establishment of SEBI. Set up in 1992 by an ordinance, the board as the chief regulator of capital markets in India was given wide jurisdiction. Amongst others, it had the power to regulate the business of stock exchanges and the workings of brokers, agents, trustees, underwriters and the like; prohibit fraudulent and unfair trade practices; review substantial acquisition or takeovers and enact related regulations.[78] The ordinance came at a time when India was jettisoning its socialist shackles, and it became necessary to provide for an independent regulator to write and implement rules regarding investor activities. But the price of hasty promulgation soon became evident. Five days after the ordinance was promulgated, SEBI knew nothing about it.[79] Chairman G. V. Ramakrishna pleaded ignorance when asked about the new law. 'I have still not got a copy . . . [but only] bits and pieces from the press', he said.[80] It later became clear that the ordinance had been drafted without due consultations and in a way that kept the board under the government's leash. The finance ministry retained both direct and supervisory control over policies, making it unlikely that the board would function efficiently or independently.[81] The effect of hasty actions became even more apparent when the government repealed the Capital Issues Control Act, 1947,[82] thereby allowing Indian companies to make public issues of capital with or without premium, so long as they made necessary disclosures to the SEBI.[83] But SEBI, once again, knew nothing of this.

[76] Anon, 'Human Rights Body to Be Set Up' *Times of India*, 30 September 1993.
[77] *Ibid.*
[78] § 11, the Securities and Exchange Board of India Act, 1992.
[79] Sucheta Dalal, 'SEBI Clueless on Ordinance' *Times of India*, 20 February 1992.
[80] *Ibid.*
[81] *Ibid.* See also Sucheta Dalal, 'Ordinance Likely on Powers of SEBI' *Times of India*, 15 January 1992.
[82] 29 of 1947.
[83] The Capital Issues (Control) Repeal Ordinance, 1992 (9 of 1992).

When asked about the necessary disclosures, authorities at SEBI could do little more than assert that disclosure rules were still being written.[84] India's capital markets, as Sucheta Dalal put it, were in a 'confused' state.[85] Here, then, was a case of a hastily promulgated ordinance that when implemented, proved embarrassing. NHRC and SEBI, in that sense, exemplify the competing challenges of relying on ordinances. When duly drafted and debated over a period of time, it undercuts the principled rationale for an ordinance. But when done hastily, it exposes the pragmatic challenges of efficiently authoring and implementing an ordinance, especially on complex matters.

Taken together, the three concentrations – nationalisation, national security and national bodies – give us a basic view of ordinances and their expansive presence in India. Clearly, both numerically and substantively, they are widely prevalent in India; so much so that without a proper study of ordinances, an assessment of India's parliamentary credentials is seems incomplete. Keeping in mind this introductory account of the substantive use of ordinances, we may now turn to the related question: How has parliament responded to these ordinances?

2. *Parliamentary Responses to Ordinances*

In theory, a cabinet resorts to an ordinance as a temporary measure when at least one house of parliament is not in session. When parliament reassembles, every ordinance, in keeping with Article 123(2), must be laid 'before both Houses'. At that point, one of four outcomes is largely possible. First, the ordinance may become an Act through the normal legislative procedure that is, from the cabinet's point of view, the best-case scenario. This must be done within six weeks of reassembly of parliament.[86] Second, the ordinance may be put to vote, but 'disapproved' or rejected by parliament, which is, from the cabinet's point of view, the worst-case scenario. In such a case, the ordinance immediately ceases to operate.[87] Third, the cabinet may, for a variety of reasons, decide against putting the ordinance to vote at all. That is to say, it may let the ordinance 'die' – or lapse. Lastly, the cabinet may 'withdraw' an ordinance.[88]

[84] Sucheta Dalal, 'Decontrol without a Framework' *Times of India*, 2 June 1992.
[85] Sucheta Dalal, 'Confusion Compounded' *Times of India*, 5 July 1992.
[86] Constitution of India, Article 123 (2)(a).
[87] Constitution of India, Article 123 (2)(a).
[88] Constitution of India, Article 123 (2)(b).

TABLE 2.9. *Parliamentary responses to ordinances*

	Became Acts	Disapproved	Lapsed	Withdrawn	Re-promulgated
1952–1959	48	–	03	01	–
1960–1969	62	–	05	–	–
1970–1979	122	–	12	01	–
1980–1989	83	–	10	–	–
1990–1999	107	–	36	–	53
2000–2009	56	–	10	–	06

These four outcomes fall into two broad categories. The first outcome is the 'successful' one: Here, an ordinance becomes an Act and acquires permanence. Although for different reasons, the remaining three outcomes share an 'unsuccessful' quality: In each of these cases, an ordinance ends as an ordinance; it does not become an Act. If unsuccessful, an ordinance 'ceases to operate' immediately on rejection by parliament, or after the expiry of six weeks from the date of reassembly of parliament if it is because of lapse or withdrawal. Parenthetically, it may be noted that a fifth outcome is also possible. If a cabinet so chooses, it may re-promulgate an unsuccessful ordinance after the reassembled parliament is no longer in session. But a re-promulgated ordinance is still an ordinance, and will eventually meet one of the four outcomes mentioned earlier.

Table 2.9 lists the ways in which parliament has responded to ordinances thus far. Of the 615 ordinances, 478 (77.7 per cent) 'succeeded'; they became Acts. Of the 'unsuccessful' ones, seventy-five (12.1 per cent) expired (or lapsed); fifty-nine (9.5 per cent) were re-promulgated and two (.003 per cent) were withdrawn. These numbers when plotted decade-wise show a marginal decline in the percentage of successful ordinances. The 1950s had the lowest number of ordinances and nearly the highest conversion rate: Fifty-two ordinances were promulgated and forty-eight of them became Acts (92.3 per cent). The success rate in the 1960s was 92.5 per cent; 90.3 per cent in the 1970s, 89.2 per cent in the 1980s and 77.7 per cent in the 2000s. The 1990s is the outlier. Of the 196 ordinances promulgated during that decade, only 107 (54.5 per cent) became Acts. As many as eighty-nine failed, of which thirty-six (18.3 per cent) expired and another fifty-three (27 per cent) were re-promulgated. These low rates of success were brought about by poor performances in several years. For example, in 1995, of the fifteen ordinances promulgated, only six became Acts. The year 1996 did worse: Thirty-two were promulgated and only nine became Acts. Similarly, in 1997, thirty-one were promulgated and only eleven became Acts. Taken together, the 1990s, in a neat contrast to the 1950s, had the most number of ordinances and the worst conversion rate.

Incidentally, the second possibility – that of a resolution by both houses disapproving an ordinance – has never materialized. Reasons for this are not too difficult to guess. First, it is highly unlikely, although not impossible, for a government to be in a minority in both houses. Second, in case of majority governments, cabinets are likely to take all precautions – including three-line whips – to avoid parliamentary embarrassment. As such, a disapproving resolution is only really likely in a situation where another government has taken office after the promulgation of an ordinance, and the new cabinet wishes to make a *political* point against the previous office holders. There are no legal reasons to bring forth a resolution. A disapproved ordinance immediately ceases to operate, in contrast, to an expired (or lapsed) ordinance that ceases to operate at the end of six weeks from the date of reassembly of parliament. Therefore, the legal consequences of a disapproving resolution and expiry are the same, except that the former brings an ordinance to an end slightly earlier in time.

Of the options that have materialised so far, some clarifications must be included here. In particular, the connection between ordinances that became Acts and the ones that expired is worth noting. They are represented in separate columns, but the distinction is not always clear. That is because, in practice, expiry can be of three kinds. First, there may be cases where an ordinance expires and nothing else happens: we may call them 'simple' expiry. Second, there may be cases where an ordinance expires, but a new Act covering the same ground is legislated into law within a short period of time: we may call them 'formal' expiry. It has happened several times. For example, the Armed Forces (Special Powers) Continuance Ordinance, 1956 was promulgated on 2 February 1964.[89] Parliament came back into session on 10 February. Six weeks later, the ordinance expired. Nonetheless, an Act with similar provisions became law on 9 May 1964.[90] The delay here, it seems, was more administrative than substantive. And because formally expired ordinances, by definition, become Acts relatively quickly, I have included them in Table 2.9, in the 'turned into Acts' category. Finally, there may be cases where an ordinance expires, and it is followed by an Act, but in the *distant*

[89] 1 of 1964.
[90] The Armed Forces (Special Powers) Continuance Act, 1964 (9 of 1964).

future: we may call them 'distant' expiry. This, too, has happened on occasion. For example, the Vajpayee cabinet promulgated the Central Vigilance Commission (CVC) Ordinance, 1998 establishing the CVC on 25 August 1998.[91] It expired. The ordinance was re-promulgated on 8 January 1999.[92] That, too, expired. Nonetheless, the cabinet finally succeeded in piloting the CVC bill through parliament, but after a period of more than *four* years. The Central Vigilance Commission Act, 2003 became law in September 2003.[93] This is a good example of distant expiry. The ordinance became law, but only after a substantial period of time. As such, in Table 2.9, I have included all cases of distant expiry in the 'expired' column. In other words, 'expired' in Table 2.9 includes all cases of simple and distant expiry; cases of formal expiry, however, are part of the 'turned into Acts' column.

In comparison to the seventy-six ordinances that have expired (in the sense that I have just defined), only two ordinances have been withdrawn. The authority to withdraw an ordinance is provided for in Article 123(2)(b): 'An Ordinance . . . may be withdrawn at any time by the President'. Once again, the reasons for the rather limited use of the withdrawal option are not difficult to guess. On one hand, to withdraw an ordinance is to implicitly agree that an ordinance was not required to begin with. That is an embarrassment that cabinets understandably want to avoid. On the other hand, the legal implications of withdrawal, it seems, are no different from expiry.[94] As with a disapproving resolution, an ordinance, if withdrawn, ceases to operate immediately. In contrast, if allowed to expire, it ceases to operate after six weeks from the date of reassembly of parliament. Given this rather limited legal effect, cabinets understandably avoid withdrawing ordinances.

The Essential Services Maintenance Ordinance, 1957[95] (ESMO) was the first ordinance ever to be withdrawn. It was promulgated on 7 August 1957 in the midst of considerable drama. Employees of the Posts and Telegraph Department, amongst others, threatened to go on strike over pay and benefits.[96] Even though the Lok Sabha was in session, Nehru planned to bring in an ordinance banning the proposed strike.[97] Speaker

91 15 of 1998.

92 4 of 1999.

93 45 of 2003. On the history of the Act, see Rajeev Dhawan, 'Protecting the Bureaucracy' *The Hindu*, 7 March 2003.

94 On interpretative issues relating to expiry, see Chapter 3, Section B.

95 5 of 1957.

96 Anon, 'Government to Rush Bill Rendering P. and T. Strike Illegal' *Times of India*, 4 August 1957.

97 Anon, 'Protest Against Essential Services Emergency Bill' *Times of India*, 4 August 1957.

M. A. Ayyangar stepped in, and counselled against it. The house, he said, should have a chance to discuss the issues involved.[98] As a result, the Essential Services Maintenance Bill, 1957 was hurriedly introduced – one that defined certain government departments to be 'essential services' and prohibited employees in such departments from going on strike. In parliament, Nehru insisted that the committee stages be bypassed, and the bill debated and voted on immediately.[99] The opposition objected to that and staged a walk out. Two days later, the bill was passed by the Lok Sabha, but Rajya Sabha was not in session and no effort was made to bring it into session. In the meanwhile, talks between the government and the labour unions inched towards failure.[100] With no negotiated solution in sight, and the bill not having become an Act, the cabinet promulgated the ESMO on 7 August, empowering itself with provisions to preemptively declare strikes illegal.[101] But against all odds, an agreement was reached at the eleventh hour. The unions called off the strike, and the government, amongst other things, agreed to revoke the ordinance.[102] Nehru kept his word. On 12 August, 'with the emergency having receded', the ESMO was withdrawn, and thereby, became the first ordinance to meet that fate.[103]

Finally, some mention should be made of re-promulgated ordinances. As Table 2.9 shows, until the 1990s, ordinances had *never* been re-promulgated. One may even argue that a convention had developed against re-promulgating ordinances.[104] But when faced with political expediency, the established practice was conveniently forgotten. Of the 196 ordinances promulgated in the 1990s, as many as 53 (27 per cent) were re-promulgated, including some that were promulgated twice or more. This sudden surge in the number of re-promulgated ordinances was partly fuelled by the rise of minority and coalition governments that became the norm during that decade, and their inability to develop

98 *Ibid.* 99 *Ibid.*

100 Anon, 'Strike Decision Stands' *Times of India*, 7 August 1957.

101 Anon, 'Govt. Assumes Emergency Powers to Prevent Strikes' *Times of India*, 8 August 1957.

102 Anon, 'Posts and Telegraphs Strike Called Off' *Times of India*, 9 August 1957; Anon, 'P. and T. Stand Explained' *Times of India*, 9 August 1957.

103 Anon, 'President Revokes Ordinance' *Times of India*, 13 August 1957. See also Anon, 'Emergency Powers Ordinance May Be Withdrawn' *Times of India*, 9 August 1957. The only other ordinance to be withdrawn was the Delhi Administration (Amendment) Ordinance, 1977 (6 of 1977).

104 Re-promulgation, as we shall see in Chapter 3, raises several challenging questions of interpretation and constitutionality.

bipartisan proposals. With fractured verdicts and irreconcilable differences, parliament nearly came to a halt and the private preferences of cabinets became 'legislation' in India.

The Essential Commodities (Special Provisions) Amendment Ordinance, 1992 was the first one to be re-promulgated at the national level.[105] It was originally promulgated on 27 August 1992 and re-promulgated on 2 January 1993.[106] Two other ordinances were part of this 'first' re-promulgation package. The Indian Medical Council (Amendment) Ordinance, 1992[107] and the Dentists (Amendment) Ordinance, 1992[108] were promulgated and later re-promulgated together. Although the trend began in 1992, re-promulgation assumed monstrous proportions in 1996 and 1997. Of the thirty-two ordinances promulgated in 1996, as many as nineteen were cases of re-promulgation or repeated re-promulgation. Take, for example, the Building and Other Construction Workers (Regulation of Employment and Conditions of Service) Ordinance, 1995.[109] It was originally promulgated on 3 November 1995, then re-promulgated on 5 January 1996,[110] then again on 27 March 1996,[111] and for a fourth time on 20 June 1996.[112] The ordinance finally became law on 19 August 1996.[113] *Several* ordinances had a similar trajectory. For example, the Depositories Ordinance, 1995[114] and the Industrial Disputes (Amendment) Ordinance, 1995[115] were promulgated four times each. Similarly, the Coal Mines Provident Fund and Miscellaneous Provisions (Amendment) Ordinance, 1996[116] and the Supreme Court and High Court Judges (Conditions of Service) Amendment Ordinance, 1996[117] were promulgated three times each. Sharing a similar trend was 1997. Of the thirty-one ordinances that were promulgated, sixteen were cases of re-promulgation, and at least seven were re-promulgated twice. In the 2000s, this number dramatically came down – only twelve out of seventy-two ordinances were re-promulgated – although it still remains a matter of concern. Re-promulgation, as we shall see in Chapter 3, raises

[105] 12 of 1984.
[106] The Essential Commodities (Special Provisions) Amendment Ordinance, 1993 (1 of 1993).
[107] 13 of 1992.
[108] 14 of 1992.
[109] 14 of 1995.
[110] 3 of 1996.
[111] 15 of 1996.
[112] 25 of 1996.
[113] The Building and Other Construction Workers (Regulation of Employment and Conditions of Service) Act, 1996 (27 of 1996).
[114] 11 of 1995.
[115] 12 of 1995.
[116] 5 of 1996.
[117] 7 of 1996.

several challenging questions of legality and interpretation, only some of which have been judicially addressed.

We now have an introductory understanding of the areas in which ordinances have tended to concentrate (the 'what' question), and the ways in which parliament has responded to them. Let us now turn to parliamentary sessions (the 'when' question), and the bearing they have on ordinances.

B. PARLIAMENTARY SESSIONS AND THE CONVENIENCE OF ORDINANCES

Because ordinances may be promulgated except when 'both Houses of Parliament are in session', two questions are worth investigating. First, does the frequency of parliamentary sessions affect their numbers? Intuitively, it would seem so: The fewer the number of sessions, greater is the likelihood of ordinances. Second, do trends justify the claim that they are generally motivated by 'convenience', not necessity? Ordinances, on many occasions, are promulgated close to the start of parliamentary sessions or immediately at their conclusion. Should such proximity matter in assessing their necessity and propriety? Taken together, these issues will give us a better view of 'when' – both empirically and normatively. Before that, however, it may be profitable to provide an explanation of the constitutional provisions, conventions and terms associated with parliamentary sessions.

1. Parliamentary Sessions: Provisions, Conventions and Interpretation

Unless dissolved earlier or extended for extenuating reasons, India's Lower House, under Article 83, ordinarily sits for five years.[118] The Constitution, however, does not mention how often any given parliament should be in session; it merely says that 'six months shall not intervene between its last sitting in one session and the date appointed for its first

[118] Constitution of India, Article 83(2) ('The House of the People, unless sooner dissolved, shall continue for five years from the date appointed for its first meeting and no longer and the expiration of the said period of five years shall operate as a dissolution of the House: Provided that the said period may, while a Proclamation of Emergency is in operation, be extended by Parliament by law for a period not exceeding one year at a time and not extending in any case beyond a period of six months after the Proclamation has ceased to operate').

sitting in the next session'.[119] By convention, India's parliament meets for three sessions annually (at least in theory): (1) the budget session (runs from February–May), (2) the monsoon session (from July–September) and (3) the winter session (from November–December).[120] Even though the provision authorises the president to 'summon each House of Parliament', in practice, decisions regarding commencement and duration of sessions are made by the cabinet, usually with inputs from the Ministry of Parliament Affairs.[121] And once summoned, a house may be brought to a close by several means; for example, it may be adjourned, prorogued or dissolved.

Adjournment is a break in parliamentary proceedings; it postpones the business of the house to another time or date in the same session.[122] Such breaks may range from short periods (including a few hours) to several weeks. In India, presiding officers often adjourn houses when members are disruptive or it becomes difficult to transact ordinary business.[123] Houses are also occasionally adjourned for longer periods; for example, by convention, parliamentarians enjoy a three-week recess during the budget session and a two-week recess during the winter session. A notice of adjournment usually includes a statement of the date and time when the house will reassemble, unless it is sine die, in which case there is no assurance that the house will meet again during that session.[124]

Prorogation is also a break in parliamentary proceedings, but one that signals the end of a session.[125] It may take place at any time either after adjournment or while a house is in session. The decision to prorogue

[119] Constitution of India, Article 85(1) ('The President shall from time to time summon each House of Parliament to meet at such time and place as he thinks fit, but six months shall not intervene between its last sitting in one session and the date appointed for its first sitting in the next session').

[120] Handbook for Members of Lok Sabha Ch. 1, r. 3 (1) (15th ed., Lok Sabha Secretariat, New Delhi, 2009). See also, V. K. Agnihotri, *Handbook on the Working of Ministry of Parliamentary Affairs* 17–18 (Ministry of Parliamentary Affairs, New Delhi, 2004).

[121] For a description of the procedure, see *id.* at 19–22.

[122] Reference by President 2002 (2002) 8 SCC 237 at para 52.

[123] Unfortunately, this pattern is all too common. See, e.g., Anon, 'Parliament Paralysed for Third Consecutive Day', *NDTV News*, 24 November 2011, *available at*: http://www.ndtv.com/article/india/parliament-paralysed-for-third-consecutive-day-152607 (accessed 15 January 2012); Vinay Kumar, 'Uproar in Lok Sabha over Telangana' *The Hindu*, 23 February 2011, *available at*: http://www.thehindu.com/news/national/article1483071.ece (accessed 15 January 2012); Anon, 'Houses Adjourned over Nandigram Deadlock' *The Indian Express*, 20 November 2007, *available at*: http://www.indianexpress.com/news/houses-adjourned-over-nandigram-deadlock/241115/ (accessed 15 January 2012).

[124] *Supra* n. 122 at para 52.

[125] *Ibid.*

is generally made by the cabinet and notified by the president. Once prorogued, a house may be called back into session by the president only; presiding officers are not authorised to do so. This is a key difference. When adjourned sine die, a house is still in session and the presiding officer, if he or she so desires, may bring it back into session.[126] But prorogation, like adjournment, does not preclude the possibility of future sessions and, therefore, unfinished business from the prorogued session does not lapse.[127] A prorogued house, in other words, is inactive but 'alive', unless it is coincident with its maximum tenure.[128]

Dissolution, in contrast, signals the end of a particular parliament, thereby necessitating new elections. All pending matters including bills lapse at the moment of dissolution.[129] Interestingly, whereas both the Lower and Upper Houses may be adjourned or prorogued, only the Lower House may be dissolved.[130] And once dissolved, it cannot be revived.[131] The Lower House has a maximum span of five years and automatically stands dissolved at the end of that tenure. But it may also be dissolved earlier.[132] A decision to prematurely dissolve a particular Lower House is made by the outgoing cabinet and carried out by the president, although the matter is not without controversy.

To summarise, then, once summoned to meet, both houses of parliament may break in a number of ways. An adjournment ends a particular *sitting* of parliament, prorogation ends a particular *session* and dissolution ends that *parliament* (i.e., the Lower House) itself.[133] These

[126] This has happened on a number of occasions. On 25 May 1987, the Lower House was adjourned sine die to mark the end of the budget session. But the house was never prorogued. Accordingly, on 27 July, it met again for the monsoon session, which was, legally speaking, a continuation of its earlier session. On 28 July, the speaker adjourned the house sine die, and on 3 September, it was finally prorogued by the president. This happened again in 1989. The monsoon session was adjourned sine die on 18 August, but never prorogued. The house again came back to session for three days starting 11 October. It was adjourned sine die and finally prorogued on 20 October 1989.

[127] *Supra* n. 122 at para 52.

[128] *Id.* at para 53.

[129] *Id.* at para 52.

[130] The Upper House, consistent with Constitution of India, Article 83 (1), is a permanent body. Constitution of India, Article 83(1) ('The Council of States shall not be subject to dissolution, but as nearly as possible one third of the members thereof shall retire as soon as may be on the expiration of every second year in accordance with the provisions made in that behalf by Parliament by law').

[131] *Supra* n. 122 at para 52.

[132] Constitution of India, Article 85(2) (The President may from time to time'(a) prorogue the Houses or either House; (b) dissolve the House of the People').

[133] See also A. R. Mukherjea, *Parliamentary Procedure in India* 61–65 (Oxford University Press, Calcutta, 1983).

distinctions are important because they determine when an ordinance may be promulgated. Recall the temporal limits in Article 123(1): 'If at any time, except when both Houses of Parliament are in session, the President ... may promulgate ... Ordinances'. The president's temporal scope to promulgate ordinances, therefore, turns on the meaning of 'in session'. Given our earlier distinctions, it is clear that parliament is not in session when either house of parliament stands prorogued, or the Lower House stands dissolved. In such circumstances, a president obviously has authority to promulgate ordinances.[134]

However, does the president have authority to promulgate an ordinance when either house of parliament stands adjourned – for example, for recess during its budget session? In an absolute – or 'literal' – sense, parliament, in such situations, is not in session. But adjournment, as we saw earlier, has a legal meaning, and an adjourned parliament is deemed to be in session, though not in sitting. The Constitution, in several of its provisions, impliedly recognises this distinction between parliament being 'in session' and 'in sitting'. Article 85(1), for example, says that 'six months shall not intervene between [the parliament's] last sitting in one session and the date appointed for its first sitting in the next session'. This distinction read in the context of Article 123(1), therefore, suggests that ordinances are impermissible when parliament is *nominally* in session; it need not be in sitting. In other words, the president may promulgate ordinances only when either house of parliament stands prorogued or the Lower House stands dissolved; an adjourned house is still in session.

Improper as it sounds, cabinets have prorogued sessions or dissolved the Lower House – or attempted to do so – just to promulgate ordinances. Earlier I mentioned the controversy surrounding Mrs Sonia Gandhi's alleged 'office of profit'. In June 2004, the Manmohan Singh cabinet created the National Advisory Council (NAC) – apparently to oversee the

[134] Because the Constitution of India, Article 123(1) authorises the president to promulgate ordinances when 'either House of Parliament' is not session, it implies that ordinances may be promulgated even if one of the house *is* in session. Although arguably undemocratic, at least on eight occasions, ordinances were promulgated when the Lower House was still in session. See, e.g., the Travancore-Cochin Appropriation (Vote on Account) Ordinance, 1956 (4 of 1956); the Essential Services Maintenance Ordinance, 1957 (5 of 1957); the Armed Forces (Special Powers) Continuance Ordinance, 1964 (1 of 1964); the Calcutta Tramways Company (Taking Over of Management) Amendment Ordinance, 1971 (10 of 1971); the Coal Mines (Nationalisation) Amendment Ordinance, 1976 (3 of 1976); the National Security (Amendment) Ordinance, 1984 (5 of 1984); the Tea Companies (Acquisition and Transfer of Sick Tea Units) Ordinance, 1985 (3 of 1985); the Swadeshi Cotton Mills Company Limited (Acquisition and Transfer of Undertakings) Ordinance, 1986 (5 of 1986).

implementation of the Common Minimum Program to which the UPA coalition partners had agreed. Mrs Gandhi was appointed its chairperson. Because of her post, she enjoyed the rank and status of a cabinet minister and received perks and benefits paid out by the central government. For nearly two years, none of this was particularly controversial.

Things changed in March 2006. Parliament was in its budget session, but had been adjourned for its three-week recess. Around that time, the NDA-led opposition started an agitation against Mrs Gandhi and her appointment, alleging that it amounted to an 'office of profit' under Article 102 – something that disqualified her from the membership to either house of parliament.[135] Unable to find fault with the opposition's legal arguments, the cabinet secretly came up with a draft ordinance to remove Mrs Gandhi's disqualifications under the law. Although not in sitting, parliament was in session and that created a hurdle. The government, therefore, got parliament adjourned sine die and recommended to the president that it be prorogued. The entire post-recess budget session was done away with – ostensibly for the benefit of a party president. But the ordinance did not materialise. As I mentioned before, an alert piece of reporting by the *Indian Express* made those plans public, and an embarrassed cabinet immediately backtracked.[136] Eventually, Mrs Gandhi resigned, only to be re-elected, and a piece of legislation later on regularised her appointment to the NAC.[137]

This failed attempt to opportunistically adjourn or prorogue parliament was not unique. In 1994, the budget session of parliament was adjourned on 13 May and both houses were notified to reassemble four weeks later. Yet, the Narasimha Rao cabinet prorogued the Lower House of parliament on 23 May, thereby paving the way for three ordinances.

[135] Constitution of India, Article 102 (1)(a) ('A person shall be disqualified for being chosen as, and for being, a member of either House of Parliament if he holds any office of profit under the Government of India or the Government of any State, other than an office declared by Parliament by law not to disqualify its holder'). Anon, 'Earlier in Day, BJP Spelt Out Her Office of Profit' *Indian Express*, 23 March 2006, *available at*: http://www.indianexpress.com/news/earlier-in-day-bjp-spelt-out-her-office-of-profit/1040/0 (accessed 13 January 2012).

[136] R. Venkataraman, 'To Stop Office-of-Profit Axe, UPA Gets Ordinance' *Indian Express*, 21 March 2006. Anon, 'Uproar in Parliament Over Ordinance "Shielding" Sonia' *Hindustan Times*, 22 March 2006.

[137] Venkitesh Ramakrishnan, 'A Masterstroke' *Frontline*, 23(6), (25 March – 7 April 2006), *available at*: http://hindu.com/fline/fl2306/stories/20060407007212900.htm (accessed 13 January 2012). See also Sujay Mehdudia, 'President Kalam Signs Office of Profit Bill, *The Hindu*, 19 September 2006, *available at*: http://www.hindu.com/2006/09/19/stories/2006091922020300.htm (accessed 13 January 2012).

The next day, two ordinances were promulgated – the Manipur Municipalities Ordinance, 1994[138] and the Punjab Municipal Corporation Law (Extension to Chandigarh) Ordinance, 1994.[139] A day later, the cabinet promulgated the third one – the New Delhi Municipal Council Ordinance, 1994.[140] Although important, these ordinances were of the 'regulatory' kind and, unlike the proposed Office of Profit Ordinance, not particularly controversial. The Manipur Ordinance, for example, established the administrative machinery for municipal bodies in the state, defined their powers and duties and required that elections be held to fill the new positions. Similarly, the Chandigarh Ordinance extended the provisions of the Punjab Municipal Corporation Act, 1976 to the Union Territory of Chandigarh, thereby putting in place a mechanism for the administration of municipalities in that city. Even though the 1994 ordinances did not generate a whole lot of controversy, these examples – both in failure and success – demonstrate the ease with which 'formal' conditions necessary to promulgate ordinances can be *created*.

This sort of legislative manoeuvring has an obvious air of impropriety. But are there legal limits to how and when the executive may prorogue parliamentary sessions to make way for ordinances? In *Re Kalyanam Veerabhadraya*, the Madras High Court said no.[141] In July 1949, the Madras Legislative Assembly was debating several amendments to the Madras Maintenance of Public Order Act, 1947.[142] Despite that, the governor prorogued the session on 2 August and promulgated an ordinance – the Madras Ordinance, 1949 – on the ground that he was 'satisfied that immediate action was necessary'.[143] The governor's action, the petitioners argued, was a fraudulent exercise of power; there was no emergency, and the legislature was prorogued solely to make an ordinance possible.[144] The High Court rebuffed that claim. 'It is open to the Governor', the judges wrote, 'to prorogue the legislature at any time he pleases'.[145] 'We do not see anything wrong in the Governor proroguing the Assembly and the Council with a view to enable himself to issue an Ordinance'.[146] 'The legislature, which is democratically constituted, is very slow to move in the matter of legislation', and, therefore, 'if the Governor has reasons to believe that immediate action is necessary, it [can] be more expedient to have resort to the power of issuing an Ordinance . . . rather than approach

[138] 6 of 1994.
[139] 7 of 1994.
[140] 8 of 1994.
[141] AIR 1950 Mad 243.
[142] 1 of 1947 (Madras).
[143] Ordinance 1 of 1949 (Madras).
[144] *Supra* n. 141 at para 21.
[145] *Ibid.*
[146] *Ibid.*

the Legislature for the necessary legislation', they said.[147] In other words, for the Madras High Court, the power to prorogue is an absolute one; presidents (and governors) may invoke it at any time and for any reason. And even if done *solely* to make an ordinance possible – as in the office of profit controversy – that, too, the High Court seemed to suggest, is lawful.

This absolute reading of prorogation was marginally disputed in *State of Punjab v. Satya Pal Dang*.[148] The facts of the case are rather peculiar. During the budget session of the Punjab State Assembly in March 1968, a resolution was moved expressing no-confidence in the speaker. The next day, the speaker declared the motion unconstitutional and deemed not to have been moved. Thereafter, he adjourned the Assembly for two months until 6 May 1968. This led to a crisis. The state budget needed to be adopted by 31 March, but the Assembly stood adjourned until May. With the speaker unwilling to resume legislative proceedings, the governor prorogued the Assembly and promulgated the Punjab Legislature Regulation of Procedure in Relation to Financial Business Ordinance, 1968 (1968 Ordinance).[149] The 1968 Ordinance, amongst other things, barred both houses of the state legislature from being adjourned until the completion of the financial business.[150] When challenged on the ground that the houses were prorogued solely to make way for an ordinance, the court sided with the governor. 'There was no abuse of power by him, nor can his action be described as mala fide', Chief Justice Hidayatullah wrote.[151] But he hedged on the larger question: 'Whether a Governor will be justified to do this when the Legislature is in session and in the midst of its legislative work is a question that does not fall for consideration here'. 'When that happens, the motives of the Governor', he added, 'may conceivably be questioned on the ground of an alleged want of good faith and abuse of constitutional powers'.[152]

Clearly, *Satya Pal Dang* is less sweeping than the view articulated by the Madras High Court, and if correct, would imply that presidents and governors do not have complete discretion in proroguing houses. The matter, however, was not affirmatively adjudicated upon. The court merely left open the possibility of judicial review without saying anything about its scope or the grounds on which such reviews may take place. Nonetheless, both decisions and their general tenor err on the side of wide

[147] *Ibid.*
[148] AIR 1969 SC 903.
[149] 1 of 1968 (Punjab).
[150] *Id.* at § 3.
[151] *Supra* n. 148 at para 14.
[152] *Ibid.*

TABLE 2.10. *Decade-wise breakdown of parliamentary session and ordinances*

Decade	Ordinances	Lok Sabha Sessions*	Lok Sabha Sitting
1952–1959	52	1350	929
1960–1969	67	1599	1165
1970–1979	135	1433	999
1980–1989	93	1405	957
1990–1999	196	1312	763
2000–2009	72	1291	710

* Here 'in session' refers to the period from the date of commencement to the date when the session is adjourned sine die, although as I mentioned earlier, technically a house remains in session until it is prorogued.

discretion and that has stark implications for Article 123. If the decision to prorogue a parliamentary session is entirely – or substantially – within the discretion of the cabinet, it follows that the temporal limit in Article 123 does not impose any real restriction. The executive, it turns out, may satisfy the 'not in session' requirement simply by proroguing parliament when it *is* in session.

2. *Proximity to Parliamentary Sessions*

With this background in mind, we may now turn to the comparison between parliamentary performance – measured by the number of 'days in session' and 'days in sitting' – and the frequency of ordinances. Because ordinances may be promulgated only when either house is not in session, does the frequency of parliamentary sessions affect the number of ordinances? That is the first question we must consider.

Two things stand out in Table 2.10. First, there is a substantial difference between the number of days the Lower House is deemed to be in session, and the number of days it is actually in sitting. Because 'days in sitting' measure the actual work done in parliament, it is, generally speaking, a better standard by which to measure parliamentary performance, although for our immediate purpose, 'days in session' obviously is the more relevant standard. Second, both numbers – relating to session and sitting – are on the decline. When broken down by individual years, it becomes clear, for example, that since 1975, with five exceptions, the Lower House has never sat for more than 100 days.[153] Contrast this

[153] Statistical Handbook, *supra* n. 1 at 52.

TABLE 2.11. *Top ten years with the largest number of sessions and corresponding ordinances*

Year	Sessions	Ordinances
1956	205	9
1967	198	9
1953	180	7
1955	178	7
1966	175	13
1954	175	9
1973	173	4
1974	172	15
1958	171	7
1970	170	5

with the fact that starting in 1952, the Lower House sat for more than 100 days *every* year until 1974.[154] This difference is evident in the averages for each decade. As the preceding table shows, compared to the 116.5 days in sitting on average in the 1960s, the Lower House in the 1990s and 2000s has managed an average of no more than 76.3 days and 71 days, respectively. And as if to illustrate this downward trend, the Lower House, in 2008, sat for a total of forty days – the lowest ever in India's parliamentary history. To anyone concerned about the gradual decay in the quality and extent of parliament's performance in India, these are ominous trends.[155]

Throughout the duration of the fifty-eight years under consideration, parliamentary sessions exhibit a statistically significant correlation with the number of ordinances. In other words, the lower the number of sessions, the greater the likelihood of ordinances. As Table 2.10 shows, in the ten years with the highest number of sessions, parliament was in session on average for 179.7 days every year. During the same period, there were 8.5 ordinances every year: substantially less than the 10.6 ordinances for the entire duration. A reverse trend is noticeable in Table 2.11 that lists the ten years with the lowest number of sessions. In those 10 years, parliament was in session on average for 102.7 days every year, and

[154] *Ibid.*

[155] Anon, 'Parliament Disruption Main Tool of Opposition: Vice President' *Indian Express*, 2 February 2011, *available at*: http://www.indianexpress.com/news/parliament-disruption-main-tool-of-opposition-vice-president/745252/0 (accessed 13 January 2012).

TABLE 2.12. *Top ten years with the smallest number of sessions and corresponding ordinances*

Year	Sessions	Ordinances
2009	91	9
2004	93	8
1999	95	10
1979	98	12
1975	100	29
1998	105	20
1985	109	8
2006	110	3
1984	113	15
1977	113	16

there were 13 ordinances every year, which is, once again, substantially more than 10.6 ordinances for the entire duration.[156]

The statistical correlation is even stronger when ordinances are compared to parliamentary sittings, rather than sessions. Therefore, as with sessions, the lower the number of parliamentary sittings, the greater the likelihood of ordinances. As Table 2.13 shows, the average of 10 years with the highest number of sittings is about 129.7 days. During the same period, there were 5.9 ordinances every year, which is nearly 50 per cent less than the number of ordinances on average for the entire duration. Conversely, Table 2.14 shows parliamentary sittings in the ten years with the least number of sittings: It amounts to an average of 60.3 days every year. During these ten years, the number of ordinances, on average, rose to 16.7 every year, which is nearly 57 per cent greater than the number of ordinances on average for the entire duration.[157]

Therefore, other things being equal, parliamentary performances measured by days in session or sitting, in sync with our intuitive expectations, have an inverse bearing on the number of ordinances. But to better understand when ordinances are promulgated in any given year, we must take a closer look at their proximity to parliamentary sessions. That will give

[156] For a regression analysis of the number of parliamentary sessions, their correlation with ordinances, and the corresponding p value, see Annex 2B.

[157] For a regression analysis of the number of parliamentary sittings, their correlation with ordinances, and the corresponding p value, see Annex 2C.

TABLE 2.13. *Top ten years with the largest number of sittings and corresponding ordinances*

Year	Sittings	Ordinances
1956	151	9
1955	139	7
1954	137	9
1953	137	7
1958	125	7
1959	123	3
1964	122	3
1963	122	0
1960	121	1
1968	120	13

us a better grasp of the second question: Do trends justify the claim that ordinances are generally motivated by reasons other than necessity?

With some notable exceptions, ordinances are promulgated at a midpoint; they come into existence after a session ends and before the next one begins.[158] For that reason, there are two points with reference to which proximity of ordinances to sessions may be measured. First, how many days *after* the termination of a session was an ordinance promulgated? Second, how many days *prior* to the commencement of the next session was the same ordinance promulgated? Resorting to an ordinance soon after the termination of a session or just before the commencement of the next session raises questions about its propriety – and possibly its legality. To be sure, close proximity, whether measured by days after or days prior to a session, does not necessarily establish bad faith. But it brings the cabinet's motive into sharp focus. Why, after all, should a cabinet promulgate ordinances close to the date of termination or commencement of sessions? Is it an attempt, for example, to undermine or circumvent parliament? Or is it an attempt to avoid parliamentary scrutiny? Or does it speak to the idea that parliament has lost its relevance as a legislative body? Whatever the reason, ordinances that are promulgated in close proximity to sessions deserve additional scrutiny.

[158] The exceptions include ordinances that are promulgated while one of the houses is already in session. With reference to the Lok Sabha, this has happened around fourteen times. In other words, at least on fourteen occasions, ordinances were promulgated when the Lok Sabha was in session, but the Rajya Sabha was not.

TABLE 2.14. *Top ten years with the smallest number of sittings and corresponding ordinances*

Year	Sittings	Ordinances
2008	46	8
2004	48	8
1999	51	10
1975	63	29
1998	64	20
2009	64	9
1997	65	31
1979	66	12
2007	66	8
1996	70	32

But 'proximity' is a relative term; there are no hard-and-fast rules by which to measure it. For our purposes, I have divided ordinances into five periods: those that came within fifteen days ('highly suspect'), those that came within sixteen and thirty days ('suspect'), those that came within thirty-one and forty-five days (less-than-suspect'), those that came within forty-five and sixty days ('less-than-suspect' again), and finally, those that came before or after sixty days ('unsuspecting'). As the terms suggest, in making this classification, I assume that ordinances that came fifteen days after a session ended or before the start of a session are particularly vulnerable to the charge of bad faith and, therefore, calls for heightened scrutiny. Those that came sixteen and thirty days of either session are also vulnerable, but less so. The least suspecting, in this scale, are those that came sixty days after or before a session. In other words, the further we get away from the date of termination or commencement of a session, the less likely that an ordinance was motivated by 'convenient' considerations.

Note an important point here. Because the scale measures days from both ends, it is possible – indeed probable – that an ordinance falls in the 'unsuspecting' and 'highly suspect' categories simultaneously. It may be 'unsuspecting' when measured from the date of termination of a session. But it may be 'highly suspect' when measured from the date of commencement of the next session. For example, let us assume that in 1990, the winter session of parliament ended on 1 December. An ordinance was promulgated on 10 February 1991. The budget session, let us

TABLE 2.15. *Decade-wise breakdown of ordinances and their proximity to terminated sessions in days*

	≤15	16–30	31–45	46–60	>60
1952–1959	8	13	16	8	7
1960–1969	11	18	10	18	10
1970–1979	10	16	24	37	48
1980–1989	11	13	27	15	27
1990–1999	54	64	46	18	14
2000–2009	11	12	16	12	21

assume, commenced on 20 February 1991. When measured with reference to the date on which the winter session was terminated, our hypothetical ordinance is 'unsuspecting'; it came more than sixty days later. But when measured with reference to the date on which the budget session began, it appears 'highly suspect', having been promulgated barely ten days before the commencement of a new session. In other words, in calculating the total number of 'highly suspect' or 'unsuspecting' ordinances using the aforementioned periods, both ends must be borne in mind.

Table 2.15 is a decade-wise break down of ordinances and their proximity to sessions – one that measures the number of days from the termination of a session after which ordinances were promulgated. Seen from this side, 241 ordinances (39.1 per cent) fall in the 'highly suspect' and 'suspect' categories, whereas 127 ordinances (20.6 per cent) fall in the 'unsuspecting' category. In other words, 39.1 per cent of all ordinances were promulgated less than thirty days after the termination of sessions, whereas 20.6 per cent of all ordinances were promulgated more than sixty days after parliamentary sessions ended. Of the former, 105 (17 per cent) are in the 'highly suspect' category – they were promulgated less than fifteen days after sessions ended, and 136 of them (22 per cent) are in the 'suspect' category – they were promulgated more than fifteen days but less than thirty days after sessions ended. Decade-wise, the 1970s had the best record: ten (only 7 per cent) were 'highly suspect'. In contrast, the 1990s had the worst record: fifty-four (27.5 per cent) fell in the same category. The 1970s also had the best record for 'unsuspecting' ordinances: forty-eight of them (35.5 per cent) were promulgated more than sixty days after sessions concluded. Expectedly, the 1990s had the worst record: fourteen (only 7 per cent) came after more than sixty days.

TABLE 2.16. *Decade-wise breakdown of ordinances and their proximity to sessions before which they were promulgated*

	≤15	16–30	31–45	46–60	>60
1952–1959	7	22	9	8	4
1960–1969	19	14	14	12	5
1970–1979	24	44	13	26	26
1980–1989	11	25	21	16	14
1990–1999	10	53	52	46	34
2000–2009	1	31	12	10	18

The Barsi Light Railway Company (Transferred Liabilities) Ordinance, 1953 was the first 'highly suspect' ordinance.[159] That year, parliament's winter session ended on 24 December, and the ordinance was promulgated seven days later on 31 December. Other examples include the Industrial Disputes (Banking Companies) Commencement of Decision Ordinance, 1954, promulgated barely three days after the budget session ended that year;[160] the Representation of People (Amendment) Ordinance, 1955, promulgated six days after the winter session ended that year;[161] the Railways (Employment of Members of Armed Forces) Ordinance, 1965 that came five days after the monsoon session ended that year;[162] the Maintenance of Internal Security (Amendment) Ordinance, 1974 that came eight days after the monsoon session ended that year[163] and the Patents (Amendment) Ordinance 1994 that came eight days after the winter session of parliament in 1994.[164]

Now consider proximity from the reverse. Table 2.16 measures the proximity of ordinances from the point of view of days before the commencement of a new session.[165] Seen from this side, 261 ordinances (43.4 per cent) fall in the 'highly suspect' and 'suspect' categories, whereas 101 of them (16.8 per cent) fall in the 'unsuspecting' category. In other words, 43.4 per cent of almost all ordinances were promulgated less than thirty days before the start of sessions, whereas 16.8 per cent of them were

[159] 7 of 1953.
[160] 7 of 1954.
[161] 7 of 1955.
[162] 4 of 1965.
[163] 11 of 1974.
[164] 13 of 1994.
[165] Note that Table 2.11 has fewer ordinances (601) compared to the total of 615. This is because I have used the Lok Sabha dates of commencements and terminations to make these calculations. And seen from this perspective, there are fourteen ordinances that were promulgated at a time when the Lok Sabha was in session, but not the Rajya Sabha.

promulgated more than sixty days before the start of sessions. Of the former, seventy-two (11.9 per cent) are in the 'highly suspect' category – they were promulgated less than fifteen days before sessions started, and 189 of them (31.4 per cent) are in the 'suspect' category – they were promulgated more than fifteen days, but less than thirty days before sessions started. Decade-wise, the 2000s had the best record: only one (1.3 per cent) was 'highly suspect', whereas the 1960s had the worst record: nineteen (29.6 per cent) fell in the same category. The 2000s also had the best record for 'unsuspecting' ordinances: eighteen of them (25 per cent) were promulgated more than sixty days before sessions began. Expectedly, the 1960s had the worst: five (only 7.8 per cent) came more than sixty days before the sessions began.[166]

Seen from this side, the Representation of People (Amendment) Ordinance, 1956 was one of the first highly suspect ordinances.[167] It was promulgated on 8 November 1956 – barely six days before parliament came back to session on 14 November that year. Other examples include the Goa, Daman and Diu (Administration) Ordinance, 1962, that was promulgated on 5 March that year, seven days prior to the start of the session on 12 March;[168] the Defence of India (Amendment) Ordinance, 1962, that was promulgated on 3 November, five days prior to the start of the session on 8 November;[169] and the Foreign Exchange Regulation (Amendment) Ordinance, 1969 that came into existence on 13 November, barely four days prior to the start of the session on 17 November.[170] Of course, amongst the most well known in this category is the Banking Companies (Acquisition and Transfer of Undertaking) Ordinance, 1969. As I previously mentioned, it was promulgated on 19 July 1969 – a day before parliament came back to session.[171] Even the second ordinance brought in to overcome the Supreme Court's objections to the first one was hardly better.[172] The Banking Companies (Acquisition and Transfer of Undertaking) Ordinance, 1970 was promulgated on 14 February, barely six days before parliament reassembled for the budget session that year.[173]

[166] Because figures in Tables 2.10 and 2.11 are based on the dates on which Lok Sabha sessions ended, they may be marginally different if calculated on the basis of Rajya Sabha sessions.

[167] 9 of 1956.

[168] 2 of 1962.

[169] 4 of 1962.

[170] 9 of 1969.

[171] 3 of 1969.

[172] The first bank nationalisation ordinance was invalidated in *R. C. Cooper v. Union of India* 1970 (3) SCR 550.

[173] 3 of 1970.

These figures, taken together, should give us pause. Although they do not establish that all ordinances are necessarily motivated by bad faith, they raise several questions. This is particularly true of the 176 ordinances that fall in the 'highly suspect' category. These ordinances, it appears, were almost invariably promulgated to avoid parliamentary scrutiny, at least initially. Cabinets rarely explained the 'immediate necessity' that led to them. Neither did they say anything to justify the specific dates on which the ordinances were promulgated. If at all, on occasions, cabinets candidly admitted otherwise.

But even in the case of ordinances that fall in the unsuspecting category, the charge of 'convenience' cannot be shrugged off easily. This is because of what I shall refer to as the 'cluster' phenomenon. On ninety-two occasions, two or more ordinances were promulgated on the *same* day. These ninety-two clusters (i.e., days on which two or more ordinances came together) has the following break-up. On one occasion (27 March 1996), eight ordinances were promulgated together – the highest ever in a single day. On another occasion – 2 January 1993 – as many as seven were brought into effect on the same day. Then there are three occasions (5 January 1996, 20 June 1996 and 23 April 1998) on which five ordinances were promulgated on the same day. There are also six occasions (22 October 1971, 8 December 1975, 26 July 1981, 16 January 1993, 25 January 1993 and 24 January 1997) when four ordinances were promulgated the same day, and another fifteen occasions when three were brought in on the same day. Finally, on as many as sixty-six occasions, two ordinances were promulgated the same day. When combined with the 'highly suspect' figures, these clusters raise the serious likelihood that a vast majority of ordinances have been motivated by convenience – administrative or otherwise – rather than any 'real' sense of legislative urgency.

Now that we have an introductory account of the 'what' and 'when' questions, I shall turn to 'who'. In other words, who – or more appropriately, which cabinets – promulgated these ordinances?

C. PRIME MINISTERS, CABINETS AND THE USE OF ORDINANCES

Ordinances are formally promulgated by presidents. In practice, prime-ministers and their cabinets are responsible for them. In this penultimate section, my objective is to describe the ordinance-related record of India's cabinets since 1952. I have already made several references to the various cabinets in discussing the 'what' question. But this section is a more detailed account of how cabinets have contributed to the rising tide of ordinances.

India has a multi-party system. Therefore, barring highly exceptional circumstances, only four types of cabinets are possible: (1) single-party majority cabinet, (2) coalition majority cabinet, (3) single-party minority cabinet and (4) coalition minority cabinet. The 'majority' point requires some clarification. Because India's Lower House has 545 seats, by majority, I have in mind a government that has the *active* support of at least 272 members. This definition, therefore, excludes governments whose majority status is dependent on parties giving 'outside' support – an arrangement where parties support a government without participating in it. For example, the Vajpayee-led NDA Government in 1998 had a bare majority in parliament, but only with the outside support of the Telugu Desam Party (TDP). As a result, the Vajpayee cabinet, for our purposes here, should be classified as a minority government.[174] To put it differently, a government is considered a majority only if representatives of parties (and independents) adding up to 272 *participate* in it. Thus far, India has had three of the four types of cabinets, with the coalition majority cabinet being the only exception.

Between 1952 and 2009, single-party majority cabinets have been in office for almost thirty-one years (i.e., 53 per cent of the total duration). In that period, they promulgated 282 ordinances (i.e., 45.8 per cent of all ordinances). As Table 2.12 shows, of these 282, Nehru promulgated sixty-six in his three tenures as the prime minister. Indira Gandhi more than doubled that number: While leading single-party majority governments, she promulgated 150 of them. In contrast, Lal Bahadur Shastri and Rajiv Gandhi were more subdued; the former promulgated nine, whereas the latter added another thirty-seven to the list.

Of the remaining two types, coalition minority cabinets have been in office for about eighteen years (31 per cent of the time) and in that period, promulgated 188 ordinances (30.5 per cent). Thus far, seven prime ministers have served eleven such cabinets. Of them, Vajpayee has been prime minister thrice and Manmohan Singh twice. In absolute numbers, Singh leads the table with thirty-six ordinances in his first term in office, closely followed by Vajpayee with thirty-three ordinances that came during the latter's second term as prime minister. Finally, single-party minority

[174] On minority governments, see Csaba Nikolenyi, *Minority Governments in India: The Puzzle of Elusive Majorities* (Routledge, London, 2009).

TABLE 2.17. *Prime ministers, cabinet types, tenures and ordinances*

Prime Minister	Cabinet type	Tenure	Ordinances
Jawaharlal Nehru	SPM	17.04.52 – 10.05.57	41
Jawaharlal Nehru	SPM	11.05.57 – 31.03.62	18
Jawaharlal Nehru	SPM	01.04.62 – 27.05.64	07
Gulzari Lal Nanda	SPM	27.05.67 – 08.06.67	–
Lal Bahadur Shastri	SPM	09.06.64 – 11.01.66	09
Gulzari Lal Nanda	SPM	11.01.66 – 24.01.66	–
Indira Gandhi	SPM	24.01.66 – 03.03.67	15
Indira Gandhi	SPP	04.03.67 – 14.03.71	38
Indira Gandhi	SPM	15.03.71 – 24 .03.77	99
Morarji Desai	CM	24.03.77 – 27.07.79	21
Charan Singh	CM	28.07.79 – 13.01.80	07
Indira Gandhi	SPM	14.01.80 – 31.10.84	56
Rajiv Gandhi	SPM	31.10.84 – 01.12.89	37
Vishwanath P. Singh	CM	02.12.89 – 09.11.90	10
Chandra Shekhar	CM	10.11.90 – 21.06.91	06
Narasimha Rao	SPP	21.06.91 – 15.05.96	108
Atal B. Vajpayee	CM	16.05.96 – 01.06.96	–
H. D. Deve Gowda	CM	01.06.96 – 20.04.97	23
Inder K. Gujral	CM	21.04.97 – 18.03.98	23
Atal B. Vajpayee	CM	19.03.98 – 12.10.99	25
Atal B. Vajpayee	CM	13.10.99 – 21.05.04	33
Manmohan Singh	CM	22.05.04 – 21.05.09	36
Manmohan Singh	CM	22.05.09 – 31.12.09*	04

* Singh's second term continues until May 2014.
SPM: Single-party majority SPP: Single-party minority CM: Coalition minority

cabinets have been in office for nearly nine years (15.5 per cent of the time) and promulgated as many as 146 ordinances (23.7 per cent). Thus far, only two prime ministers have led single-party minority cabinets (Mrs Gandhi and Narasimha Rao), and Mrs Gandhi is the only prime minister to have led both single-party majority and single-party minority governments, respectively. In this capacity, Mrs Gandhi promulgated thirty-eight ordinances whereas Rao greatly outpaced her with 108 of them. Gulzari Lal Nanda, twice-acting prime minister, is the only one not to have ever promulgated any ordinance.

All things being equal, a single-party majority government should yield *fewer* ordinances compared to a minority government of either kind. After all, a single-party majority government, by definition, has the numbers to see its legislation through parliament. The record of fifty-eight years suggests that this is mostly correct. As I mentioned previously, single-party

TABLE 2.18. *Top ten years with the smallest number of ordinances and corresponding cabinet types*

Year	No. of ordinances	Cabinet type
1963	00	SPM
1960	01	SPM
1982	01	SPM
1989	02	SPM
1959	03	SPM
1961	03	SPM
1964	03	SPM
2006	03	CM
1952	04	SPM
1973	04	SPM

SPM: Single-party majority SPP: Single-party minority
CM: Coalition minority

majority cabinets held office for 53.8 per cent of the time, but promulgated 45 per cent of the ordinances. Coalition minority cabinets were in office for 31 per cent of the time and responsible for 30.5 per cent of ordinances. Finally, coalition minority cabinets were in office for 15.5 per cent of the time, but promulgated 23.7 per cent of all ordinances. The figures for single-party majority and single-party minority cabinets are not strictly proportional, but the wedge is not an insignificant one. This is further corroborated by the relationship between single-party majority cabinets and ordinances in the top-ten years with the most and least numbers of ordinances and the corresponding cabinet types. As Table 2.18 shows, the ten years with the least number of ordinances had single-party majority governments with the exception of 2006, which had a coalition minority cabinet. In contrast, of the ten years with the most number of ordinances listed in Table 2.19, five had single-party minority or coalition minority cabinets or a combination of the two. Of the remaining five, three of them had exclusively single-party majority cabinets, and the remaining two years had both single-party majority and minority cabinets.

With various components now in place, we may finally ask the 'endemic' question: Why are there so many ordinances? With the exception of 1963, they have been promulgated every year. With the exception of religious affairs and related fields, there are substantial numbers of ordinances in most areas of law broadly defined. With the

TABLE 2.19. *Top ten years with the largest number of ordinances and corresponding cabinet types*

Year	No. of ordinances	Cabinet type
1993	34	SPP
1996	32	SPP – CM
1997	31	CM
1975	29	SPM
1971	23	SPP – SPM
1992	21	SPP
1998	20	CM
1980	19	SPM
1976	16	SPM
1977	16	SPM – SPP

SPM: Single-party majority SPP: Single-party minority
CM: Coalition minority

exception of Gulzari Lal Nanda, every prime minister has promulgated ordinances. Why, to pose the question once again, are there so many ordinances?

D. WHY ORDINANCES ARE WIDELY USED: AN ARGUMENT

Our analysis thus far makes it clear that no one factor can explain why ordinances are commonplace in India. In this section, I will argue that historical, empirical and attitudinal reasons must be marshalled together to make sense of their widespread nature.

First, a reason from the past: the convenience of precedent. Nehru's contributions in nurturing India's parliamentary institutions are well known. But less well understood is his parallel eagerness to rely on anti-parliamentary methods to introduce legislation. By the time he ceased to be India's prime minister, Nehru set an ordinance-related precedent that successive prime ministers have gleefully followed – and at times, expanded on. As I mentioned earlier, G. V. Mavalankar, India's first speaker, had urged caution. In a letter written in 1954, he reminded Nehru of the first parliament's precedent-setting responsibility: 'It is not a question of present personnel in the Government, but [one] of precedents'. If ordinances 'were not limited by convention only to extreme and very urgent cases', the result, he said, 'may be that, in future, the government may go on issuing ordinances giving the Lok Sabha no option, but to rubber-stamp'.[175] His concerns were brushed aside.

When Indira Gandhi took over, ordinances reached new heights. She introduced vast reforms, which by themselves may have had merit. But in relying on ordinances, it is not readily clear that her method had any merit. Later, when the Janata Party and its coalition partners formed the first non-Congress government in New Delhi, they promised a new start. They brought in legislative and constitutional changes and undid several of Mrs Gandhi's emergency-related excesses.[176] But reversing the precedent on ordinances was not one of them. Morarji Desai and Charan Singh held office for nearly three years and in that period, promulgated twenty-eight ordinances. Thus, by the time Mrs Gandhi came back to office in January 1980, ordinances had a bipartisan record – and things have not changed since then. If anything, the bipartisan consensus has grown stronger.

In 1969, Vajpayee was critical of the Bank Nationalisation Ordinance, 1969, especially because it was, as he put it, a sign 'that the government was afraid of facing Parliament in a straightforward manner'.[177] Three decades later, he conveniently forgot that charge. Under his leadership, the NDA cabinet promulgated the Prevention of Terrorism Ordinance, 2001, barely five weeks before parliament was to convene for its winter session, and in full knowledge that the government lacked the numbers to turn the ordinance into an Act. Several opposition parties – including the Congress Party – criticised the government, but adopted a strange line of attack. It had been brought in, they said, 'without consultations'.[178] Note the nature of the claim. To the Congress, the offence was not so much that the NDA cabinet had promulgated an ordinance. Rather, it had to do with the fact that it was brought in without *their* inputs. And when the UPA cabinet promulgated the Unlawful Activities (Prevention) Amendment Ordinance, 2004, the BJP took ordinance-related criticism one step further: it offered none. Party spokesman Arun Jaitley was scathing in his assessment of the provisions of the new law, but said nothing about the

[175] Presidential Ordinances, *supra* n. 1 at vi.

[176] As Austin put it, the Janata government was remarkably successful 'in repairing the Constitution from the Emergency's depredations, in reviving open parliamentary practice through its consultative style when repairing the Constitution, and in restoring the judiciary's independence'. *Supra* n. 25 at 403–404.

[177] *Supra* n. 38 *ibid.*

[178] Anon, 'Sonia Gandhi Cracks the Whip, Partymen Fall in Line on POTO' *Times of India*, 20 November 2001. See also Anon, 'Congress Firm on Opposition to POTO, but Ranks Appear Confused' *Times of India*, 24 November 2011.

ordinance per se. That the amendments were brought in by an ordinance did not matter *at all*.[179] Jaitley's approach is a telling reminder of how far we have normalised ordinances. They are part of our parliamentary way of life and hardly tied to any notion of 'immediate necessity'.

Nevertheless, this 'precedent' argument cannot explain why successive cabinets kept up with ordinances. After all, various cabinets have opted not to follow several worthwhile precedents in other areas. This is where a set of empirical reasons become relevant. In this chapter, I looked at parliament's performance and its bearing on ordinances. Parliament's performance, as I previously argued, may be measured by the number of Acts legislated in a given year, the number of days it is in session in the given year and the number of days it is sitting in a given year. From the earlier Tables (2.3 and 2.4), it is clear that the inverse relationship between Acts and ordinances, if any, cannot be positively asserted. In other words, there is no data to make the claim that ordinances rise with the fall in the number of parliamentary legislation and vice-versa. However, Tables 2.10 and 2.11 suggest that there is a statistically significant correlation between parliament's performance measured by the number of days the Lower House is in session and the number of ordinances that may be promulgated; in other words, the lower the number of days in session, the greater the likelihood of ordinances. Lastly, Tables 2.12 and 2.13 suggest that the correlation between parliament's performance measured by the number of days the Lower House is in sitting and the number of ordinances is even stronger. That is to say, the lower the number of days in sitting, greater is the likelihood of ordinances. These two findings – the relevance of sessions and sittings to ordinances – should not be surprising. The very mechanism of ordinances, in a sense, is an incentive to keep parliament out of session, and the fact that they require neither debate nor justification makes them even more 'valuable'. This is especially true of cabinets struggling to cobble together legislative majorities, and yet keep up the appearance of a functioning legislature.

But this argument about the inverse relationship between parliament's performance and the number of ordinances cannot be the full story, either. By definition, a single-party majority cabinet has a legislative majority and, therefore, lacks any incentive to keep parliament out of session or promulgate ordinances. And yet, as Table 2.17 shows, 45 per cent of all ordinances promulgated thus far came from single-party majority cabinets. This is where a set of attitudinal reasons become relevant. They

[179] Anon, 'New Bill Will Weaken Fight on Terror: BJP' *Times of India*, 24 September 2004.

are qualitative in nature, and refer to the attitudes a cabinet may hold towards parliament. For our purposes, attitudinal reasons, I will argue, may be of two kinds.

First, cabinets may look upon parliament as a cumbersome institution. Parliamentary legislation necessarily calls for some measure of transparency, deliberation and scrutiny, and a cabinet that wishes to avoid these 'constraints' – for whatever reasons – may take recourse to ordinances. The Bank Nationalisation Ordinance, 1969 and the proposed Office of Profit Ordinance in 2006 are good examples. I have discussed them earlier and will avoid rehearsing the facts again. Suffice it to say, both ordinances had different intentions underlying them. The 1969 Ordinance had to do with the internal politics of the Congress Party and Mrs Indira Gandhi's emergence as the undisputed leader of the government and the party. The proposed 2006 ordinance had to do with validating Mrs Sonia Gandhi's seat in parliament by removing her disqualification. Despite those immediate differences, they had something in common: the idea that legislation involves a degree of deliberation and scrutiny that are best avoided, at least initially. Empirically speaking, these ordinances were not necessary; the respective cabinets had the numbers to get an Act through parliament.

Second, cabinets may have outright contempt for parliament and ordinances may result from that attitude. This is different from the first, and can reveal itself in at least five ways. First, a cabinet may promulgate an ordinance in the full knowledge that it does not have the numbers to eventually enact it into law. The original and the re-promulgated versions of the Prevention of Terrorism Ordinance, 2001 are good examples. When the Vajpayee cabinet promulgated the ordinance in October 2001, several of its allies openly opposed the law.[180] Later, when parliament reconvened for its winter session, it became abundantly clear that the government would not introduce the bill: they lacked the numbers. And yet, the cabinet chose to re-promulgate the ordinance with slight modifications. That a majority in parliament, albeit impliedly, had rebuffed the need for such a law did not matter.

Next, a cabinet may promulgate an ordinance when either house of parliament is already in session. There are several cases where this has happened. The Tea Companies (Acquisition and Transfer of Sick Tea

[180] Smita Gupta, 'Naidu Wants POTO Amended to Protect Press Freedom' *Times of India*, 18 November 2001.

Units) Ordinance, 1985 is one such case.[181] It was promulgated at a time when the Lower House was in session, but the Upper House was not. Another example is the promulgation of the Swadeshi Cotton Mills Company Limited (Acquisition and Transfer of Undertakings) Ordinance, 1986.[182] Once again, the Lower House was in session, but not the Upper House. The point to note is that in all such cases, rather than create conditions whereby both houses can properly enact a piece of legislation, cabinets prefer to make the *functioning house* irrelevant.

Third, a cabinet may promulgate an ordinance even after a bill has been introduced in parliament. This, too, has happened on several occasions. For example, the Armed Forces (Special Powers) Continuance Ordinance, 1964 was promulgated after a similar bill was pending in parliament.[183] In other words, parliament was already seized of the issue. But rather than leave the matter to parliament, the cabinet promulgated the ordinance on the ground that it was immediately necessary. This is also true of the Requisitioning and Acquisition of Immovable Property (Amendment) Ordinance, 1968.[184] It was promulgated in June 1968, and at a time when a similar bill was already pending before the Lok Sabha.[185] In such cases, ordinances have the effect of making *deliberations* in the two houses irrelevant.

Fourth, a cabinet may promulgate an ordinance after it has already been passed by one house of parliament. In August 1998, the Vajpayee cabinet promulgated the Prasar Bharti (Broadcasting Corporation of India) Amendment Ordinance, 1998 to undo the changes introduced by the previous regime.[186] It reintroduced parliamentary oversight of the corporation and brought in several other changes to the composition of the board. The ordinance, however, was promulgated after it had already been passed by the Lower House, and was pending in the Upper House.[187] The government lacked the number there, and rather than face embarrassment, chose to avoid the vote entirely by bringing in an ordinance. In other words, it made the pending *bill* irrelevant. The opposition charged

[181] 3 of 1985.

[182] 5 of 1987.

[183] 1 of 1964.

[184] 4 of 1968.

[185] See also the Public Premises (Eviction of Unauthorised Occupants) Amendment Ordinance, 1968 (5 of 1968); the Indian Patents and Designs (Amendment) Ordinance, 1968 (8 of 1968).

[186] 16 of 1998.

[187] Ashish Mullick, 'Centre's Decision Paves Way for Gill's Exit' *Times of India*, 28 August 1998.

the government with 'subverting democracy'.[188] Expressing predictable outrage, Congress spokeswoman Girija Vyas said that the government had handled the issue in an 'undemocratic manner' because a 'bill had already been passed by the Lok Sabha and had become a property of Parliament'.[189] On its own, the criticism has considerable merit. By promulgating an ordinance, the cabinet truncated the legislative procedure rather than take it to its logical conclusion. But it is unclear if partisan criticisms of such kind are meant to be – or can be – taken seriously. The Congress's track record, after all, is hardly better.

Finally, in the most egregious case of contempt towards parliament, a cabinet may promulgate an ordinance after parliament has formally rejected a bill. This is different from the first instance of contempt I explained earlier: There, the cabinet promulgates an ordinance in the *knowledge* that it does not have the numbers to enact a law. The events surrounding the abolition of Privy Purses – a pension granted to India's former ruling princely houses – by presidential order is a good example. In 1970, Mrs Gandhi's government tabled a bill to abolish these pensions. After much constitutional haggling, the government succeeded in getting the bill through the Lower House by the slimmest of margins, but it was defeated in the Upper House. Unwilling to give up, Mrs Gandhi achieved the same result by issuing a directive. To be sure, there was no ordinance involved; the president issued an 'order' derecognising the titles.[190] But the facts exemplify the broader point I have in mind: A cabinet can wilfully disregard parliament's stated intent by simply bringing in an ordinance.

Together, these attitudinal reasons – along with the empirical and precedential reasons – give us a better understanding of the prevalence of ordinances in India. Whereas the empirical side of the equation measures parliament's performance and the likelihood of ordinances, the attitudinal side speaks to a cabinet's attitude towards parliament. Ordinances are more likely when the houses perform poorly, but they are as likely when cabinets treat parliament as a hindrance or view it as an expendable body. In other words, precedents, performances and personalities – or some combination of the three – hold the key to ordinances in India.

If correct, this analysis negates part of the reason for which a provision for ordinances was included in India's Constitution. In the Constituent Assembly, Dr Ambedkar defended draft Article 123 as a necessary evil.

[188] Anon, 'Opposition Parties Decry Prasar Bharti Ordinance' *Times of India*, 31 August 1998.

[189] *Ibid.*

[190] *Supra* n. 25 at 220–233.

But he partly justified the extraordinary arrangement on the ground that misuse was unlikely. In the face of persistent criticisms from the likes of Kamath, Kunzru and Shah, Ambedkar insisted that future presidents and cabinets would be responsible in their reliance on ordinances, and that the fear of misuse was unfounded. That original expectation clearly stands belied, and the data in this chapter is compelling evidence of that.

E. CONCLUSION

Included in the Constitution as an 'exceptional' arrangement, the mechanism of ordinances has, in the course of sixty years, become just another legislative arrangement. Indeed, in many ways, it has become a *parallel* arrangement, and often, the preferred legislative arrangement. To cabinets opposed to even elementary measures of transparency or scrutiny, ordinances are a comfortable alternative: they require no discussion, debate or vote. Although this explains the political use of ordinances, what about its legality? In the next three chapters, I shall turn to the law of ordinances and particularly focus on Article 123. How have courts interpreted Article 123? How should they interpret it? I shall discuss a range of interpretative questions, and in doing so, defend the view that much of the political practices associated with ordinances are unconstitutional. Despite words to the contrary, Acts and ordinances, I will argue, do not have the 'same force and effect', and that substantial constraints on a cabinet's reliance on ordinances is constitutionally defensible.

ANNEX I

Regression analysis is the standard method by which to measure the relationship between a dependent variable and one or more independent variables. In this chapter, I have tried to assess the relationship between ordinances on one hand and parliamentary Acts, parliamentary sessions and parliamentary sittings on the other hand. Of the numbers in the following Tables, most relevant for our purposes is the p value that helps us ascertain the statistical significance of the findings. Conventionally, a finding is statistically significant if the p value is lower than .05. Table 2A measures the relationship between ordinances and Acts. Because the p value (.55) is greater than .05, one may say that ordinances and Acts are not statistically correlated. Strictly speaking, even that cannot be asserted. In formal terms, given the p value, one may only say with 95 per cent confidence that the hypothesis that ordinances and Acts have no bearing on each other cannot be rejected. The *p* value in Table 2B is .04. Because it is less than .05, it is, conventionally speaking, considered statistically significant. In other words, one may say with 95 per cent confidence that the hypothesis that ordinances and parliamentary sessions have no bearing on each other *can* be rejected. Similarly, because the *p* value in Table 2C is less than .05, one may say with 95 per cent confidence that the hypothesis that ordinances and parliamentary sittings have no bearing with each other *can* be rejected. Note that the *p* value does not 'prove' anything. If less than .05, it merely suggests that the relationship between two factors cannot be dismissed as one of chance.

2A. Ordinance and Acts

	Coefficients	Standard Error	*t* Stat	*P*-value	Lower 95%	Upper 95%
Intercept	12.62052045	3.508011365	3.597628155	0.000680328	5.593129297	19.64791161
No. of Acts	−0.033743925	0.056222996	−0.600180125	0.550807344	−0.146372118	0.078884269

2B. Ordinance and parliamentary sessions

	Coefficients	Standard Error	*t* Stat	*P*-value	Lower 95%	Upper 95%
Intercept	21.93865169	5.561028201	3.945071108	0.000224555	10.79857364	33.07872974
No. of Sessions	−0.077895948	0.037626885	−2.07022045	0.043054876	−0.153271656	−0.00252024

2C. Ordinance and parliamentary sittings

	Coefficients	Standard Error	*t* Stat	*P*-value	Lower 95%	Upper 95%
Intercept	20.79702466	3.939681592	5.278859261	2.1878E-06	12.90489413	28.68915519
No. of Sittings	−0.105331807	0.039507147	−2.666145594	0.010009663	−0.184474132	−0.026189481

Part II

Law and Interpretation

3

Negotiating the Text: Ordinances, Article 123 and the Interpretative Deficit

When the Constitution says that the ordinance making power is legislative power and an ordinance shall have the same force as an Act, an ordinance should be clothed with all the attributes of an Act of legislature carrying with it all its incidents, immunities and limitations under the Constitution. It cannot be treated as an executive action or an administrative decision.

Justice Y. V. Chandrachud, in *T. Venkata Reddy and Others v. State of A.P.* AIR 1985 SC 724 at para 15.

We have already seen that Article 123 authorises the president to promulgate ordinances 'except when both Houses of Parliament are in session'. Such recourse to ordinances, however, requires that the president be 'satisfied that circumstances exist which render it necessary for him to take immediate action'. The mechanics of an ordinance, at first sight, appear simple. Once promulgated, it has 'the same force and effect as an Act of Parliament'. The ordinance must 'be laid before both Houses' after parliament reassembles, and unless properly enacted into an Act, 'it shall cease to operate at the expiration of six weeks' from the date of reassembly. But an ordinance, as I discussed in Chapter 2, may also cease to operate prior to the expiry of six weeks 'if resolutions disapproving it are passed by both Houses' or if it is 'withdrawn by the President'. And Article 123(3) clarifies that the president may promulgate ordinances only on matters in which parliament is competent to enact laws; transgressions beyond that are declared void.[1]

[1] Constitution of India, Article 123(3) ('If and so far as an Ordinance under this Article makes any provision which parliament would not under this Constitution be competent to enact, it shall be void').

This description appears simple and comprehensive. The simplicity, however, is more apparent than real. Article 123 raises a range of analytical questions that cannot be accounted for by its simple recital, something one might refer to as the text's 'interpretative deficit'. It is especially evident in situations where the normative content of the provision is itself under challenge. For example, what does it mean to say that the president may promulgate ordinances except when both houses are 'in session' – a question we considered previously. Similarly, what does it mean to say that an ordinance 'ceases' to operate? Or that the president may promulgate only on matters in which parliament has 'competence' to enact? These questions challenge the very meaning of Article 123 and, therefore, cannot be resolved by simply reciting the provision. We need something more – a standard – by which to make sense of it.

Some of these questions have been called into controversy earlier, and the interpretative deficit has been mostly filled by syllogistically equating ordinances with Acts. Recall that ordinances are declared to have the 'same force and effect' as Acts of parliament. Understanding the scope and effect of ordinances, it is often said, is about understanding the scope and effect of Acts – one leads to the other. The Supreme Court, especially, is keen on this equivalence. There is no qualitative difference, the court says, 'between an ordinance issued by the president and an act passed by parliament'.[2] And because the president's power in Article 123 is coextensive with the power of parliament to make laws, limitations cannot be read into it.[3] Both are products of legislative power and 'equally subject to the limitations which the Constitution has placed upon that power'.[4] Ordinances, therefore, 'should be clothed with all the attributes of an act of legislature carrying with it all its incidents, immunities and limitations under the Constitution'.[5] Here, then, is the standard by which the Supreme Court has tried to make sense of Article 123: when in doubt about ordinances, refer to Acts. The standard also has authorial appeal. H. M. Seervai, for example, stridently argues 'that except as to the limit put on the duration of an Ordinance . . . there is no other limitation on the legislative power of the president . . . if the condition precedent for the enactment of an Ordinance is fulfilled'.[6] Or, as he later put it, 'nothing

[2] *R. K. Garg v. Union of India* (1982) 1 SCR 947 at para 7.

[3] *Ibid.*

[4] *A. K. Roy v. Union of India* AIR 1982 SC 710 at para 14.

[5] *T. Venkata Reddy v. State of A.P.* AIR 1985 SC 724 at para 14.

[6] H. M. Seervai, *Constitutional Law of India* Vol. II, 1114 (N.M. Tripathi, Bombay, 1968).

is excluded from the scope of an Ordinance which is not excluded from the scope of an act of parliament'.[7]

In this chapter, I will critically discuss five analytical questions central to ordinances, arguing that the court's syllogistic template is incorrect – it cannot resolve the interpretative deficit. More specifically, I will argue that the template, in some respects, is too narrow; it *does not* capture the complexity of ordinances. In other respects, the template is irrelevant; it *cannot* perform its intended function. The overarching effect of the two arguments will lead us to a counterintuitive position: Article 123 does not mean what it says. Despite language to the contrary, Acts and ordinances, I will argue, cannot have the same force and effect. The syllogistic template must, therefore, be abandoned. But what should we replace it with? Making sense of ordinances, I will argue, requires a 'robust understanding' of Article 123, the policy embedded therein and the context through which it presents itself. Equally, it requires a thoroughgoing command of the history of use and abuse through which ordinances have become an integral part of India's parliamentary system, something I discussed in Chapter 2. For that reason, simply equating Acts with ordinances without an analytical or empirical grounding is bound to lead us astray.

A. HIDDEN LAWS: THE 'PUBLIC' REQUIREMENT OF ORDINANCES

Take the case of legal effect. At what point in time do ordinances take effect? This is a matter on which the Supreme Court is yet to adjudicate. But the court's syllogistic template would suggest that Acts and ordinances come into force in a similar manner. The General Clauses Act, 1897 (the 1897 Act), s. 5, provides for the commencement of Acts: 'Where any Central Act is not expressed to come into operation on a particular day, then it shall come into operation on the day on which it receives the assent'. Note that publication of the law or even its notification is not a requirement; Acts come into operation on the very day they are assented. If ordinances are analogously read with this provision, it implies that they also come into effect on the day of assent, irrespective of publication. A. P. Pandey made this argument earlier. 'Reading [the] provision *mutatis mutandis* in relation to an ordinance, it appears that an ordinance also comes into operation on the date on which it is

[7] *Ibid.*

promulgated', he said.[8] But promulgation, he reminds us, is not synonymous with publication; the latter is only a record that promulgation had indeed taken place.[9]

There are two immediate problems with the argument: one semantic, the other, legalistic. Semantically, to promulgate something may mean 'to make [something] widely known, to publish'.[10] This was the view held by Thomas Macaulay, the first law member to the Governor-General's Council in 1834. To the question 'what does promulgation mean', he wrote, 'it means, if I understand its sense, the publication of a law in an authentic form'.[11] And so it is conceivable that when ordinances are said to come into force when they are promulgated, it implies that they come into force when they are published. But, legally speaking, Pandey's recourse to s. 5 is especially untenable. The 1897 Act, s. 30, provides that 'the expression Central Act wherever it occurs, *except* in section 5 . . . shall be deemed to include . . . an Ordinance promulgated by the president under Article 123 of the Constitution'. In other words, the provision on commencement of central Acts is not meant to apply to presidential ordinances. Interestingly, having made s. 5 inapplicable to ordinances, the 1897 Act does not specify how they should come into force.

Legally, three options are open. First, as with Acts, an ordinance may come into force when it is promulgated by the president – narrowly understood as 'assented to'. Second, it may come into force on the date on which the promulgation (i.e., assent) is *notified* in the official gazette. Or, it may come into force on the date on which the full ordinance is *published* in the gazette. Which of these options should apply to ordinances? The 1897 Act, s. 30, discounts the first option. Of the remaining two, only the third, I will argue, is legally defensible. That is to say, an ordinance – unlike an Act – may come into effect only when it is published in the gazette. More strongly, any rule of commencement short of full publication would be unconstitutional. The rest of this section attempts to explain why that is so.

As I mentioned in the Introduction, Acts, at least in theory, are products of a public and deliberative process. Proposals for Acts originate in specific departments and at the pre-drafting stage, move through a maze

8 A. P. Pandey, 'Hundred Years of Ordinances in India: 1861–1961', 10 *Journal of Indian Law Institute* 259, 289 (1968).

9 *Ibid.*

10 *The Essential Law Dictionary*, 352 (1st ed., Sphinx Publication, Illinois, 2008).

11 Thomas Macaulay, Minute No. 5 (14 June 1835) referred in Law Commission of India, 32nd Report on Section 9 of the Code of Criminal Procedure (May 1967).

of consultations before being presented to the cabinet for consideration.[12] Once approved by the cabinet, the Ministry of Law and Justice turns the proposal into a draft bill. Once introduced in parliament, a bill tends to have a long shelf life. It may be referred to various committees for consideration, or if tentatively approved, it may go through several readings, amendments and debates before being voted on. If both houses of parliament approve it by the requisite majority, the bill is sent to the president for assent. The process generates a degree of publicity and reporting that makes the commencement of Acts immediately on assent, at least, *minimally* acceptable.

But ordinances are different, both in theory and practice. For obvious reasons, they are not subject to parliamentary scrutiny prior to promulgation. Once provisionally agreed upon by the cabinet that an ordinance is needed, a bill is drafted. And subject to final approval, it is sent to the president for assent. Shailaja Chandra, a former joint secretary to the Union Government shared her experiences about the promulgation of an ordinance.[13]

> It was August 1992. Mr. Narasimha Rao was the Prime Minister... On August 27 morning, I was sent for by the Health Secretary and told that an ordinance was to be promulgated that evening. I was dispatched to the Ministry of Law where the ordinance was dictated line by line by an Additional Secretary.
>
> I came to know only through him that the ordinance was intended to thwart the Chief Minister of Andhra Pradesh for wantonly granting permission to establish around 20 medical colleges... Bringing an ordinance was the brainchild of Prime Minister Narasimha Rao, a former Chief Minister of Andhra Pradesh. At 6 pm, the legal officer handed over a typewritten draft to me and I rushed back to Nirman Bhavan... Late that night, the president's assent to promulgate the ordinance was obtained... Overnight, the Central Government had wrenched all powers from States to give permission to establish new colleges, increase seats or introduce post-graduate courses in medical colleges.[14]

[12] *Manual of Parliamentary Procedures in the Government of India* ch. 9 (Ministry of Parliamentary Affairs, New Delhi, 2004).

[13] The Indian Medical Council (Amendment) Ordinance, 1992 (13 of 1992).

[14] Shailaja Chandra, 'Abolish MCI, Councils' *The Pioneer*, 3 September 2009. Such instances are not unheard of. As I discussed in the Introduction, during the heated 'office of profit' controversy in 2006, there were reports in the media that the Union Cabinet had abruptly sent parliament into recess to be able to promulgate an ordinance that had been drafted overnight.

Three things are worth noting. First, not all ordinances are promulgated in this manner. But this experience is largely emblematic of the secrecy associated with the process. By its very nature, ordinances are held to a different standard; they do not have public requirements similar to Acts. Although Chandra's experience involved a regulatory ordinance designed to administer medical schools, the implications are particularly egregious when 'non-public' actions create offences or impose other burdens.[15] Second, of course, one can find instances where Acts have been legislated with remarkable haste and without public debate such that it makes a mockery of parliament's deliberative expectations. A report by the PRS Legislative Research group suggests that in 2007, the Lower House passed 41 per cent of bills (not including financial bills) with little or no discussion. And it further claims that in the three years between 2004 and 2007, the percentage of bills passed with almost no discussion increased from 17 per cent to 41 per cent.[16] Although this trend is unfortunate, note that this does not, by itself, legitimise ordinances. By their very nature, Acts are guaranteed a minimum degree of public presence (introduction in parliament, a motion to vote etc.) that is not true with respect to ordinances. Also, the comparison must be relevant. Even though the trend towards enacting laws without elaborate parliamentary discussion and debate is disappointing, the legislative process, at its best, still remains deliberative. In contrast, ordinances at their best are still a secretive, executive-driven, non-participative fiat. Lastly, it is conceivable that given its low premium on publicity, the provision on commencement of Acts is itself unconstitutional. But assuming that it is not, the rule should not apply to ordinances.[17]

With respect to the procedure by which they become law, ordinances are entirely different from Acts and, therefore, should not attract the implications of the 'same force and effect' provided for in Article 123. To put it differently, Acts and ordinances may have the same force and effect, but they are different with respect to procedure and, therefore, should be subject to different rules on commencement. Acts may come into force immediately on presidential assent, but ordinances, I would argue,

[15] See, e.g., The Prevention of Terrorism Ordinance, 2001 (9 of 2001) (now repealed).

[16] Anon, 'Vital Stats: Legislative Activity in Parliament', *available at*: http://www.prsindia.org/parliamenttrack/vital-stats/legislative-activity-in-parliament-2008–421/ (accessed 16 November 2011). See also C. V. Madhukar, 'House This for Debate?' *The Indian Express*, 3 January 2007.

[17] For discussion on the 'publication' requirement, see Law Commission of India, 60th Report on the General Clauses Act, 1897 (May 1974) at pp. 30–33.

must be published before they can commence. Any other interpretation would be tantamount to imposing legal burdens based on non-public legislation. But what is the status of this 'publication' requirement? Is it one of mere expediency to be done away with when inconvenient? Or is it a *constitutional* requirement that cannot be dispensed with? I will argue that it is of the latter kind, and a 'rule of law' framework may help explain why that is so.

'Rule of law' as a legal term of art is not in India's Constitution. Nevertheless, public law analyses are often done in its name.[18] Even though its precise role in constitutional interpretation is suspect, its hermeneutic presence straddles across the broad sweep of legislative,[19] executive[20] and even constituent power.[21] Almost nothing seems immune from it, if only in words.[22] In *Kartar Singh v. Punjab*,[23] Sahai J., while evaluating the constitutionality of the now repealed Terrorist and Disruptive Activities Act, 1985, suggested that 'democratic accountability should be so maintained that *every* action of the Government be weighed in the scale of rule of law'.[24] Recently, in *Sudhakar v. A.P.*,[25] Kapadia J. held that even the president's prerogative powers were not immune from judicial review on rule of law grounds.[26] Discretionary executive power, even prerogative powers, must be 'subject to the rule of law' and they 'cannot be compromised on grounds of political expediency'.[27] And similar language is easily available in matters dealing with constitutional amendments. In *P. Sambamurthy v. A.P.*,[28] the Supreme Court invalidated Article 371 D (5) in the Constitution on the ground that the provision violated the rule of law – something it said was 'clearly a basic and essential feature of the Constitution'.[29] Authorising state governments to defy or annul

[18] See Upendra Baxi, 'Rule of Law in India' in Randall Peeerenboom et. al. (eds.), *Asian Discourses of Rule of Law* 328 (Routledge, London, 2004). See also Richard H. Fallon, 'The Rule of Law as a Concept in Constitutional Discourse', 97 (1) *Columbia Law Review* 1 (1997); Michel Rosenfeld, 'Constitutional Adjudication in Europe and the United States: Paradoxes and Contrasts', 2 *International Journal of Constitutional Law* 633 (2004).

[19] See, e.g., *Maneka Gandhi v. Union of India* AIR 1978 SC 597.

[20] See, e.g., *Satwant Singh Sawhney v. Assistant Passport Officer* AIR 1967 SC 1836.

[21] See, e.g., *Indira Nehru Gandhi v. Raj Narain* AIR 1975 SC 2299.

[22] The centrality of this 'rule of law' rhetoric in legal discourse is hardly jurisdiction specific. For its increasing references in diverse international instruments, see Randall Peerenboom, 'Human Rights and Rule of Law: What's the Relationship?' 36(4) *Georgetown Journal of International Law* 809, 810–815 (2005).

[23] (1994) 3 SCC 569.

[24] *Id.* at para 442. (emphasis added).

[25] AIR 2006 SC 3385.

[26] *Id.* at para 7.

[27] *Id.* at para 6.

[28] (1987) 1 SCR 879.

[29] *Id.* at 889.

decisions of administrative tribunals, the court said, was inconsistent with the 'basic principle of the rule of law . . . that the executive is bound by law'.[30] These decisions could be easily multiplied. But the point is essentially the same: whatever its analytical purchase, rule of law has become a catholic – and possibly convenient – term of art through which to analyse the exercise of public power.

How does this help with the argument that ordinances unlike Acts *must* be published to come into force? Here is the simple point: If rule of law is pervasively present in India's Constitution in the way the Supreme Court suggests it is, then the president's power to promulgate ordinances cannot be exercised in a manner that diminishes the former. But does that concept require that citizens be subject to only 'public' legislation? The question takes us to the debate on what rule of law really means – a matter on which legal theorists and political philosophers have had, and still have, vast disagreements.[31]

Twentieth-century debates on the rule of law have largely centred around two versions: those advocating a 'thin' or narrow understanding versus those preferring a 'thick' or wide one. The narrow version restricts the rule of law to features that make law, irrespective of its content, efficacious.[32] The wider version rejects this content-neutral understanding of the term.[33] Although there is a large body of literature defending these separate, but sometimes, overlapping positions, almost everybody agrees that rule of law, whatever else it might mean, at a minimum requires that citizens be subject to *public* legislation.[34] Proposed by Fuller in his argument about the 'inner morality of law', law's public requirement and its connection to the rule of law now enjoy near-universal appeal.[35]

[30] *Ibid.*

[31] For an introduction to the rule of law, see Brian Tamanaha, *On the Rule of Law: History, Politics, Theory* (Cambridge University Press, Cambridge, 2004).

[32] See, e.g., Joseph Raz, *The Authority of Law: Essays On Law and Morality* 210–232 (Oxford University Press, Oxford, 1979).

[33] See, e.g., Roberto Unger, *Law in Modern Society* 176–181, 192–223 (Free Press, New York, 1976); R. Dworkin, *A Matter of Principle* 11–18 (Harvard University Press, Cambridge, MA, 1985); Sir John Laws, 'The Constitution: Morals and Rights', *Public Law* 622 (1996); Luc Tremblay, *The Rule of Law, Justice and Interpretation* (McGill-Queen's University Press, Montreal, 1997); T. R. S. Allan, *Constitutional Justice: A Liberal Theory of the Rule of Law* (Oxford University Press, Oxford, 2001); David M. Beatt, *The Ultimate Rule of Law* (Oxford University Press, Oxford, 2004).

[34] For a summary of the important competing positions, see *supra* n. 22 at 826–834; Paul P. Craig, 'Formal and Substantive Conceptions of the Rule of Law: An Analytical Framework', *Public Law* 467 (1997).

[35] L. Fuller, *The Morality of Law* ch. 2 (Yale University Press, New Haven, 1964).

This public requirement, Jeremy Waldron has recently argued, should be understood not in the sense that every last member of the community must know about the laws, but 'in the sense of being *available* to anyone who is sufficiently interested and available in particular to those who make a profession of being public norm-detectors and who make that expertise available to anyone who is willing to pay for it'.[36]

What this unanimity regarding the public requirement tells us is that non-public ordinances are inconsistent with the most elementary demands of the rule of law. If rule of law requires anything at all, it *at least* requires that laws be public. This must apply to ordinances as well. Without the benefit of a nominally deliberative process, ordinances, I would argue, may come into effect only when they are published, or more robustly, only after they have been duly publicised.[37] It is in this sense that the publication requirement is not merely pragmatic or expedient – it is legal. Pandey, therefore, is incorrect; contrary to Acts, ordinances may come into effect only after they are officially published (and perhaps publicised).[38]

The argument is really one of common sense. However, its real effect, I believe, is to open up the possibility that Article 123 does not mean what it says. If Acts and ordinances must commence differently, then, despite language to the contrary, they cannot have the 'same force and effect'. Once this possibility is recognised – albeit through an uncontroversial application – it opens the door to further situations where Acts and

36 Jeremy Waldron, 'The Concept and the Rule of Law', 43(1) *Georgia Law Review* 1, 26 (2008) (emphasis in original).

37 Even the Statute of Proclamations, 1539 (mentioned earlier) – the so-called height of Tudor despotism – provided for an elaborate mechanism to ensure the publicity of proclamations. Keeping in mind that the 'King's subjects should not [be] ignorant of his proclamations', the Statute provided that 'every sheriff or other officer and minister to whom any such proclamation should be directed by the King's writ under his Great Seal, shall proclaim or cause the same to be proclaimed within fourteen days after the receipt thereof, in four several market towns if thee be so many, or else in other towns or villages within the limit of their authority; and they to cause the said proclamations to be fixed and set up openly upon places convenient in every such town, place or village, upon pain and penalty of such sum and sums of money or imprisonment of body as shall be contained in the said proclamation or proclamations'.

38 It is worth pointing out that the Nagpur High Court in *Laxmibai v. State of M.P.* AIR 1951 Nagpur 94 came to the conclusion that an ordinance promulgated under the provisions of the Government of India Act, 1935 (26 Geo 5 Ch. 2) came into effect on its publication. But in that case, judges had the benefit of a provision – § 3 – of the Central Provinces General Clauses Act, 1914 (1 of 1914) that provided rather clearly that a 'Governor's act comes into operation on the date on which it is first published in the official Gazette'.

ordinances may not have the same force and effect. In the rest of this chapter, I shall discuss several controversial situations that exemplify this larger point.

B. 'PARALLEL' CHALLENGE: THE PERMISSIBILITY OF RETROSPECTIVE AND PROSPECTIVE PROVISIONS

We may now turn to the question of the *date* of commencement. Ordinarily, an ordinance should come into force on the day on which it is published. But, on occasions, presidents may specify an alternative date for commencement. An ordinance, for example, may provide for retrospective effect. Or conversely, it may provide for prospective effect. Because Article 123 says nothing about the date of commencement, the permissibility of retrospective and prospective ordinances is not immediately obvious.

With certain limits, Acts can have unlimited retrospective effect.[39] That much is beyond argument. But despite its common use, defining retrospectivity is not easy.[40] Nor is it any easier to justify why it should be allowed; arguments grounded in 'necessary evil,' 'efficiency' or even 'rule of law' are not sufficient to account for its various uses.[41] Judicial decisions in India do not overtly rely on any of these reasons; rather, they ground it in the idea that retrospectivity is a necessary incidence of parliament's original legislative power. Legislative power conferred on a 'Sovereign Legislature', the Supreme Court has said, 'carries with it authority to enact a law either prospectively or retrospectively, unless there can be found in the Constitution itself a limitation on that power'.[42]

[39] For an introduction to the theory and practise of retrospective legislation, see Charles Sampford, *Retrospectivity and the Rule of Law* (Oxford University Press, Oxford, 2006).

[40] For analytical efforts at defining retrospective legislation, see Elmer A. Driedger, 'Statutes: Retroactive Retrospective Reflections', 56 *Canadian Bar Review* 268 (1978); Stephen Munzer, 'A Theory of Retroactive Legislation', 61 *Texas Law Review* 425 (1983); Michael J. Graetz, 'Retroactivity Revisited', 98 *Harvard Law Review* 1820 (1985); Jill E. Fisch, 'Retroactivity and Legal Change: An Equilibrium Approach', 110 *Harvard Law Review* 1056 (1997).

[41] *Supra* n. 39 at 229–256.

[42] *M.P.V. Sundararamier & Co. v. State of Andhra Pradesh* (1958) SCR 1422, 1460. See also *J.K. Jute Mills Co. v. State of Uttar Pradesh* AIR 1961 SC 1534 ('The power of a legislature to enact a law with reference to a topic entrusted to it, is... unqualified subject only to any limitation imposed by the Constitution. In the exercise of such a power, it will be competent for the legislature to enact a law, which is either prospective or retrospective').

A syllogistic template would, therefore, suggest that ordinances may also have retrospective and prospective effects.

In *Prabhakar Kondaji Bhapkar v. Emperor*,[43] Chief Justice Beaumont proposed this view for the first time. Because an 'ordinance is to have the like force of law as an act passed by the Indian Legislature', it followed that an ordinance may also be retrospective.[44] Echoing this, Chagla J. clarified that the power to promulgate ordinances was subject to two limitations only: that there be an emergency and that an ordinance be effective only for a period of six months.[45] This was reiterated in *Jnan Prosanna v. Province of West Bengal*.[46] According to Chief Justice Harries, 'if the Governor [had] a right to legislate . . . then . . . inherent in that right [was] the right to legislate retrospectively'.[47] In other words, the syllogistic template suggests that ordinances, like Acts, can have unlimited retrospectivity. But this view, I would argue, is incorrect. The template fails to account for the legislative architecture around which Article 123 is constructed.

1. *The Limits of Retrospective Operation*

I will argue that temporally speaking, an ordinance – contrary to an Act – can only go so far back in time; it may only have *limited* retrospectivity. The point is best made using a hypothetical set of facts. Assume that India is facing a budget crisis with national expenditure far outweighing sources of revenue, and made worse by high inflation and currency concerns. Despite debating several proposals, consensus was hard to come by. The crisis, in the meanwhile, reached a tipping point. With parliament not in session, the president promulgated an ordinance – The (Special) Estate Duty Ordinance, 2011 (Estate Ordinance 2011) – imposing 70 per cent duty on 'taxable estate' to increase revenue. Even though the ordinance was promulgated on 1 January 2011, it was deemed to have come into effect on 1 April 2010. The ordinance, in other words, was made retrospectively applicable to taxable estates by three-quarters of a calendar year. But parliament, let us assume, was in session on 1 April

[43] AIR 1944 Bom. 119.

[44] *Id.* at 119.

[45] *Id.* at 120. See also, *Emperor v. Sreekant Pandurang Ketkar* AIR 1943 Bom. 169.

[46] 53 CWN 55.

[47] *Id.* at 71. See also *The United Provinces v. Atiqa Begum* 1940 FCR110 (F.B.); *King-Emperor v. Benoari Lal* 72 Ind. App. 57; *Hirji Laxmidas v. Fernendez* (1945) FLJ 119; *Ahmed Khan v. Emperor* AIR 1948 Lah. 120; *In Re Velayudm* 1950 (1) MLJ 508.

2010. Does that affect the legality of the retrospective provision in the Estate Ordinance 2011?

Because it was given retrospective effect from 1 April 2010, it implies that the ordinance effectively came into force at a time when parliament was in session. This, however, potentially goes against Article 123: 'If at any time, *except when both houses of parliament are in session*, the President is satisfied that circumstances exist which render it necessary for him to take immediate action, he may'. The president could *not* have promulgated the ordinance on 1 April 2011. For that reason, the retrospective commencement of the Estate Ordinance 2011 seems to indirectly achieve that which could not be directly achieved. Should that be allowed?

In *Jnan Prosanna*, Chief Justice Harries said yes. When pointed out that retrospective commencement in certain situations – as in the facts of that case, or in our hypothetical example – would be tantamount to 'legislating when the legislature was in session', he was unimpressed.[48] 'If the Governor has power . . . to legislate retrospectively, then it is immaterial', he said, 'whether the legislation is made to take effect from a time when the legislature was in session'.[49] 'The important point of time is the date of the promulgation of the Ordinance. If the legislature was not then in session then the Ordinance [is] valid, no matter what retrospective effect it had'.[50] In other words, once allowed, there are no further limits to retrospectivity in ordinances. An Act can be made to go back any number of years; ordinances, therefore, may do the same.

This view is incorrect; syllogistic references to the nature of parliament's legislative power, I will argue, are insufficient in deciding the scope of retrospectivity in ordinances. Although parliament's legislative power is a good starting point, the scope of the president's powers to promulgate must ultimately be in sync with Article 123 and its surrounding architecture. And that is where these decisions fall short.[51] In deciding the proper scope of retrospectivity, two competing considerations must be borne in mind. On one hand, there is the challenge of legislative *exceptionality*. The president's legislative powers in Article 123 are not parallel; they are exceptional. This is particularly true in the sense that ordinances may originate only at moments when Acts are impossible. But as the hypothetical example shows, indefinite retrospectivity

[48] *Id*. at 72.

[49] *Ibid*.

[50] *Ibid*.

[51] Although many of the decisions referred to here are pre-1950, the Constitution's textual similarity with previous legislation from where ordinances were important make these decisions a relevant starting point.

undermines this exceptionality; it validates ordinances even at points in time when Acts were possible. On the other hand, there is the concern about legislative *flexibility*. Presidential legislative power will lose relevance if it is burdened with stringent temporal limits. For it to remain relevant, that power must have sufficient prospective and retrospective latitudes. In short, retrospectivity, widely read, undermines Article 123 in the first sense. But narrowly read, it undermines Article 123 in the second sense. How then should we read it?

These competing demands are best resolved by what I will refer to as the 'known cause' test. In my view, two questions make up the test. First, was parliament ever in session from the date on which an ordinance is deemed to have come into effect? If no, then retrospective operation is valid without further review. This is so because it suggests that by definition, parliament had no opportunity to consider the matter. However, if parliament *was* in session on the date on which the ordinance is deemed to have come into effect or at any time since, then the second question becomes relevant: did parliament know about the cause of action – the so-called legislative emergency – while it was in session? If it did not, then retrospectivity in ordinances, even from a date on which parliament was in session, is constitutional; it suggests that parliament had no opportunity to consider the matter. To disallow retrospectivity in these circumstances would undermine legislative flexibility. However, if parliament had knowledge of the cause of action, retrospective operation of an ordinance is unconstitutional – it suggests that parliament, despite knowledge that a new law is needed, chose not to act. To allow retrospectivity in these situations would undermine legislative exceptionality. In other words, retrospective operation is valid if parliament was never in session from the date on which an ordinance was deemed to have come into effect, or parliament, despite being in session, did not know about the legislative emergency on which the president purports to rely. However, if parliament was in session at any point from that date and knew about the emergency, retrospective operation must be invalid. This manner of accounting for retrospectivity in ordinances upholds both exceptionality and flexibility.

Bhupendra Bose v. State of Orissa is a classic example.[52] The petitioner challenged the results of an election to a local municipal body on the grounds that procedural requirements were not followed. The High Court agreed, and invalidated the result. Alarmed by the possibility that

[52] AIR 1962 SC 945.

elections to other municipal bodies may also be invalidated, the governor promulgated an ordinance; electoral laws were retrospectively amended to override the High Court's reasoning and judgment. By the terms of the known-cause test, this retrospectivity is valid even if the ordinance was deemed to have come into effect at a point in time when the state legislature was in session, or had been in session at some point since that date. The legislature did not know the cause of action – the High Court's invalidation of electoral results – and could not possibly have known it. Similarly, consider the retrospective validity of our hypothetical Estate Ordinance 2011. We assumed that the ordinance was deemed to have come into effect at a point in time when parliament was in session. Its validity would, therefore, depend on the 'novelty' of the budget crisis. Was that something parliament knew of in April 2010 or at any point after that while in session? If so, retrospective effect is unconstitutional; it undermines legislative exceptionality.

Apart from explaining how the test works, these two examples also point to its weakness. The test appears to work well with 'episodic' causes, that is, causes like in *Bhupendra Bose* that occur on identifiable dates. But its utility with 'continuous' causes is suspect, that is, causes that are often the culmination of a series of socio-political moments. In such cases, it is difficult to precisely identify points at which certain things become 'known'. The Estate Ordinance, 2011 – and the financial crisis to which it responded – are good examples. A financial crisis is almost always a work in progress. It is the product of several decisions spanning many years, and identifying the precise moment of crisis is not easy. In particular, it may be difficult to identify the point at which action on the issue could no longer be deferred. And in such circumstances, the known-cause test may not be entirely useful.

However, two things must be said in reply. The non-episodic nature of legislative causes of action is a general problem for *all* retrospective legislation; it is not peculiar to our discussion of ordinances. A strong reading of the non-episodic nature of legislative events will lead to the conclusion that all legislation – or at least a significant number of legislation – are retrospective by definition. Secondly, how the known-cause test should be applied will depend, in part, on the standard of proof demanded in judicial review proceedings. If judges prefer a relatively non-intrusive standard of review, then the fact that some aspects of the legislative cause of action were known at a point in time when parliament was in session would not make an ordinance fatal. For these reasons, the test, despite some difficulties, I would argue, is useful in separating valid cases of retrospective ordinances from ones that are not. To summarise, although both Acts and ordinances may enact retrospective legislation, different limits apply to them. Parliamentary Acts may go back in time indefinitely; ordinances, however, may go only so far back as the previous session of parliament – subject, of course, to the known-cause test.

2. *The Limits of Prospective Operation*

Now consider the converse: Can ordinances have *prospective* effect? The 1897 Act, s. 5, makes it clear that parliament may determine the date on which an Act is to commence. As with retrospectivity, parliament has near complete discretion in determining the date of prospective commencement. For example, it may authorise an Act to come into effect several weeks, months or even years later. Presumably, ordinances may also provide for prospective commencement, but are there any limits to this?

The two concerns identified earlier – exceptionality and flexibility – apply here as well. First, authorising an ordinance to come into effect, say, ten months into the future would, under normal circumstances, undermine legislative exceptionality. By then, parliament would have been in session for a period of time, or may be in session at that very moment. Secondly, with prospective effect, there is the need to additionally account for Article 123(2) (a): 'Every . . . Ordinance shall be laid before both Houses of Parliament and shall cease to operate at the expiration of six weeks from the reassembly of Parliament, or, if before the expiration of that period resolutions disapproving it are passed by both Houses, upon the passing of the second of those resolutions'. So, if an ordinance provides for prospective operations to come into effect six months after a session of parliament is over, it would fall foul of the limits prescribed in Article 123(2). In other words, although both Acts and ordinances may provide for prospective effect, there are certain differences. With Acts, there are no limits. They may come into effect at any point of time in the future. Ordinances, however, have limits: their prospectivity is limited to periods prior to the commencement of the next parliamentary session.

Apart from the date of commencement, we may also consider the duration of ordinances here. Whereas prospective effect determines when Acts and ordinances come into existence, sunset clauses determine when they formally cease to exist. Without any sunset provision, an Act remains in force for an indefinite duration, or at least until it is amended or repealed.[53] But an Act may also be self-expiring; parliament may define its tenure. By its own provisions, an Act may cease to exist after several months or years. Arguments for sunset provisions, both in constitutions and legislation, are often grounded in concerns that have to do with intergenerational consent, legislative oversight or regulatory efficiency.[54] Frequently employed by legislatures, sunset provisions, some argue, force legislative and executive bodies to periodically engage in public conversation and re-examine the basis for its authority.[55] This is particularly beneficial in policy contexts where information deficits exist or has the effect of distributing political power, costs and risks across branches of government.[56]

Whatever the benefits in the case of Acts, I will argue that ordinances should have a limited capacity for sunset provisions. The concerns here are same as before: balancing legislative exceptionality and flexibility while remaining grounded in Article 123, its architecture and context. As with prospective effect, ordinances may provide for sunset clauses only for a period of time in the future that is *prior* to the commencement of the next legislative session. In other words, sunset clauses cannot extend beyond the term of a forthcoming session of parliament. A contrary view would be inconsistent with the requirement in Article 123(2) that such an ordinance 'cease to operate at the expiration of six weeks from the reassembly of parliament', unless properly enacted into law. Therefore, irrespective of the duration provided for in the provisions of an ordinance, it will cease to exist six weeks from the date on which parliament reassembles. This would be true even in situations where an ordinance has a self-denied tenure of, say, five years.

Let me explain the practical import of the argument with the provisions of the now-repealed Prevention of Terrorism Ordinance, 2001,

[53] See Jacob E. Gersen, 'Temporary Legislation', 74 *University of Chicago Law Review* 247 (2007).

[54] See, e.g., Jefferson to Madison, 6 September 1789, reprinted in Julian P. Boyd et al. (eds.) *The Papers of Thomas Jefferson XV*, 396 (1958), The Federalist No. 26 (Alexander Hamilton), *available at*: http:// thomas.loc.gov/home/histdox/fed_26.html (accessed 16 November 2011).

[55] See, e.g., Peter Margulies, 'Judging Terror in the "Zone of Twilight": Exigency, Institutional Equity and Procedure After September 11', 84 *Boston University Law Review* 383 (2004). For a comparative study of sunset clauses in terrorism legislation in the common-law world, see John E. Finn, 'Sunset Clauses and Democratic Deliberation: Assessing the Significance of Sunset Provisions in Antiterrorism Legislation', 48 *Columbia Journal of Transnational Law* 442 (2010).

[56] *Supra* n. 53 at 248–280.

(POTO). Promulgated in October 2001 in the aftermath of the 11 September attacks in New York City, the 2001 Ordinance, s. 1(6), provided that 'it shall come into force at once and shall remain in force for a period of five years from the date of its commencement'. Here is an ordinance with a sunset clause that claims to have a self-defined life of five years. But this is unconstitutional beyond a particular period. Despite this provision, the ordinance could not have operated beyond six weeks from the date of reassembly of parliament. And its self-defined tenure of five years may be permissible only in highly exceptional situations where parliament does not convene for that duration. Short of that, the sunset clause, and indeed the entire ordinance, must cease to operate immediately on the expiry of six weeks from parliament's reassembly.

As with the very act of commencement, our discussion regarding the date and duration of commencement reiterates my argument that the Supreme Court's syllogistic template is incorrect. The argument demonstrates that a range of architectural limits specifically apply to ordinances – limits that the court's syllogism cannot identify. For that reason, the scope and effect of ordinances cannot be determined simply by analogising them with Acts; a fuller view must be grounded both in Article 123 and the related architecture that makes the provision possible.

The weakness of the syllogistic template aside, arguments regarding retrospectivity and prospectivity also suggest that the commonly held view about the duration of ordinances is incorrect. Note that Article 123 does not prescribe the maximum duration of ordinances. The commonly held view is that an ordinance may have a maximum life of seven-and-a-half months.[57] Article 85 enjoins parliament to meet once every six months, and an ordinance, once promulgated, must cease to exist six weeks after the reassembly of parliament in accordance with Article 123(2). When put together, the two imply that an ordinance may be in operation for no more than seven-and-a-half months.

To understand why this view is incorrect, we must distinguish between the 'tenure' of an ordinance and its 'validity'. Tenure refers to the period of time for which an ordinance is in the legislative digests; that is, the period during which an ordinance will show up in the compendium of legislation. Validity, in contrast, refers to the duration for which an ordinance is in *operation*; that is, the duration for which an ordinance is in effect. Note that tenure and validity do not necessarily go together. Legislation may

[57] See, e.g., *D. C. Wadhwa v. State of Bihar* AIR 1987 SC 576 at para 6; *T. Venkata Reddy v. State of AP* AIR 1985 SC 724 at para 13.

have tenure (i.e., may be present in the statute books) but may not have validity (i.e., may not be in effect). Conversely, there may be unusual cases where a piece of legislation, through some legal fiction, has validity but not tenure. The argument that an ordinance may be in effect only for seven-and-a-half months is incorrect; both its tenure and validity may far exceed that period.

First, consider tenure. Because Article 123 does not provide for a maximum duration for ordinances, it can only be determined by references to the frequency of parliamentary sessions. Ordinarily, parliament must convene at least once every six months, or more specifically in the words of Article 85 'six months shall not intervene between its last sitting in one session and the date appointed for its first sitting in the next session'. The provision, however, has exceptions, and the Supreme Court's opinion in *Reference by President* (No. 1 of 2002)[58] is useful in explaining why that is the case. Whereas Article 85 enjoins parliament to meet every six months, Article 83(2) limits the tenure of the Lower House to five years, unless dissolved sooner.[59] What is the effect of reading Article 85(1) into Article 83(2)? Does Article 85(1) operate as an implied limitation on Article 83(1)? The following set of hypothetical facts may help in clarifying the questions.

Assume that the Lower House holds its first sitting in June 2006. Ordinarily, its tenure is valid until May 2011. The house meets in January 2009, and is thereafter adjourned. It should reconvene no later than July 2009; that is the mandate of Article 85(1). Now assume that an ordinance is promulgated in February 2009. This ordinance, under Article 123(2), is valid for a maximum duration of six weeks from the date of reassembly of the house. By implication, the ordinance is valid until mid-September 2009. Now assume that the president dissolves the Lower House in June 2009 and calls for new elections. However, Article 85(1) requires that six months not intervene between two sessions. Does it imply that electoral formalities must be completed within a month, and a new house constituted by July 2009? In 2002, President Kalam turned to the Supreme Court for advice on that point.[60]

[58] (2002) 8 SCC 237.

[59] Article 83(2) ('The House of the People, unless sooner dissolved, shall continue for five years from the date appointed for its first meeting and no longer and the expiration of the said period of 5 years shall operate as a dissolution of the House').

[60] *In Reference by President* (2002) 8 SCC 237. The following facts led the matter to be referred to the Supreme Court. In July 2002, the Gujarat Legislative Assembly was dissolved by the governor on the recommendation of the Council of Ministers. However,

The six-month clause in Article 85(1), it turns out, might be understood in at least two ways. Bear in mind that every five years, the Lower House is newly reconstituted based on a new electoral verdict. One way of reading Article 85(1) is to limit its applicability to *intra*-house sessions. That is to say, the six-month clause applies to a Lower House seeking to complete its full tenure. But once the Lower House is dissolved, the mandate in Article 85 does not apply. The other way of reading Article 85(1) is to make the six-month clause also applicable to *inter*-house sessions as well. That is to say, after a particular Lower House is dissolved, six months should not intervene between the last sitting of that house and the first sitting of the next house, the composition of which is contingent on new elections. In *Reference by President*, the Supreme Court favoured the former reading.[61] Article 85(1), the court said, 'is mandatory in nature and relates to *an existing and functional* (Parliament or) Legislative Assembly and not to a dissolved Assembly whose life has come to an end and ceased to exist'.[62] The six-month clause, in other words, does not apply to a dissolved parliament. Therefore, to return to our hypothetical facts, the July 2009 deadline does not apply to the constitution of a new house.

How does all this affect the tenure of the February 2009 ordinances? Ordinances are valid until six weeks after the reassembly of parliament, which ordinarily must meet at least once every six months. That limitation, we now know, does not apply to a dissolved parliament. If elections are not held for any reason, a new Lower House cannot be constituted. Indeed, as the Supreme Court itself acknowledged, there is no time constraint on the conduct of elections: 'Obviously, neither the Constitution nor the Representation of People Act, 1951 prescribes any time limit for the conduct of election after the term of the Assembly is over either by premature dissolution or otherwise'.[63] In other words, if parliament is dissolved – as in our hypothetical facts – and elections cannot be conducted for an extended period of time, an ordinance, once promulgated, may enjoy *tenure* for a period that easily exceeds seven-and-a-half months.

the last sitting of the assembly was held in March 2002. Under Article 174(1), six months should not intervene between two sessions of an assembly. Accordingly, it was required that the new assembly be in session at the latest by October 2002. Despite acknowledging that the requirement of Article 174(1) is mandatory in character, the Election Commission pleaded its inability to complete electoral formalities by the due date. It was under those circumstances that the president, in exercise of the powers conferred under Article 143(1), referred the matter to the Supreme Court for advice.

[61] *Id.* at para 85.

[62] *Id.* at para 85 (emphasis added).

[63] *Id.* at para 106 (per Balakrishnan J.).

That is to say, an ordinance, once promulgated, will remain in the compendium of legislation until a new parliament is constituted or it is withdrawn by the president.[64]

But there can also be less exceptional circumstances where an ordinance has *validity* rather than tenure for a period exceeding seven-and-a-half months. The obvious case is one of an ordinance with retrospective effect. Our hypothetical Estate Ordinance 2011, for example, although promulgated in 1 January 2011 is deemed to have come into effect on 1 April 2010. Consequently, although the ordinance's formal tenure may be limited to a few months – it may be in the statute books for, say, six months – its legal *effect* extends far beyond that period. Taken together, these examples demonstrate why the claim that an ordinance's term is limited to a maximum period of seven-and-a-half month duration is too simplistic. Both in ordinary and exceptional ways, an ordinance may far exceed that duration.

C. TEMPORARY FIATS, PERMANENT LAWS: THE LEGAL EFFECT OF 'FAILED' ORDINANCES

With the manner, date and duration of commencement out of the way, we may now turn to the *effect* of ordinances. Once promulgated, an ordinance may encounter one of the four fates I explained previously. It may be enacted into law – the best-case scenario. Or conversely, it may be disapproved by a majority resolution in parliament. But an ordinance may also lapse; that is, it may 'wither away' without facing any form of parliamentary scrutiny. And finally, the president has the option of withdrawing an ordinance at any time prior to its parliamentary disapproval or lapse. Recall that these four possibilities fall into two broad categories. The first possibility (ordinance enacted into law) transforms an ordinance into an Act of parliament. As a result, the ordinance and its legal effects become permanent. But the remaining three possibilities (disapproval, lapse or withdrawal) do not achieve this. In all these cases, an ordinance ends as an ordinance; it does not become an Act. Thus, that raises the troubling prospect of a 'failed' ordinance. Do transactions initiated or completed at a point in time when an ordinance was validly in force continue to enjoy legal effect after it ceases to operate?

64 See also Rakesh Bhatnagar, 'All Eyes on the Supreme Court to Resolve Gujarat Tangle' *Times of India*, 26 August 2002.

Our hypothetical Estate Ordinance 2011 and related facts will help clarify the question. Promulgated on 1 January 2011 with the ostensible objective of raising revenues to overcome a financial crisis, the ordinance, let us assume, provokes an outcry. With the public mood sternly against it, political parties refuse to support the initiative. The cabinet decides not to introduce it as a bill. Consequently, it fails and in the language of Article 123, 'ceases to operate' six weeks from the date of parliament's reassembly. However, during the twelve weeks or so during which the ordinance had the force of law, revenue authorities went about imposing duties on properties that fell within its scope. What is the legal status of duties already imposed? Should the state return the duties collected? Or do completed transactions acquire a degree of permanence even under a lapsed ordinance?

At the outset, it is worth pointing out that the benefits of the 1897 Act is not available to ordinances. That Act, in s. 6, provides that

> Where . . . any Central Act . . . repeals any enactment hitherto made . . . then, unless a different intention appears, the repeal shall not . . . (c) affect any right, privilege, obligation or liability acquired, accrued or incurred under any enactment so repealed; or (d) affect any penalty, forfeiture or punishment incurred in respect of any offence committed against any enactment so repealed; or (e) affect any investigation, legal proceeding or remedy in respect of any such right, privilege, obligation, liability, penalty, forfeiture or punishment as aforesaid.

If applicable, the provision would resolve the controversy: All duties collected and all properties processed during the pendency of the Estate Ordinance 2011 remain valid beyond its formal tenure. Note, however, that the provision applies only to a *repeal*. Earlier, I pointed out that the manner of promulgating ordinances, by its very nature, is different from the way legislation is enacted. But an ordinance as a product, by its very nature, is also different from an Act in one respect: *only* ordinances and bills lapse. An otherwise valid Act ceases to have legal effect if and only if it is repealed, either by a separate Act or by the terms of the Act itself. Of course, an Act may fall into disuse. A state of disuse, however, is not the same as being legally invalid.[65] In contrast, an ordinance ceases to have effect (i.e., lapse after six weeks from the date parliament reassembles), unless it is enacted into legislation.

[65] See Peter Benson Maxwell, *On the Interpretation of Statutes* 380–383 (Fred Rothman and Co., Colorado, 1991). See also *White v. Boot* 2 TR. 274; *Leigh v. Kent* 3 TR 362; *R. v. Wells* 4 Dowl. 562.

Lapse, however, is not the same as repeal. Repeal is an affirmative action; to repeal an Act is to deliberately remove it from the statute books. Lapse, on the other hand, involves inaction; to let an ordinance lapse is to let it drift into a state of legal invalidity. Put another way, in case of repeal, legislators agree that a piece of legislation is no longer required. In contrast, lapse usually signifies a failure to secure a legislative approval to include a piece of legislation in the statute books. This distinction is important in so far as the 1897 Act provides for the continuity of rights, privileges and obligations *only* in cases of repeal. Indeed, there is nothing in that Act that can explain the continuing validity of actions initiated or completed under a lapsed ordinance; it says nothing about it. Therefore, in resolving the question of continuing validity of actions under a failed or lapsed ordinance, we are left with so-called general principles of statutory interpretation and their effect on the overall architecture of Article 123.

In *Bhupendra Bose,* the Supreme Court turned to those very general principles in addressing the matter. As I mentioned earlier, the petitioner challenged the results of an election to a local municipal body on the ground that procedural requirements were not followed. The High Court agreed, and declared the election void. Worried that similar challenges may invalidate other elections, the cabinet promulgated an ordinance nullifying the High Court's decision. When the state legislature came back into session, it refused to enact the ordinance into law. Consequently, the ordinance lapsed. Did the lapse revive the High Court's earlier decision invalidating the elections? The Supreme Court said no. With the interpretative benefits of the 1897 Act unavailable to them, judges turned to general principles of statutory interpretation to resolve the matter.

Based on a quick survey of three English decisions,[66] Chief Justice Chandrachud concluded that no inflexible rule could be laid down regarding the effects of a temporary act.[67] As he put it, at least in some cases, 'repeal effected by a temporary Act would be permanent and would endure even after the expiration of the temporary act'.[68] The precise nature of the effect, he said, 'must depend upon the nature of the right or obligation resulting from the provisions of the temporary act and upon their character whether the said right and liability are enduring or not'.[69] Keeping in mind 'the object of the Ordinance and the right created by the

[66] See *Steavenson v. Oliver* 151 ER 1024; *Warren v. Windle* 102 ER (KB) 578; *Wicks v. Director of Public Prosecutions* (1947) A.C. 362.

[67] AIR 1962 SC 945 at para 22.

[68] *Id.* at para 22.

[69] *Id.* at para 21.

validating provisions', the court concluded that it 'must be held to endure and last even after the expiry of the Ordinance'.[70]

The reasoning was reiterated in *Venkata Reddy v. State of A.P.*[71] The governor promulgated the Andhra Pradesh Abolition of Posts of Part-Time Village Officers Ordinance, 1984, to abolish the post of part-time Village Officers and to create a new category of posts referred to as Village Assistants. The ordinance, despite a series of re-promulgation, lapsed; the Andhra Pradesh State Assembly refused to enact it. The petitioner, then a part-time Village Officer, argued that because the ordinance lapsed, his earlier post stood revived. The Supreme Court rejected the argument. Once again, Chief Justice Chandrachud came to the conclusion that failed ordinances do not become void retrospectively. Article 123(2) says that a failed ordinance 'shall cease to operate', and that, he said, 'only means that it should be treated as being effective till it ceases to operate on the happening of the events mentioned in [the provision]'.[72] The part-time posts stood abolished on the date on which the ordinance was promulgated, and 'its effects were irreversible except by a new legislation', he added.[73] To be sure, parliament and state legislatures were not powerless to undo the effects of failed ordinances, but only a proper legislation with retrospective effect could achieve a turnabout. And that, Chief Justice Chandrachud concluded, is the only way to revive 'closed or completed transactions' generated under a failed ordinance.

1. Bhupendra Bose*: A Critique*

The reasoning in both of these cases is flawed and the syllogistic template is primarily at fault. First, they proceed on the premise that ordinances are analogous to temporary Acts. They are not. A temporary Act is like any other Act, except that it is self-expiring in nature. That is, it is an Act with a sunset clause. Whereas ordinary Acts remain in force until amended or repealed, a temporary Act has complete discretion to define its own tenure. For example, a temporary Act may expire at the end of three years, and yet all rights, duties and obligations created by it may endure in perpetuity. Or it may determine that the effects of the law will remain in effect for a further period of three years and then expire. As a product of parliament's plenary legislative power, a temporary Act has complete discretion in designing itself. But none of this applies to an

[70] *Id.* at para 23.
[71] AIR 1985 SC 724.
[72] AIR 1985 SC 724 at para 18.
[73] *Ibid.*

ordinance. It cannot provide for the endurance of its rights and duties. As the Supreme Court itself pointed out, such enduring provisions would run counter to the cessation requirement in Article 123.[74] Therefore, to equate ordinances with temporary Acts is to confer greater legitimacy on the former than it deserves.

Second, because the court interprets the effects of lapsed ordinances through the prism of temporary Acts, it has the implied effect of privileging presidential 'fiat' over parliamentary legislation. In *Venkata Reddy*, for example, the post of part-time Village Officer was created by an Act.[75] An ordinance abolished that, and despite its subsequent lapse, generated a permanent state of affairs. Only a new Act, the court says, can undo that state of affairs. This view of lapsed ordinances creates a paradox: The executive can undo legislative rights and duties merely by issuing an ordinance, but their effects can be undone and status quo restored only by another legislation. This hierarchy is obviously inconsistent with the scheme of legislative powers in India's Constitution. Although the president, I believe, has significant legislative powers in the Constitution, it does not extend to undoing the effects of parliamentary legislation willy-nilly.

Third, the court's approach does not fit into the architecture of Article 123. Ordinances are time sensitive; they 'cease to operate' six weeks after parliament reassembles. In concluding that lapsed ordinances generate enduring effects, Chief Justice Chandrachud pointed to the language in Article 123. A lapsed ordinance merely ceases to operate, and that, to him, 'only [meant] that it should be treated as being effective till it ceases to operate on the happening of the events mentioned in [the provision]'.[76] However, consider the facts in *Bhupendra Bose*. With the electoral ordinance upheld, in what sense does it cease to operate? It does not cease to operate for the petitioner; *his* loss is permanent. Nor does it cease to operate for those who benefitted from the retrospective validation of election results; *their* benefits are permanent. And it certainly does not cease to operate for all future contestants to whom the changed regulations will apply. The facts in *Venkata Reddy* have a similar effect. With the lapsed ordinance having permanently destroyed the part-time posts, for whom does the ordinance cease to operate? The petitioner has irreversibly lost his job; conversely, those appointed to the newly created posts benefit

[74] AIR 1962 SC 945 at para 19.
[75] Madras Hereditary Village Offices Act, 1895 (III of 1895).
[76] AIR 1962 SC 945 at para 18.

forever. In what sense, then, does a failed ordinance cease to operate? Given the court's interpretation, ordinances cease to operate only in the sense that they are no longer part of the statute books in India. After it has lapsed, anyone looking up the compendium of legislation in India would not find it there. But this limited cessation, I would argue, is insufficient. To say that it ceases to operate prospectively is to make it valid for all times to come and, therefore, negates the temporal dimensions in Article 123.

2. *The Semantic Possibilities of Article 123*

Semantically, 'ceases to operate' in Article 123 is capable of at least two meanings. To understand them, we must go back to the earlier distinction between 'tenure' and 'validity'. 'Ceases to operate' can have a formal or narrow meaning limited to tenure; ordinances cease to operate in the sense that they are no longer part of the statute books. But it can also have a more substantive or wide meaning that incorporates its validity; here ordinances cease to operate in the sense that they wipe out all legal traces such that they never existed. In other words, 'ceases to operate', in the latter sense, includes both tenure and validity: the law *and* its effects – past and present – cease to operate. Which of the two should one prefer? As I have tried to explain, in both *Bhupendra Bose* and *Venkata Reddy*, Chief Justice Chandrachud preferred the narrow view. More importantly, he presented his argument in a matter-of-fact manner as if a simple recital of Article 123 necessarily led to that conclusion. That is clearly not the case. Article 123 is capable of bearing at least two meanings and we need a measure by which to arbitrate between them; simply reciting the provision does not achieve anything.

Given these semantic possibilities, what should be the legal effect of the 'ceases to operate' clause? In determining this, appeals to consequential and policy reasons are inevitable. I have already shown that a narrow reading of that clause produces a paradoxical hierarchy; the executive can permanently undo the deliberated effects of the legislature such that a further legislation is necessary to revive the status quo. But a narrow interpretation is also suspect for policy reasons. Currently, ordinances have minimum, if any, legal costs. The executive can conveniently resort to ordinances without worrying about its future possibilities. If they succeed in legislating it into an Act, they obviously succeed. But failure also counts as 'success'; their efforts will nevertheless generate permanent effects. The empirical record bears this out. As I argued in Chapter 2, ordinances have grown exponentially in recent times; they are a convenient fall-back option for the executive. During their most egregious years, ordinances were treated as a parallel legislative route.[77] Even though a reduced number of parliamentary working days and the emergence of unstable coalition governments amongst others are at fault, judicial interpretations also bear responsibility for the executive's cavalier approach. Courts, after all, have made it all too easy for the executive.

Admittedly, undoing the effects of completed administrative and judicial actions under a lapsed ordinance is an arduous task. It can be a legal nightmare with potential for infinite complexities, but that is a good thing. Prior knowledge regarding the potential complexities – unless it succeeds in securing legislative approval in the future – will (and should) weigh heavily on the executive in assessing if circumstances really exist that make an ordinance necessary. Presumably, a legal requirement to undo completed transactions under a lapsed ordinance will promote responsible practices while dramatically reducing its usage.

Finally, examples from three different contexts should drive home the point that a wide reading of Article 123 is a better option. Consider the legal effects of our hypothetical Estate Ordinance 2011. Assume that duties on several properties were imposed under the ordinance prior to its lapse. Because of the narrow interpretation, these duties will remain valid forever. To those who had to pay the estate duty, the ordinance never really ceases to operate. Even though the ordinance may cease to exist as law, it leaves behind a trail of permanent effects. This scenario is mostly similar to the facts in *Bhupendra Bose* and *Venkata Reddy*.

To understand the startling implications of the narrow interpretation in the context of an ordinance, consider the case of Mohammad Afroze and his prosecution under the dreaded POTO. Promulgated by the Vajpayee cabinet, POTO came into effect on 24 October 2001. Parliament reconvened four weeks later on 19 November 2001, and remained in session for thirty-one days. The ordinance, however, did not become an Act: the government lacked the requisite votes in parliament. Consequently, a slightly amended version was re-promulgated by the president on 30 December 2001.[78] This re-promulgated version remained in effect until

[77] By parallel, here I mean statistically parallel. That is to say, there have been occasions where the president has promulgated almost the same number of ordinances in a year as the number of acts legislated in that same year.

[78] The Prevention of Terrorism (Amendment) Second Ordinance, 2001 (12 of 2001) (now repealed).

the ordinance was enacted into law by an extraordinary procedure on 26 March 2002.[79]

In the light of these facts, consider the case of Mohammad Afroze. Afroze was arrested in Mumbai on 2 October 2001. During the raid, the police recovered from his possession a passport with the immigration seals of several countries, international credit cards and a global-roaming mobile phone.[80] Although initially charged with robbery under the provisions of the Penal Code, the police later changed track. They claimed that he was an *Al-Qaida* agent who had received extensive training in terrorist camps and was involved in the planning of several high-profile attacks.[81] Amongst other charges, he was accused of plotting to crash a plane into the British House of Commons, and of similar daring acts in India and Australia. To unearth the details of what the Mumbai police claimed was an 'international conspiracy', senior officers were sent to the United States, UK and Australia for further investigations. On 1 March 2002, Afroze was formally charged under the re-promulgated POTO, thereby making him the first person to be charged under the anti-terror ordinance in the State of Maharashtra.[82]

Less than four weeks later, the public prosecutor requested the trial court that POTO charges against the accused be dropped.[83] He claimed that there was insufficient evidence to prosecute him under the provisions of that ordinance. That same day, Scotland Yard categorically dismissed claims by the Mumbai police of a plot to attack the British parliament. And with no corroborating evidence to back up Afroze's so-called confession, the police admitted to a 'bona fide error of judgment'.[84] He was later released on bail while the police continued its investigation on charges of alleged sedition. Eventually, the robbery charges were also dropped.

There are a number of troubling aspects to this entire episode, but I shall restrict the discussion to the effects of a lapsed ordinance. Recall that the re-promulgated POTO became law only on 28 March 2002. Up

[79] B. L. Shankar and Valerian Rodrigues, *The Indian Parliament* 311–315 (Oxford University Press, New Delhi, 2011).

[80] Ranjit Khomne, 'Afroze Likely to Be Booked Under POTO' *Times of India*, 3 January 2002.

[81] Anon, 'Afroze Was Part of Al Quida Hit Squad' *Times of India*, 28 March 2002.

[82] Anon, 'Afroze Is the First to Be Booked under POTO in State' *Times of India*, 9 March 2002.

[83] Anon, 'Public Prosecutor Says Police Didn't Consult Him about POTO Charges' *Times of India*, 27 March 2002.

[84] Anon, 'Afroze Finally Gets a Taste of Freedom' *Times of India*, 10 April 2002.

until then, there was a real possibility that the Vajpayee cabinet would fail to get POTO enacted into law for a second time. What if the ordinance had failed again? Because of the court's narrow interpretation, POTO's lapse for a second time would have made no difference to Afroze. As several legal counsels rightly pointed out, the government's failure to enact POTO into law would not have affected cases already under way.[85] Law Minister Arun Jaitley repeated this view; the lapse of the ordinance notwithstanding, prosecutions already initiated would continue as if they were still in force.[86] Afroze, in other words, could be arrested, tried, and even sentenced to death or life imprisonment in pursuance of a 'fiat' issued by the cabinet so long as the process began while the ordinance was still in force. None of this unfolded because the police gave up on those charges. But if the Vajpayee cabinet had failed to get POTO enacted into law and the police had persisted with those charges, the striking consequences of the narrow interpretation would have come into sharp focus.

Apart from the permanent effect of the kind that could have been brought about by Afroze's case, the court's narrow interpretation can produce permanent effects in an entirely different sense. Take the case of a university. In India, a university can only be established by an Act.[87] An ordinance, therefore, can also establish a university.[88] Hypothetically, assume that the ordinance lapses six months later because parliament refuses to enact it. Also assume that the university had achieved several things in those six months. It may have, for example, put in place an academic infrastructure sufficient to commence functioning, secured approvals for some courses, completed the first round of admissions and started introductory classes. What would be the legal effect of the ordinance lapsing? Nothing, if the Supreme Court is correct. The university will continue as if the ordinance is *permanently* valid. The same would be true of administrative or regulatory bodies established by ordinances. In Chapter 2, I discussed a large number of cases where ordinances were used to establish national-level bodies.[89] If the Supreme Court's narrow

85 Ranjit Khomne, 'Cases under POTO Will Stay Even if the Bill Is Defeated' *Times of India*, 22 March 2002.

86 Arun Jaitley, 'POTO Pin-Up' *Times of India*, 13 December 2001.

87 See *Prem Chand Jain v. R.K. Chhabra* (1984) 2 SCR 883.

88 See, e.g., the Manipur University Ordinance, 2005 (2 of 2005). Note that this was a case of converting a state university into a central university, not a proper case of an ordinance establishing a new university entirely.

89 See, e.g. Securities and Exchange Board of India Ordinance, 1992 (5 of 1992); National Commission for Backward Classes Ordinance, 1993 (23 of 1993); Protection of Human Rights Ordinance, 1993 (30 of 1993); Central Vigilance Commission Ordinance, 1999 (4 of 1999).

interpretation is correct, then these bodies will continue to exist permanently despite the 'cease to operate' requirement in Article 123.

Lastly, consider the effect of repeal by an ordinance. Parliament in the exercise of its legislative power can repeal legislation; ordinances, therefore, may also do so.[90] Assume that an ordinance repeals an existing piece of legislation, and eventually lapses.[91] Does the lapse revive the repealed Act? A temporary Act, on its expiry, does not revive the repealed law unless specifically provided for in the Act itself.[92] Therefore, if an ordinance is legally equivalent to a temporary Act, as the Supreme Court says it is, a lapse will have no effect. The repealed Act remains permanently repealed, unless subsequently revived by a new Act. The implication is obvious: the *executive* can permanently repeal a valid piece of legislation.

Both temporally and schematically, the Supreme Court's narrow interpretation is problematic. Temporally speaking, there are two ways in which ordinances do not cease to operate as a result of this interpretation. There can be cases where an ordinance ceases to operate (i.e., enjoy the status of law), but leaves behind a trail of permanent effects, especially with reference to transactions already completed. With reference to those affected by it, these ordinances, it may be said, are partially in operation. The Estate Ordinance 2011, *Bhupendra Bose*, *Venkata Reddy* and, most importantly, the facts involving Mohammed Afroze are examples of this kind. But in some cases, ordinances, despite their lapse, do not cease to operate even in this nominal sense; they are permanently in operation. The university ordinance is one such example. Here, the lapsed ordinance, for all intents and purposes, remains in the statute books forever. The university will continue to function – recruit faculty, admit students, impart education and offer degrees – in a way that makes it appear that the ordinance never lapsed. Also, all future legal disagreements must be resolved with reference to the provisions of that ordinance

[90] See *King-Emperor v. Benoarilal* 72 Ind. App. 57 ('Assuming that the condition as to emergency is fulfilled, the Governor-General . . . may repeal or alter the ordinary law . . . just as the Indian Legislature itself might do'). Some doubts were raised on the permissibility of repeal through ordinances in *Sib Nath Banerjee v. King-Emperor* AIR 1943 Cal. 344. But later decisions have put to rest this controversy. See, e.g., *Jnan Prosanna v. W.B.* 53 CWN 55 ('The Provincial Legislature could undoubtedly amend the existing Provincial law and that being so the Governor can do so by Ordinance if circumstances exist justifying the promulgation of such Ordinances').

[91] As I pointed out in Chapter 2, there are several instances were ordinances have been used to repeal existing legislation. See, e.g., Saurashtra (Abolition of Local Sea Customs Duties and Imposition of Port Development Levy) Repealing Ordinance, 1952 (4 of 1952); Parliamentary Proceedings (Protection of Publication) Repeal Ordinance, 1975 (25 of 1975).

[92] *S. Krishnan v. The State of Madras* AIR 1951 SC 301.

and in that sense it remains a valid source of law. The narrow interpretation, therefore, has effectively written off the 'cease to operate' clause into non-existence. However, the consequences of that interpretation go beyond the temporal concerns. Schematically speaking, it privileges the executive in ways that are inconsistent with the arrangement of legislative powers in the Constitution. The power to promulgate ordinances in moments of legislative urgency has morphed into a parallel power to legislate, such that India's executive can permanently repeal valid laws without parliamentary involvement. For these reasons, the narrow interpretation is erroneous. In contrast, the more substantive or wide interpretation described earlier does a better job of accounting for these challenges.

3. Two Improved Versions Reconsidered

Some progress has been made in this regard. In *Krishna Kumar Singh v. State of Bihar*,[93] Sujata Manohar J., for example, broke away from the received view and suggested a slightly different formulation. The State of Bihar had taken over the management and control of non-governmental educational institutions, thereby turning the previous employees into government employees under the new management.[94] Eventually, the ordinance failed. Contrary to the prevailing narrow interpretation in the Supreme Court, Manohar J. cautioned against permanent effects. 'One should not readily assume that an Ordinance has a permanent effect, since by its very nature it is an exercise of a limited and temporary power given to the Executive', she said.[95] According to her,

> [such] a power is not expected to be exercised to bring about permanent changes unless the exigencies of the situation so demand. Basically, the effect of an Ordinance can be considered as permanent when that effect is irreversible or possibly when it would be highly impractical or against public interest to reverse it e.g. an election which is validated should not again become invalid. In this sense, we consider as permanent or enduring that which is irreversible. What is reversible is not permanent.[96]

Relying on this standard based on reversibility, practicality and public interest, she reversed the employees to their precious non-governmental status.[97] Even though this version of the 'ceases to operate' clause is an

[93] AIR 1998 SC 2288.
[94] *Id.* at para 16.
[95] *Id.* at para 31.
[96] *Ibid.*
[97] *Id.* at para 37.

improvement over the narrow interpretation, it does not go far enough. Note that her opinion does not revise the narrow interpretation in any major way; at best, it slightly moderates the pendulum away from permanent effects. Rather than the presumptive permanence the Supreme Court conferred on failed ordinances, Manohar J. is willing to engage in some form of heightened scrutiny. Its effect, however, is not readily obvious. Her 'irreversible, impractical or public interest' tests are wide enough to satisfy most situations arising out of lapsed ordinances. A conviction, she would presumably argue, cannot be undone. Or a university, once established, cannot presumably be torn down. Or even a piece of legislation once repealed, cannot presumably be reversed. And although she did reverse the status of employees in *Krishna Kumar*, Manohar J. is approving of the court's conclusion in *Bhupendra Bose*. An election once validated, she says, 'should not again become invalid'.[98] Her revised version, then, is more apparent than real.

The only meaningful reform to the narrow interpretation rule was proposed in *Mahanta v. State of Assam*.[99] This little-known decision from the Gauhati High Court is the nearest judges have come to approving the wide interpretation I have defended here. The petitioner belonged to a community that had previously been notified as an 'Other Backward Class' (OBC) in the state.[100] Wanting greater protection in jobs and admission, the community insisted that they be declared 'Scheduled Tribes' (ST) under the Constitution.[101] That would have guaranteed further benefits under the Constitution. Parliament not being in session, the president promulgated an ordinance effectively declaring them an ST community. Meanwhile, the state withdrew the existing notification conferring OBC status on the community. But when the ordinance lapsed, the community was left with no 'protection'. Their OBC status had been withdrawn and the ST status had lapsed. Should it still benefit from reservations in government colleges intended for those belonging to ST communities? In other words, should the effect of the lapsed ordinance endure?

Refusing to treat the lapsed ordinance as a temporary Act, and lapse as analogous to repeal, Ramakrishna J. pointed out that 'no action has been

[98] *Ibid.*

[99] AIR 1999 Gau 32.

[100] *Id.* at para 5.

[101] Constitution of India, Article 342(1) ('The President may with respect to any State or Union territory, and where it is a State, after consultation with the Governor thereof, by public notification, specify the tribes or tribal communities or parts of or groups within tribes or tribal communities which shall for the purposes of this Constitution be deemed to be Scheduled Tribes in relation to that State or Union territory, as the case may be'.).

taken by the parliament to make a law pursuant to the rights conferred on certain citizens under the Ordinance with a view to enable those citizens to continue to enjoy such rights'.[102] And 'unless and until the competent authority enacts such a law . . . to confer such benefits afresh . . . it is not possible to hold that as a right has already accrued, that right has to be saved,' he said.[103] But he accepted the petitioner's argument in the alternative that the rights created by the state notification conferring OBC status on the community in 1975 has become permanent and stood revived on the lapse of the ordinance.[104] The efflux of twenty-five years had created permanent rights, and allowing the unfortunate turn of events to continue 'without considering the legitimate rights of the petitioners', he thought, would 'result in serious injustice to them'.[105] For those reasons, although the community could not claim ST benefits under the lapsed ordinance, their OBC rights remained valid in law.[106] To be sure, the opinion is not analytically grounded. Ramakrishna J. does not explain why the wide rule with respect to the 'cease to operate' clause is better. And despite his clear statement against enduring rights, the point on retrospective invalidation remains ambiguous. These shortcomings aside, *Mahanta* is a useful starting point for reassessing the utility of a wider rule of interpretation.

To summarise the argument, an ordinance, by its nature, is different from an Act. Earlier, I drew attention to a procedural difference; an ordinance is different from an Act in the way it is promulgated into law. But here the difference pertains to the product – the very thing we call ordinance. An ordinance, unlike an Act, can lapse; it ceases to operate if it is withdrawn by the president or if it is not enacted into law through normal parliamentary procedure. In contrast, an Act ceases to operate if and only if it is repealed, expressly or by implication. And because of these differences, ordinances, contrary to the language in Article 123, cannot have the 'same force and effect as an Act of Parliament'.

D. ORDINANCE RAJ: THE LEGALITY OF RE-PROMULGATING ORDINANCES

Because ordinances may lapse on occasion, it leaves open the possibility that they may be *re-promulgated* after a parliamentary session ends.

[102] AIR 1999 Gau 32 at para 26.
[103] *Id.* at para 26.
[104] *Id.* at para 30.
[105] *Id.* at para 32.
[106] *Id.* at para 34.

Article 123 states the conditions under – and the method by – which ordinances may be promulgated, but says nothing about the possibility of re-promulgation. Can the same ordinance be re-promulgated? Are there limits to the number of times it can be re-promulgated, if at all? This is the question that I will address in this section.

Between 1967 and 1981, the State of Bihar promulgated 256 ordinances that 'were kept alive for periods ranging between one and fourteen years by repromulgation from time to time'.[107] Re-promulgated mechanically and strategically, the authorities ensured that the ordinances did not outlive their prescribed tenure.[108] In *D. C. Wadhwa v. State of Bihar*,[109] the Supreme Court concluded that the practice was unconstitutional. Four steps made up most of the court's reasoning: (1) The lawmaking function in the constitution is entrusted to the legislature, (2) it is contrary to democratic norms that the executive should have the power to make law, (3) the power to issue ordinances to tide emergent situations over is exceptional and, therefore, of necessity to be limited in point of time and (4) a contrary view – of allowing the executive to usurp legislative functions – is opposed to India's 'constitutional scheme'.[110] Given how little these steps engage with the text of Article 123 (or its state counterpart in Article 213), one wonders why the court abandoned its syllogistic template on this occasion, opting for an analysis grounded in the 'norms' and 'schemes' embedded in Article 123, something I earlier referred to as the provision's architecture.

The court's conclusion, even though defensible, is far from uniform. On two separate occasions, the Patna High Court interpreted Article 213 in favour of re-promulgative powers.[111] Referring to the permissibility of re-promulgation, in *Mathura Prasad Singh v. State of Bihar*,[112] Singh J. concluded that

> [The] Constitution having vested the Governor with power to promulgate Ordinance when Legislature is not in session and such an Ordinance is given the same force and effect as an act of Legislature . . . it [was] not for

[107] *Supra* n. 57 at para 4.

[108] For a copy of a circular letter advising re-promulgation, see *id.* at para 5. For the detailed description of the assiduous manner in which legislative sessions were timed, and their implications for keeping ordinances alive, see D. C. Wadhwa, *Re-promulgation of Ordinances: A Fraud on the Constitution of India* 8–17 (Orient Longman, New Delhi, 1983).

[109] AIR 1987 SC 579.

[110] *Id.* at para 6–7.

[111] *Chakardharpur Biri and Tobacco Merchants' Association and Others v. State of Bihar* 1973 Tax LR 2132; *Mathura Prasad Singh and Others v. State of Bihar* AIR 1975 Pat 29.

[112] AIR 1975 Pat 295.

> the Court to declare such an Ordinance ultra vires on this score. It is for the Legislature of the State to disapprove of it, if the State is sought to be ruled by successive Ordinances, as and when it meets, or for the electorate to disapprove of the conduct of its accredited representatives for having ruled the State by means of Ordinances and reject them at the next poll.[113]

Professor S. P. Sathe was sympathetic to this sort of reasoning. Referring to Wadhwa's petition to the Supreme Court, he wrote: 'Although the matter he brought before the Court was of great importance, it should have been brought before the legislature because such clandestine repromulgation of ordinances was an affront to the legislation and the legislature alone should have corrected it and reprimanded the government'.[114] But Wadhwa himself saw it differently. 'The political approval of a measure by the Legislature on the one hand and the need for legal compliance with constitutional requirements on the other hand are two different things', he argued.[115] The Patna High Court judgment, he felt, attributed importance only to the former, putting the latter in a low key or even in a negative key.

Where, then, did Wadhwa and Sathe disagree? At issue here is the appropriate scope of judicial remedy in redressing unconstitutional practices. Both Sathe and Wadhwa were in agreement that re-promulgation was constitutionally wrong. However, Wadhwa further believed that the wrong had a judicial remedy; Sathe believed it did not. 'The only justification for the Court's intervention was that such fraudulent re-promulgation of ordinances was a gross violation of the Constitution', Sathe wrote. And because Article 32 is specifically provided for being used against violations of fundamental rights, he wondered if the Court had conceded that Wadhwa had a 'fundamental right that he should be governed according to the Constitution'.[116] Although valid in the context of the particular petitioner, Sathe's arguments might carry less weight in situations where the petitioner is more closely tied to the legislative (mal)practice, or if need be, directly affected by it.[117] At that point, he

[113] *Id.* at para 16.
[114] S. P. Sathe, *Judicial Activism in India* 124 (Oxford University Press, New Delhi, 2002).
[115] *Supra* n. 108 at 33. [116] *Ibid.*
[117] Beyond that, there are other avenues through which the matter may have been 'appropriately' decided. For example, the matter may have been decided in exercise of the Supreme Court's appellate powers while hearing matters originally decided by the High Courts in exercise of their writ jurisdictions. The scope of the writ jurisdiction of the High Courts under Article 226 is considerably wider than that of the Supreme Court under Article 32. See Constitution of India, Article 226(1) ('Notwithstanding anything

might be constrained to agree with Wadhwa that a judicial remedy is indeed appropriate.

1. The Re-promulgative Exceptions

Two aspects in *D. C. Wadhwa* have attracted wide attention and criticism. First, there was a mismatch between the court's hortatory denunciation of the practice and its formal order. At various points, Chief Justice Bhagwati was scathing in his assessment of the re-promulgative practice. He considered the 'enormity of the situation . . . startling'[118] at one point; elsewhere, he anointed the practice as 'nothing short of usurpation',[119] a clear 'subverting of the democratic process',[120] a 'subterfuge',[121] as 'reprehensible'[122] and finally, as 'a fraud on the Constitution'.[123] Nevertheless, the litany of linguistic censures did not translate into forceful remedies. Except for invalidating one of the three ordinances specifically under challenge, the court fell back on 'hope and trust that such practice shall not be continued in the future'.[124] It said (or did) nothing about the endemic practice that had otherwise taken roots in Bihar. According to Upendra Baxi, the narrative of subversion, subterfuge and fraud was inconsistent with the court's eventual 'hope and trust' kind of order.[125] 'Both "hope" and "trust" are singularly misplaced', he argues, 'in a context where a state has usurped unconstitutionally the power of the elected representatives of the people'. Baxi adds: 'It is abundantly clear that the exceedingly brief judgment in this case altogether surrenders the pedagogic function of social action litigation and jurisprudence. Their Lordships denounce, rightly, a pattern of ordinance-prone behavior of the State of Bihar. But they make no visible attempt to understand let alone explain its original epidemiological dimensions'.[126]

Secondly, the court's conclusion that re-promulgation is unconstitutional leaves certain matters unclear. For example, is re-promulgation

in Article 32, every High Court shall have power, throughout the territories in relation to which it exercises jurisdiction, to issue to any person or authority, including in appropriate cases, any Government, within those territories directions, orders or writs, including writs in the nature of habeas corpus, mandamus, prohibition, quo warranto and warranto and certiorari, or any of them, for the enforcement of any of the rights conferred by Part III and *for any other purpose*') (emphasis added).

[118] *Supra* n. 57 at para 4.
[119] *Id.* at para 6.
[120] *Ibid.*
[121] *Ibid.*
[122] *Id.* at para 7.
[123] *Id.* at para 6.
[124] *Id.* at para 7.
[125] Baxi, *supra* n. 18 at lxxxvi.
[126] *Id.* at lxxxvii

always unconstitutional? That is unlikely: Chief Justice Bhagwati listed circumstances in which the executive may be compelled to re-promulgate an ordinance.

> Of course, there may be a situation where it may not be possible for the government to introduce and push through in the legislature a bill containing the same provisions as in the ordinance, because the legislature may have too much legislative business . . . or the time at the disposal of the legislature . . . may be short, and in that event, the governor may legitimately find that it is necessary to re-promulgate the ordinance.[127]

Note that there is nothing in the four steps outlined earlier that requires – or validates – this exception. Nonetheless, what the exception suggests is that the court merely invalidated *mechanical* re-promulgation of ordinances, not re-promulgation per se. Promulgation (or re-promulgation), as an exercise of legislative powers, requires an application of mind, not just clerical approval. If emergent conditions persist alongside adequate reasons for failing to legislate an ordinance into law, re-promulgation may be valid. Unlike promulgation, the validity of re-promulgation, therefore, is predicated both on the persistence of emergent conditions *and* the availability of reasons as to why an ordinance was not transacted in the intervening legislative session.

Our focus must then be on 'adequate reasons' that would justify re-promulgation. Chief Justice Bhagwati pointed out two. First, if the volume of legislative business in the intervening session were such that the government failed to push a bill through, re-promulgation would be acceptable. Second, if time were too short during an intervening session to enact an ordinance into law, re-promulgation would be acceptable. Both of these options, to some extent, belie the fundamental requirement that an 'emergent situation' must exist for re-promulgation. If a legislative emergency truly persists, with a make-do ordinance brought in to tide it over, why should such a matter be treated with low priority? If parliament does not prioritise ordinance-related matters for reasons of volume or duration, that alone may be a ground to doubt the existence of emergent conditions.

Unsurprisingly, the exceptions were greeted with scepticism. A. G. Noorani was personal in his criticism: 'When Justice P. N. Bhagwati retired as the Chief Justice of India even those who had made it their vocation in recent years to extol his qualities had to concede that when

[127] *Supra* n. 57 at para 6.

it came to great power, timidity was his watchword'.[128] The exemption carved out by Chief Justice Bhagwati, Noorani thought, was 'wholly gratuitous and [robbed] the judgment of merit and value'. For him, 'it was a case of interpretation and the exception, based on pure legislative convenience, [derived] no sanction from Article 213'.[129] It was, as he put it, devoid of any justification.[130] Anil Nauriya, in his more measured analysis, pointed out the potential incoherence of the propositions.[131] Given that the decision outlawed 'only successive repromulgations indulged in as a practice', Nauriya argued that the court had, in effect, upheld three contradictory propositions. 'The first, that the subjective satisfaction of the president as to whether an ordinance is necessary remains outside judicial scrutiny. The second, that in some cases repromulgation may be constitutionally justifiable, and finally, that successive repromulgation would be bad'.[132] If the first and second propositions are valid, the third does not stand up to scrutiny.

Nauriya, in other words, is not so much concerned with the exceptions alone. Rather, he is interested in how the exceptions compete with the other strands of reasoning – particularly those relating to judicial review – in *D. C. Wadhwa*. For him, the incoherence is obvious: the propositions do not add up. But he does not argue that the incoherence, or what he refers to as 'judicial creativity combined with judicial coyishness', is totally useless.[133] Lest his analysis is read too strongly, he is quick to add: 'It should not be assumed that we are deploring this phenomenon, for a restrained form of judicial artistry may well be necessary if the court is to uphold essential democratic principles and yet survive'.[134] I shall return to the question of judicial review in greater detail in Chapter 4.

But Noorani's views are different. Adamant that the exceptions are unjustified, he prefers every case of re-promulgation to be invalidated. Unlike Nauriya, he has no time for 'artistry', 'creativity' or 'coyishness'. And yet, despite his belligerence, Noorani's arguments are remarkably empty. He gives no reason for opposing all forms of re-promulgation, except to make the rather banal point that 'the exception . . . derives no

[128] A. G. Noorani, 'Supreme Court and Ordinances', 22(9) *Economic and Political Weekly* 357–358 (1987).

[129] *Id.* at 357.

[130] *Ibid.* See also Jill Cottrell, 'Re-Promulgation of Ordinances in India: A Note', 37(4) *International and Comparative Law Quarterly*, 1044–1045 (October 1988).

[131] Anil Nauriya, 'Indian Judicial Renascence: The Lines Not Crossed', 22 (6) *Economic and Political Weekly* 239–242 (7 February 1987).

[132] *Id.* at 239.

[133] *Ibid.*

[134] *Ibid.*

sanction from Article 213'.[135] It is one thing to state that the exceptions do not adequately engage with the text; it is entirely something else to rest one's critique solely on the basis that a piece of text does or does not 'include' something. Texts are more malleable than Noorani is willing to admit, at least in this instance. And it is unclear how much of Indian constitutional law will meaningfully survive if we rely on Noorani's textual standards, whatever they are. Is the 'reasonableness doctrine' of equality borne out by the text of Article 14? Is the expansive array of fundamental rights borne out by the text of 'life and personal liberty' in Article 21? Is the doctrine of 'basic structure' borne out by the text of Article 368(1)? These examples could be easily multiplied.

Nonetheless, the 'textual argument' retains some appeal. Wadhwa himself made a similar point recently.[136] A host of English and Indian decisions on statutory interpretation helped him to the conclusion 'that courts cannot add words into a statute if the language of the Statute is clear and unambiguous'.[137] The language of Article 213, he felt, was 'very clear and unambiguous' and re-promulgative exceptions, therefore, had no textual basis for him. These purportedly text-based arguments are relatively unhelpful. Clarity or ambiguity of the text depends heavily on the reader, and it is only understandable that Dr Wadhwa with his long years of dedicated research should find in the text of Article 213 a strong justification for prohibiting an undemocratic practice. Whatever the strength of his textual arguments, Dr Wadhwa does have credible arguments against re-promulgation. He responded to the twin exceptions carved out by Chief Justice Bhagwati saying that 'if the time at the disposal of the legislature in a particular session is short, the solution does not lie in the repromulgation of an Ordinance'. Rather, 'it lies in extending the duration of the session of the legislature'.[138] After all, there is no upper limit fixed in the Constitution for the duration of a session of the legislature.[139] This may yet be the strongest argument against the specific exceptions in *D. C. Wadhwa*.

If the Supreme Court insists on a limited set of exceptions to the general rule against re-promulgation, what other reasons apart from those in *D. C. Wadhwa* might validate re-promulgation? Once again, take the case of POTO. Promulgated barely five weeks before the winter session

[135] *Supra* n. 128 *ibid*.
[136] D. C. Wadhwa, *Endangered Constitutionalism: Documents from a Supreme Court Case* 259–262 (Gokhale Institute of Politics and Economics, Pune, 2008).
[137] *Id*. at 262.
[138] *Id*.
[139] *Id*. at 263.

of parliament in 2001, the ordinance, as I discussed earlier, created predictable outrage. When parliament reassembled for its winter session, the cabinet decided against introducing the ordinance for parliamentary approval. There was little consensus amongst political parties on the need for the ordinance, and the government lacked the numerical support, particularly in the Upper House of parliament, to get the law passed.[140] With the Lower House eventually adjourned sine die, the Vajpayee government decided to re-promulgate the ordinance – the Prevention of Terrorism (Second) Ordinance, 2001 – with some changes.[141] Is the absence of legislative support an adequate reason for re-promulgating an ordinance? If anything, the absence of legislative support was an indication that legislators disapproved of the law, irrespective of whether the executive considered it necessary. The acceptability of the lack of legislative support as evidence of 'adequate reasons' partly depends on how expandable the latter is; *D. C. Wadhwa* provides no guidelines in this regard. And it is unclear if Chief Justice Bhagwati's two exceptions should be read as a closed category.[142]

2. *The Challenge of Contiguous Texts*

Also, *D. C. Wadhwa*'s insistence on adequate reasons points towards a higher justificatory burden in cases of re-promulgation. It raises an additional question: When is an ordinance 'the' ordinance? Consider, once again, both versions of POTO. Three provisions included in the first ordinance – a five-year sunset clause in s. 1(6), the disclosure of journalists' sources of information regarding terrorist activities in s. 3(8) and forfeiture of properties belonging to terrorists in s. 6(2) – were particularly objectionable to many political parties.[143] When promulgating it for the second time, the Vajpayee government deleted the provision relating to the compulsory disclosure of journalists' sources of information, reduced the sunset clause to three years and provided a judicial mechanism for

[140] V. Venkatesan, 'POTO and a Stand-Off' *The Frontline*, 22 December 2001 *available at*: http://www.hindu.com/fline/fl1826/18260190.htm (accessed 16 November 2011).

[141] Anon, 'POTO Promulgated with Amendment's' *The Tribune*, 1 January 2002 *available at*: http://www.tribuneindia.com/2002/20020101/nation.htm#3 (accessed 16 November 2011).

[142] For a less-than-persuasive argument that the re-promulgation in this case was unconstitutional, see D. Nagasaila and V. Suresh, 'Repromulgation of POTO: Is It Legal?' 37(5) *Economic and Political Weekly* 371–372 (2002).

[143] Anon, 'POTO Receives President's Nod for Second Time' *Times of India*, 1 January 2002.

forfeiture of property belonging to convicted terrorists. These amendments, important but presumably not definitive, raise the 'difference' question. How different should the second ordinance be for it to stay clear of the shadows of the first? Or as I put it before, when is an ordinance no longer 'the' ordinance? If (mechanical) re-promulgation is constitutionally impermissible, we need a standard by which to distinguish between contiguous ordinances. The two terrorism-related ordinances did not raise the issue. The government admitted that it was re-promulgating the earlier ordinance. However, what happens when the government insists that the changes to the text of an ordinance are sufficient to regard its second version not as an instance of re-promulgation, but a *new* promulgation?

We may think of contiguous ordinances on a spectrum. At one end are ordinances with nearly identical texts; the changes, if any, are merely cosmetic. At the opposite end are ordinances whose re-promulgated versions include significantly revised provisions. The revised provisions, for example, may include new definitions, new agencies, different remedies or alternate punishments. And if the court finds good reason to believe that such ordinances are 'new' ones rather than re-promulgated versions of the earlier texts, it may decide the government has overcome the *Wadhwa* objections to mechanical re-promulgation.[144] However, most cases of re-promulgation are likely to fall somewhere in between. Like with POTO, important changes to the existing text may lead to claims that it is a new promulgation rather than a case of re-promulgation and, therefore, permitted.

How far textual comparisons will help us in this regard is not readily clear. What we ideally need is a test that allows us to distinguish between levels of continuity and change such that there is some meaningful basis for arguing that certain levels of change would transform an ordinance into a new one. Dr Wadhwa's recent suggestion for a constitutional amendment, although important, is not particularly helpful for interpretative purposes.[145] He suggests the following amendment to Article 123: 'Notwithstanding any provision contained in this Constitution and notwithstanding any judgment of any court, no Ordinance promulgated

[144] Note, however, that we may still have to deal with situations where a sufficiently differently worded text achieves the same result as the first ordinance. Therefore, our efforts should be directed less towards the text and more towards what it seeks to achieve.

[145] *Supra* n. 135 at 292–293.

by the president shall be repromulgated by him nor any Ordinance reproducing substantially the provisions of the repealed or lapsed Ordinance shall be promulgated by him under any circumstances'.[146] Although it is a good start, I doubt its eventual utility. After all, 'substantial similarity' is precisely the point of contention. To partially get around this difficulty, rather than compare texts, we may be better off looking at the Seventh Schedule and the legislative *entry* in which a given promulgation – and its latter version – is situated. In other words, if the original ordinance and the 'new' version are traced to the same legislative entry, irrespective of changes to the text, it should raise a presumption that the latter is really a case of disguised re-promulgation. The amended POTO, on this account, was clearly a case of re-promulgation, and possibly unconstitutional.

In the final section of this chapter, I will expand this discussion on legislative entries into a broader discussion of promulgative competence. In other words, does the president lack competence to promulgate ordinances on certain matters? Or is the president competent to promulgate them on every matter on which parliament is authorised to enact legislation?

E. UNDERSTANDING COMPETENCE: SUBSTANTIVE LIMITS ON ORDINANCES

At first glance, Article 123(3) seems to provide a straightforward answer to the question of legislative competence: 'If and so far as an Ordinance under this article makes a provision which parliament would not under this Constitution be competent to enact, it shall be void'. In other words, the president may promulgate ordinances on all matters on which parliament is authorised to legislate. Article 246(1) explains parliament's legislative authority: 'Notwithstanding anything in clauses (2) and (3), parliament has exclusive power to make laws with respect to any of the matters enumerated in List I in the Seventh Schedule (in this Constitution referred to as the "Union List")'. In addition, parliament, under Article 246(2), has jurisdiction to legislate on the forty-seven matters listed in the Concurrent List: 'Notwithstanding anything in clause (3), parliament ... [has] power to make laws with respect to any of the matters enumerated in List III in the Seventh Schedule (in this Constitution referred to as the "Concurrent List")'. Therefore, Articles 246(1) and

[146] *Id.* at 293.

123(3) together suggest that the president may promulgate ordinances on all matters except those listed in the State List.

However, that is an understatement; parliament may enact legislation on matters in the State List, especially 'to make any law . . . for implementing any treaty, agreement or convention with any other country or countries or any decision made at any international conference, association or other body'.[147] Parliament, in other words, has legislative jurisdiction on matters listed in the Union and Concurrent Lists and on matters in the State List for the narrow purpose of implementing international treaties and conventions. I shall refer to all three together as the parliament's 'ordinary' legislative power. Therefore, when Article 123(3) authorises the president to promulgate ordinances on matters on which parliament is 'competent to enact,' it arguably includes all three previously mentioned components.

This view was disputed in *A. K. Roy v. Union of India*.[148] The Union Cabinet promulgated the National Security Ordinance, 1980 to 'provide for preventive detention in certain cases and for matters connected therewith'. The ordinance was challenged inter alia on the ground that the president lacked competence to do so and the petitioner argued that the right to life and personal liberty guaranteed in Article 21 may be restricted only by a parliamentary Act; ordinances cannot restrict fundamental rights because they are not sufficiently 'established' to claim the status of law. In other words, some matters, despite falling within the entries enumerated in the Union and Concurrent Lists, were excluded from the purview of ordinances. A majority in *Roy*, rightly rejected that argument. Based on a survey of the legislative scheme in the Constitution and the debates in the Constituent Assembly, Chief Justice Chandrachud developed his syllogistic template: 'The Constitution makes no distinction, in principle, between a law made by the legislature and an ordinance issued by the president'.[149] I have argued in this chapter that this claim is too wide and simplistic to be applicable to all aspects of ordinances; however, it is correct on the narrow question of subject-matter competence. Indeed, there is nothing in the Constitution that suggests that the president's *subject-matter* competence to promulgate ordinances is

[147] Constitution of India, Article 253 ('Notwithstanding anything in the foregoing provisions of this Chapter, Parliament has power to make any law for the whole or any part of the territory of India for implementing any treaty, agreement or convention with any other country or countries or any decision made at any international conference, association or other body'.).

[148] AIR 1982 SC 710.

[149] *Ibid.* at para 14.

limited in comparison to the parliament's power to enact legislation. To put it differently, on the limited question of competence, ordinances and acts *are* syllogistic: presidents may promulgate ordinances on all matters on which parliament has 'ordinary' legislative power in the way I defined it earlier.[150]

To be sure, on occasion, arguments have been made against ordinances on particular topics. On 22 February 1952, Lok Sabha Speaker G. V. Mavalankar, arguing against the use of ordinance powers to promulgate what was essentially a money bill said, 'it is only in extreme cases that an Ordinance should be issued'.[151] And again in 1956, he noted his preference against imposing taxes using ordinance: 'so far as taxation measures are concerned, the power to issue Ordinances ought not to be invoked'.[152] But these claims appeal to propriety: there are no legal grounds on which to make the argument that taxes or anything else on which parliament has ordinary legislative power are excluded from the president's power to promulgate ordinances. In 1971, Dr D. S. Dhillon, the speaker at the time, made a similar point when he argued against taxation-related ordinances in strong terms. But in reply to those who urged that there be some legal distinction between financial and non-financial, or tax and non-tax ordinances, he pleaded helplessness. 'There is nothing in my knowledge,' he said, 'on which I can base [that] ruling'.[153]

Nonetheless, apart from its 'ordinary' legislative powers, parliament also has a range of legislative powers that together may be referred to as its 'extraordinary' legislative powers. These 'extraordinary' legislative powers, I will argue, do not follow the syllogistic template. In other words, certain types of subject-matter competence enjoyed by parliament are not 'transferrable;' it does not authorise the president to promulgate ordinances on these matters. To understand why that is so, consider Articles 249, 250 and 252. Article 249 authorises parliament to make laws with respect to matters enumerated in the State List provided 'the Council of States has declared by resolution supported by not less than two-thirds of the members present and voting that it is necessary or expedient in the national interest that parliament should make [such] laws'. Such resolutions, under Article 249(2), remain in force for a period not exceeding one year as may be specified therein, although a new resolution may extend it by one year. Next, Article 250 provides that 'parliament shall, while

[150] For a dissenting, but rather unconvincing, view that ordinances have subject-matter limitations, see, Gupta J. in *supra* n. 4 at para 116–122.

[151] *Presidential Ordinances 1950–1996* v (Lok Sabha Secretariat, New Delhi, 1996).

[152] *Id.* at iv.

[153] *Ibid.*

a Proclamation of Emergency is in operation, have power to make laws for the whole or any part of the territory of India with respect to any of the matters enumerated in the State List'. Finally, under Article 252, if two or more state legislatures find it desirable that parliament should have the power to make laws on matters enumerated on the State List, 'it shall be lawful for parliament to pass an act for regulating that matter'. But parliament may do so only if resolutions to that effect are passed by legislatures that prefer parliamentary involvement in state matters, and any act so passed shall apply only to such states. These three provisions, read together, are extraordinary in three ways. First, they relate to the parliament's authority to enact on matters reserved exclusively for the States. Second, they are conditioned on the happening of specific events and third, they are temporary in nature.

How do these provisions affect the president's subject-matter competence to promulgate ordinances? Recall that the president's power to promulgate ordinances extends to all matters on which parliament is 'competent to enact'. It turns out that parliament has both 'ordinary' and '*extraordinary*' competence to enact legislation. On 'ordinary' matters, the president's subject-matter competence to promulgate ordinances, I have argued, is indeed syllogistic with parliament. But that should not apply to parliament's 'extraordinary' competence. Because 'extraordinary' competence is about enacting legislation on matters that are otherwise reserved for states, it is imperative that the Council of States, as their 'national representatives' (at least in theory), are retained in the legislative process. Without some say by the Council of States in the legislative process, the states' legislative jurisdiction, whether given up voluntarily (e.g., Article 252) or taken away involuntarily (e.g., Article 249) or coercively (e.g., Article 250), would be left without a 'national advocate'. For that reason, when Articles 249, 250 and 252 provide that 'parliament' may enact on state matters under specific circumstances, the term should be understood in its constitutional sense, which in Article 79 means the president, the Lower House and the Upper House jointly.[154]

To put it differently, when Article 123(3) says that the president may promulgate ordinances on matters on which parliament is 'competent to enact', the provision must be read to say that the president may promulgate ordinances on matters on which parliament is *ordinarily* 'competent

[154] Constitution of India, Article 79 ('There shall be a Parliament for the Union which shall consist of the President and two Houses to be known respectively as the Council of States and the House of the People'.).

to enact'. Authorising the president to promulgate ordinances on matters on which parliament has both ordinary and extraordinary competence would be an unwarranted intrusion into the states' legislative competence. As with some other analytical questions, even on matters of legislative competence, the syllogistic template, therefore, applies only partially.

F. CONCLUSION: DOING AWAY WITH THE SYLLOGISTIC TEMPLATE

In this chapter, I began by arguing that in assessing the scope of ordinances, the Supreme Court has erred in employing the syllogistic template. That template, based on the 'same scope and effect' clause in Article 123, treats Acts and ordinances as identical, and aspires to resolve interpretative deficits in the latter by referring to Acts. But when understood *in context*, a complex account emerges from Article 123. In some respects, Acts and ordinances are similar. For example, on issues of substantive competence, ordinances and Acts are indeed alike: the president may promulgate ordinances on all matters on which parliament has 'ordinary' legislative power. In other respects, they are entirely different. For example, with respect to commencement and lapse, Acts and ordinances are different. Unlike Acts, ordinances, I have argued, may commence only when they are fully published, and lapsed ordinances – again, unlike Acts – should retrospectively wipe out all legal traces of its temporary existence. Then there are cases where Acts and ordinances are moderately similar. For example, both Acts and ordinances may include provisions that have prospective or retrospective effect, but greater limits apply to ordinances. A provision in an ordinance with prospective effect can only go so far into the future, and similarly, an ordinance with retrospective effect can only go far into the past. Once these differences are accounted for, the argument points us in one direction – towards the claim that Acts and ordinances are not alike and cannot be treated as such. Even though both are products of 'original' legislative power, that feature by itself cannot determine the full scope and effect of ordinances. For this reason, Article 123 does not mean what it says; despite language to the contrary, Acts and ordinances do not have the same scope and effect. Indeed, given their contexts, they cannot have that.

The key to understanding the differences lies in the context. Article 123 is not a self-contained provision: it is necessarily implicated in a broader architecture of presidential powers, parliament's legislative powers and the cabinet's executive powers. For example, interpreting lapsed ordinances as generating permanent effects effectively authorises the executive to repeal parliamentary legislation, or conversely, authorises the executive to generate permanent rights. Or, including parliament's 'extraordinary' competence, for example, within the president's subject-matter competence in Article 123(3), has the effect of dramatically intruding into the states' legislative competence. Because of these contextual consequences, what ordinances can or cannot achieve must be grounded not only in Article 123, but also its architecture and the ways in which these two interact with associated provisions in the Constitution and (currently accepted) principles of public law. This is where the syllogistic template falls short. It elevates the 'same scope and effect clause' into a heuristic absolute, but fails to account for the context in which ordinances operate. The Supreme Court should abandon the template for interpretative purposes.

Also, it is worth clarifying that the analytical challenges pointed out in this chapter cannot be remedied through statutory amendments. Because arguments limiting the scope of ordinances are embedded in the Constitution's text as well as its architecture and context, statutory amendments reversing ordinances would themselves be unconstitutional. For example, amending the 1897 Act to provide for indefinite retrospectivity or prospectivity, or conferring permanent effect on failed ordinances would contravene Article 123. The limits are constitutional and, therefore, outside parliament's legislative powers.

In Chapter 2, I argued that precedents, performances and personalities – when taken together – can explain why ordinances are common in India. Now we are in a position to supplement that analysis with an additional observation: Judicial perspectives, it turns out, has had a (substantial) role in this. Because of uncharacteristically lax interpretations, the law, as it stands today, imposes little or no cost on the executive. It makes recourse to ordinances legally easy and, worse, expects nothing in return. Not surprisingly, cabinets have taken this as an invitation to indulge in ordinances. They are, in other words, both politically and legally convenient – and that clearly is an unacceptable state of affairs.

4

Reading Minds: Presidential Satisfaction and Judicial Review of Ordinances

The Constituent assembly conferred upon the executive the power to legislative not of course intending that the said power should be used recklessly or by imagining a state of affairs to exist when, in fact, it did not exist; nor, indeed, intending that it should be used mala fide in order to prevent the people's elected representatives from passing or rejecting a bill after a free and open discussion which is the essence of [a] democratic process.

Chief Justice Y. V. Chandrachud, in *A. K. Roy v. Union of India* AIR 1982 SC 710 at para 16.

In this chapter, I turn to the important question of judicial review: Is the president's satisfaction that an ordinance is necessary to take immediate action subject to judicial review? Put differently, when a president, for whatever reason, promulgates an ordinance into law, is it open to the courts to review that assessment? Consider a parliamentary analogy. When parliament enacts legislation, courts – in India and elsewhere – frequently review their constitutionality. But parliament's assessment that an Act is needed is generally considered *outside* the scope of judicial review.[1] On that, courts express no opinion. With ordinances, the president partially surrogates for parliament. Should courts, then, review a president's satisfaction that circumstances made it necessary to take immediate action?

In addressing that question, I will begin by arguing that syllogistic references to presidential satisfaction in other provisions of the Constitution – a common starting point – are analytically misguided. Thereafter, I will identify three argumentative strategies through which judicial review

[1] See *State of A.P. v. McDowell and Co.* AIR 1996 SC 1627; *Nayar v. Union of India* AIR 2006 SC 3127.

may be interpreted, and in the process introduce the concept of an 'intermediate legislative power' – a category that is neither fully executive nor fully legislative, but incorporates important components of both. In the rest of the chapter, I will explain the implications of this concept while examining how Indian decisions have either rejected or impliedly relied on it. And the concept, I hope, will provide a critical account of the power to promulgate ordinances through which to better understand the inadequacies of the syllogistic template discussed in Chapter 3.

A. PRESIDENTIAL SATISFACTION IN ARTICLE 356: A FALSE START?

It is common to begin discussions on the reviewability of presidential satisfaction in Article 123 with references to Article 356 in India's Constitution. The latter provision says that 'if the President . . . is satisfied that a situation has arisen in which the Government of the State cannot be carried on in accordance with the provisions of this Constitution', a proclamation may be made to that effect. Such proclamations have a debilitating effect on state governments because the president may assume 'all or any of the functions of the government of the state';[2] 'declare that the powers of the Legislature of the state shall be exercisable by . . . Parliament'[3] and 'make such incidental . . . provisions . . . including provisions for suspending in whole or in part the operation of any provisions of [the] Constitution'.[4] The Supreme Court in *Bommai v. Union of India*,[5] partly reversing its earlier decision in *Rajasthan v. Union of India*,[6] concluded that the president's satisfaction in Article 356 is judicially reviewable.

A bench of nine judges produced six separate or joint opinions running into 700-odd pages. Even though they disagreed on the appropriate scope of judicial review, they were all in agreement on the basic question of such review. A mere claim of satisfaction is insufficient, the court said; the president must be *justified* in his or her satisfaction. In other words, a 'personal whim, wish, view or opinion' is insufficient; a president's satisfaction has to be based on 'a legitimate inference drawn from the material . . . relevant for the purpose'.[7] And there must be 'sufficient proof of information with regard to . . . the state of things indicating

[2] Constitution of India, Article 356(1)(a).
[3] Constitution of India, Article 356(1)(b).
[4] Constitution of India, Article 356(1)(c).
[5] (1994) 3 SCC 1.
[6] (1977) 3 SCC 592.
[7] (1994) 3 SCC 1 at para 74 (per Sawant J.).

that the situation in question has arisen'.[8] This view was reiterated in *Rameshwar Prasad v. Union of India* – another instance where presidential satisfaction in Article 356 was challenged on the ground of extraneous considerations.[9] Chief Justice Sabharwal concluded that the president's satisfaction 'can be challenged on the ground that it is *mala fide* or based on wholly extraneous and irrelevant ground'.[10] Although courts would not attribute bad faith or motive to the president lightly, a president's decision to invoke Article 356 may be invalidated if adequate materials are shown to exist.

This approach to judicial review, it seems, relies on an objective – or realist – nature of presidential satisfaction in Article 356. For the Supreme Court, circumstances that may properly count as situations 'in which the government of the state cannot be carried on in accordance with the provisions of this Constitution' are specific and limited. And presidential satisfaction is valid if it tallies with one of the predetermined situations. That is to say, the satisfaction is valid only if it is of the right *kind*.[11] There are four senses in which presidential satisfaction must be 'right'. First, it must be of the right kind in the sense that the president himself or herself must come to that satisfaction. It should not be a vicarious one. For example, it would be unlawful if the president's relatives, for example, came to that satisfaction and the president merely acted on their advice. Second, it must be of the right kind in the sense that the satisfaction must be for purposes compatible with the 'proper scope' of Article 356. A president may dismiss a state government under Article 356 for indulging in horse trading – that is, buying and selling votes to secure majorities in legislative chambers. But is horse trading evidence that the 'government of the state cannot be carried on in accordance with the provisions of the Constitution'? If not, a dismissal on that basis is unlawful. Article 356, the argument goes, has limits; not all purposes are compatible with it. In *Bommai*, Ahmadi J. (as he was then) offered an example: 'Merely because a different political party is elected to power at the Centre, even if with a thumping majority, is no ground to hold that' a situation has arisen in which the government of the state cannot be carried on in accordance with the provisions of this Constitution'.[12] To dissolve state assemblies solely on the ground of a new political party having come to power at the

[8] *Ibid.*

[9] (2006) 2 SCC 1.

[10] *Id.* at para 147 (per Sabharwal CJ.).

[11] For a general discussion, see *Barium Chemicals Ltd. v. Company Law Board* AIR 1967 SC 295.

[12] (1994) 3 SCC 1 at para 31 (per Ahmadi J.).

centre with a sweeping majority would 'betray intolerance on the part of the Central government clearly basing the exercise of power under Article 356(1) on considerations extraneous to the said provision'.[13] In other words, dismissing state governments based on a national verdict in favour of a different party, he felt, was not a good reason to invoke Article 356(1), and in that sense, was outside the proper scope of the provision. Third, it must be of the right kind in the sense that the satisfaction is a product of legitimate inference drawn from *relevant* materials. An inference of legislative instability may be correct. But innuendos, gossip, hear-say evidence or partisan reporting are not proper bases on which to draw that inference; they do not qualify as 'objective materials'.[14] Fourth, it must be of the right kind in the sense that the satisfaction is a product of *legitimate* inference drawn from relevant materials. A president, for example, cannot draw an inference about legislative instability in the state assembly from reports about a mining scam implicating ministers in a state government. Reports of a mining scam may tell us something about the corrupt nature of the administration, but a mining scam has nothing to do with legislative stability and an inference of instability based on the former is not 'legitimate'. In short, only right conclusions by the right person based on right materials for the right purposes, the Supreme Court in *Bommai* and *Rameshwar Prasad* held, may count as 'proper satisfaction' in Article 356.

However, not all judges were on board with these four components of judicial review in Article 356; namely, the formal ('was the *president* satisfied?'), the purposive ('was the satisfaction within the *proper scope* of Article 356?'), the material ('was it based on *objective* materials?') and the inferential (were *proper inferences* drawn out of those objective materials?'). Jeevan Reddy J. and Agarwal J., Sawant J. and Kuldip Singh J., and Ratnavel Pandian J. in their opinions argued that all components were relevant in deciding the proper exercise of presidential satisfaction in Article 356.[15] But Ramaswamy J., Ahmadi J., and Verma J. and Dayal J. together restricted the scope of judicial review to the formal and purposive only.[16] The objectivity of materials and the correctness of inferences on which satisfaction is premised, they argued, were not amenable to judicial standards. Presumably, then, for the majority, only certain kinds of materials and inferences counted as valid, as opposed to the minority

[13] *Ibid.*

[14] (1994) 3 SCC 1 at para 59 (per Sawant J.).

[15] *Supra* n. 5 at 347 (per Reddy J.).

[16] *Id.* at para 201 (per Ramaswamy J.).

who chose not to limit the president's discretion in these matters.[17] The majority, in other words, advocated a *fully* objective review. In contrast, the minority preferred a *moderately* objective review; according to the latter, some – but not all – aspects of presidential satisfaction are judicially reviewable.

Despite these disagreements, there was complete unanimity regarding the general conclusion – namely, that a president's satisfaction in Article 356 is judicially reviewable. It is fashionable to use this conclusion to exhaust the discussion on the reviewability of presidential satisfaction in Article 123. The argument goes like this: (1) president's satisfaction (e.g., in Article 356) is judicially reviewable; (2) ordinances (in Article 123) involve president's satisfaction and (3) therefore, president's satisfaction in Article 123 is judicially reviewable. This argument is incorrect: The syllogism misleadingly assumes a kind of homogeneity.

When presidents act in pursuance of Article 356, they do so as India's executive head. In Article 123, they (partially) substitute themselves for parliament and act in their original *legislative* capacity. In *R. K. Garg v. Union of India*, Chief Justice Chandrachud clarified that Article 123 confers 'legislative power... on the president'.[18] The power to promulgate ordinance is a power to enact primary legislation, and Articles 13 and 367 in their enumeration of law clarify this 'legislative' label.[19] Article 13(3), for example, explains the term 'law' as including 'any Ordinance' and Article 367(2) insists that references 'to Acts or laws of, or made by, Parliament... shall be construed as including a reference to an Ordinance made by the President'. In *Nagaraj v. State of Andhra Pradesh*,[20] this point was repeated. 'The power to issue an ordinance', the court confirmed, 'is not an executive power but is the power of the executive to legislate' and therefore, plenary within its field.[21] And because the president's power to promulgate ordinances is a legislative power, reviewability of presidential satisfaction in Article 123, the court says, will depend on the principles of judicial review applicable to *legislative* power. That explains why a syllogistic reference to Article 356 is a false start. Article 123 confers a different kind of power and arguments for judicial review of legislative satisfaction under that provision must rest on reasons independent of arguments applicable to Article 356. But as

[17] *Id.* at para 35 (per Ahmadi J.). See also Soli Sorabjee, 'Decision of the Supreme Court in S. R. Bommai v. Union Of India', 3 *Supreme Court Cases (Jour)* 1(1994).

[18] (1982) 1 SCR 947 at para 6.

[19] See *A. K. Roy v. Union of India* AIR 1982 SC 710 at para 14.

[20] AIR 1985 SC 551.

[21] *Id.* at para 31.

I will demonstrate later in this chapter, the law on the reviewability of presidential satisfaction in Article 356 is not entirely irrelevant, for it can help sharpen our understanding of the issues in Article 123.

B. TEXT AND MOTIVE: TWO CHALLENGES TO OVERCOME

Because the reviewability of presidential satisfaction in Article 123, according to the Supreme Court, depends on the principles of judicial review ordinarily applicable to legislative power, a number of challenges lie ahead. To appreciate them, consider the following set of hypothetical facts. A sudden economic recession has put three of India's leading financial institutions at risk. There is a prospect of bankruptcy that, if it materialises, will have a cascading effect on the economy, adding to unemployment and financial losses running into the billions. Parliament is not in session. The president promulgates the Bank Nationalisation Ordinance, 2013 (BNO) with the stated objective of nationalising banks at risk to save them from potential bankruptcy. To assume that presidential satisfaction in Article 123 is subject to judicial review would imply that courts may invalidate the BNO on the ground that the president wrongly came to the satisfaction that it was necessary. In other words, the law is unconstitutional because it is 'unnecessary'. That conclusion would be novel in India, but also analytically challenging for two reasons.

First, Article 245 states parliament's legislative power as 'Subject to the provisions of this Constitution, Parliament may make laws'. Relying on this provision, the Supreme Court in *Indira Nehru Gandhi v. Raj Narain*[22] explained that an Act is valid provided parliament has subject-matter competence to enact it, and does so without violating provisions of the Constitution.[23] In *State of A.P. v. McDowell and Co.*,[24] Chief Justice Ahmadi put it more strongly: 'A law made by the Parliament can be struck down by Courts on two grounds *and two grounds alone* (1) lack of legislative competence and (2) violation of any of the fundamental rights . . . or of any other constitutional provision'.[25] There is no third ground, he insisted.[26] But notice the ground for invalidating the BNO. The argument is that the ordinance is unconstitutional because it is 'unnecessary'; the president wrongly came to the satisfaction that nationalisation of financial institutions was necessary to take immediate

[22] AIR 1975 SC 1590.
[23] *Id.* at para 691.
[24] AIR 1996 SC 1627.
[25] *Id.* at para 45 (emphasis added).
[26] *Ibid.* See also *State of Karnataka v. Union of India and Others* AIR 1978 SC 68; *Nayar v. Union of India* AIR 2006 SC 3127.

action. If accepted, the argument, contrary to previous decisions, would add another ground on which to review the exercise of legislative power.

To appreciate the significance of 'necessity review', consider the legislative procedure ordinarily applicable to Acts. Every legislative proposal – the *Manual of Parliamentary Procedure* says – is rooted in necessity. At the pre-drafting stage, concerned departments may formulate their 'legislative proposals in consultation with all the interests and authorities concerned . . . [and] include a discussion on the necessity for the proposed legislation'.[27] Subject to further advice from the Ministry of Law and Justice 'on the necessity or desirability of such legislation in the light of the existing laws'[28] and approval from the cabinet, a formal draft may be attempted based on an office memorandum.[29] The memorandum must include complete details of the legislative proposals, the entire background material, all other details relevant to the proposed bill and a draft note for the cabinet.[30] The draft note must once again 'state the legislative proposals, bringing out clearly the need, scope, and object of the proposed legislation; incorporate the views of other concerned departments . . . set out all [its] implications . . . and include the draft of the proposed bill'.[31] If approved by the cabinet, the bill may be formally introduced in parliament.[32] Thus, clearly a corpus of materials attesting to a bill's necessity is generated prior to its enactment (or promulgation).[33] To add necessity as a ground of review is to possibly imply that courts may rely on these (and other) preparatory materials to invalidate a law. But doing so presumably runs counter to Article 245: legislation (and, therefore, ordinances also) are subject to the *provisions* of the Constitution only – nothing else.

Second, adding necessity as a ground of review would invariably require judges to consider questions of motive.[34] Why did parliament enact a piece of legislation? Or, with ordinances, why did the president

[27] See *Manual of Parliamentary Procedures in the Government of India* (Ministry of Parliamentary Affairs, New Delhi, 2004) ch 9, r. 9. 2(a).

[28] *Id.* at ch. 9, r. 9. 2(b).

[29] *Id.* at ch. 9, r. 9. 3.

[30] *Id.* at ch. 9, r. 9. 2(b).

[31] *Id.* at ch. 9, r. 9. 5.

[32] On parliamentary procedure, see A. R. Mukherjea, *Parliamentary Procedure in India* 232–276 (Oxford University Press, Bombay, 1983).

[33] Similarly, whenever a bill seeking to replace an ordinance with or without modification is introduced in the Lower House, there has to be placed before the Lower House along with the bill a statement explaining the circumstances that had necessitated immediate legislation by ordinance. See Subhas Kashyap, *Parliamentary Procedure: Law, Privileges, Practice and Precedents* 351 (Universal Publishers, Delhi, 2006).

[34] See Francis Bennion, *Bennion on Statutory Interpretation* 484–486 (LexisNexis, London, 2008).

promulgate an ordinance? This leads us to the second hurdle: namely, assessing the constitutionality of legislation on grounds of motive. Parliamentary motives, the Supreme Court has repeatedly held, are irrelevant to the question of constitutionality. In *Deo v. State of Orissa,* the court concluded that legislative competence 'does not involve any question of *bona fides* or *mala fides* on the part of the legislature'.[35] Constitutionality is always a question of power and so 'the motives which impelled [the legislature] to act are really irrelevant'. This was reiterated in *Dutt v. Union of India.*[36] The government had taken over the functioning of a partially publicly funded 'non-official, non-political and non-profit organization' through an Act.[37] When challenged on the ground that it was principally motivated by political malice towards the patrons of the council, the court rejected the plea.[38] 'If the legislature is competent to pass a particular law, the motives which impelled it to act are really irrelevant', Justice Lahoti said.[39] On the other hand, 'if the legislature lacks competency, the question of motive does not arise at all'.

The Indian position on legislative motive is a straightforward adaptation of English law. In *Edinburgh v. Wauchope*,[40] Lord Campbell objected to the idea that courts may enquire into the proceedings of an Act. 'All that a Court of Justice can do is to look to the Parliamentary roll', he said.[41] If an Act is obtained improperly (for reasons of motive, non-application of mind or otherwise), it is for the legislature to correct it by repealing it.[42] The position is no different even in cases where a legislature is deceived, and there is proof to that effect: 'If a mistake has been made, the legislature alone can correct it'.[43] Lord Atkinson repeated that view in *Hollinshead v. Hazleton*.[44] 'The motives which influence the legislature in passing any particular enactment, or the purposes or objects it desired to effect, can only be legitimately ascertained from the language of the enactment', he said.[45] In other words, legislative motive, if any, must be located in the words of an Act.

[35] (1954) 1 SCR 1 at para 9.

[36] AIR 2004 SC 1295 at para 16.

[37] *Id.* at para 1.

[38] *Id.* at para 16.

[39] *Ibid.* See *Kerala v. People's Union for Civil Liberties* (2009) 8 SCC 46.

[40] (1842) VIII Clark and Finnelly 710.

[41] *Id.* at 725.

[42] *Lee v. Bude* (1870–1871) LR 6 CP 576, 582 (per Willes J.).

[43] *Labrador Co. v. The Queen* (1893) AC 104, 123 (per Hannen LJ.). See *British Railways Board Appellants v. Pickin* (1974) AC 765.

[44] (1916) 1 AC 428.

[45] *Id.* at 438. See *Tukino v. Aotea District Maori Land Board* (1941) AC 308. See also *Halsbury's Laws of England*, 3rd ed., Vol. 36 (1961) para. 560.

The Indian and English positions, however, are in contrast to the law in the United Sates. In a recent article,[46] Caleb Nelson argues that the use of motive in assessing constitutionality of legislation in the United States has gone through four phases. The first period stretched from the early years of the republic until the1870s,[47] the second period from the 1870s–1930s,[48] the third period from the 1930s–1970s[49] and finally, from the 1970s–present.[50] Despite acknowledging purpose-based limits on constitutional provisions, the first phase, Nelson argues, was characterized by a refusal to enquire into legislative motives.[51] And even though the antebellum courts were willing to set aside statutes that either candidly acknowledged their unconstitutional purposes or otherwise foreclosed any innocent explanation by their very language, most statutes that said nothing about their goals were effectively insulated from purpose-based judicial review.[52]

In the second phase, judges were willing to draw upon materials other than the express words of a statute in deciding if it was vitiated by an impermissible purpose, including public facts eligible for judicial notice.[53] But they also began to tinker with the applicable standard of proof. Instead of giving the legislature every conceivable benefit of the doubt, they were willing to impute impermissible purposes to statutes even in cases where alternate explanations were possible.[54] The third phase saw a measured return to the jurisprudence of antebellum courts. Chief Justice Warren wrote the seminal opinion of this period in *United States v. O'Brien*,[55] one that effectively shut the door on internal legislative deliberations as a guide to Congress' impermissible motivations. 'Inquiries into congressional motives or purposes are a hazardous matter', the Chief Justice said. 'What motivates one legislator to make a speech about a statute is not necessarily what motivates scores of others to enact it, and the stakes are sufficiently high for us to eschew guesswork'.[56] There is, in other words, no collective motive with which to unlock the parliamentary mind behind a statute. And consistent with this approach, courts in this phase were inclined to return to the earlier standard of proof, thereby

[46] Caleb Nelson, 'Judicial Review of Legislative Purpose', 83 *New York University Law Review* 1784 (2008).

[47] *Id.* at 1795–1811.

[48] *Id.* at 1812–1834.

[49] *Id.* at 1835–1849.

[50] *Id.* at 1849–1858.

[51] *Id.* at 1796.

[52] *Id.* at 1803.

[53] *Id.* at 1813.

[54] *Ibid.*

[55] 391 U.S. 367 (1968).

[56] *Id.* at 383–384.

granting legislature the widest possible benefit of the doubt in matters of motives.[57]

From the 1970s, the law, Nelson says, has changed once again. Powell's J. majority opinion in *Village of Arlington Heights v. Metropolitan Housing Development Corporation*[58] is instructive of how far courts have come in this regard. In determining invidious discriminatory purposes, he said that judges may consider the 'sequence of events leading up to the challenged decisions', the 'legislative or administrative history' and in extraordinary cases, may even summon individual legislators 'to testify concerning the purpose of the official action'.[59] The opinion's influence is hard to overestimate: legislative motive analyses have taken over vast swathes of constitutional law.[60] Although the proper method of accounting for conflicting motives – or aggregating them – remains a challenge under current law, legislative motive is a relevant object of study in the United States and an acceptable basis on which to invalidate legislation.

How would our hypothetical BNO fare in the three systems? Irrespective of the motives that may have animated the ordinance, given current law, presidential satisfaction would not be reviewed in India or England. Courts in both jurisdictions are resolutely set against the idea that the exercise of legislative power may be voided on the ground of alleged motive. Nor would the ordinance be reviewed in Nelson's first and third periods. Depending on the alleged motives and the kind of evidence adduced to substantiate them, the argument might receive a sympathetic hearing in the second and fourth periods. The success of motive arguments, however, is hard to predict. Thus far, there is no case in the United States where a statute has been successfully challenged *solely* on grounds of impermissible motives.

To summarise then, legislative power in India is subject to two conditions only – parliamentary motives not being one of them. And because the Supreme Court has tied Acts and ordinances to the same string of legislative power – the classic 'syllogistic template' explained in Chapter 3 – expanding judicial review in one case (say, ordinances) leads to an expansion in the other (Acts). Therefore, if a president's legislative satisfaction in Article 123 is to be subject to judicial review, we will need a different analysis by which to account for it. In the rest of this chapter,

57 *Supra* n. 46 at 1841.
58 429 U.S. 252 (1977).
59 *Id.* at 267–268.
60 See *Nixon v. Administrator of General Services.*, 433 US 425 (1977); *DiMa Corp. v. Town of Hallie*, 185 F.3d 823 (7th Cir. 1999); *Smithfield Foods, Inc. v. Miller*, 367 F.3d 1061 (8th Cir. 2004); *Allstate Ins. Co. v. Abbott*, 495 F.3d 151 (5th Cir. 2007).

I will introduce three competing strategies for reviewing presidential satisfaction while arguing that there are good reasons to avoid tying Acts and ordinances to the same string of judicial review. The argument is an extension of the earlier theme – as with other analytical issues, the syllogistic template with respect to judicial review of presidential satisfaction must be abandoned.

C. A SILENT TEXT: THREE STRATEGIES FOR JUDICIAL REVIEW

Once again, consider Article 123(1): 'If at any time, except when both Houses of Parliament are in session, the President is satisfied that circumstances exist which render it necessary for him to take immediate action, he may promulgate such Ordinances as the circumstances appear to him to require'. Three elements comprise Article 123: (1) The exercise of original legislative power (2) by the executive (3) at its discretion. This exercise of legislative power is based on three further conditions: (1) at least one of the houses is not in session, (2) the president is satisfied of some legislative emergency and (3) immediate action is necessary. In other words, president's legislative power is *conditional*; three conditions must be satisfied prior to its use. But this conditional exercise of legislative power in Article 123 is different from Article 245 that defines parliament's legislative power: 'Subject to the provisions of this Constitution, Parliament may make laws for . . . India'. The latter, as should be obvious, is subject to one condition only: namely, that the exercise of such legislative power be 'subject to the provisions of the Constitution'. Because both presidential and parliamentary legislative powers are conditional, it would be misleading to emphasize 'conditionality' as the distinguishing feature of the former. Therefore, recasting a president's legislative powers as *circumstantially* conditional may be a more apt description. That is to say, whereas Article 123 specifies the particular circumstances in which a president's legislative power may be invoked, Article 245 is silent about it; it leaves it to the discretion of parliament. With this difference in mind, we may turn to three competing strategies by which to think about judicial review of presidential satisfaction in Article 123.

The first strategy might be to *equate* judicial review of Acts (i.e., ordinary legislative power) with those of ordinances (i.e., circumstantially conditional legislative power) while maintaining that both are reviewable on identical grounds. We know Acts in India cannot be reviewed based on motive. Therefore, ordinances cannot be reviewed based on motive, either. We also know parliament's decision to enact a piece of legislation cannot be reviewed. Therefore, a president's decision to promulgate an ordinance cannot likewise be reviewed. The strategy requires an emphasis on the legislative nature of both powers, but that they are prefaced by different conditions is relatively immaterial. We may refer to this as the 'negative' approach to judicial review of presidential satisfaction.

The second strategy might be to *disassociate* the review of Acts from ordinances, by emphasizing the circumstantial conditions that distinguish the former. Here, differences are highlighted rather than underplayed. And it may be put in the following form: Although both ordinances and Acts are products of legislative power, they are prefaced by different conditions, thus making them distinct categories of legislative power. Therefore, ordinances may be reviewed on grounds normally inapplicable to legislation. The fact that both share the same narration of legislative power is relatively immaterial here. We may refer to this as an 'intermediate' approach to judicial review.

The third strategy might be to equate Acts with ordinances, while arguing that both should be reviewed on expanded grounds. The argument is a two-step process and may be put in the following form. Thus far, courts have erred in refusing to review the constitutionality of Acts based on, say, legislative motive. If unjustifiably vitiated by animus towards a person or group, an Act *should* be invalidated on that ground. And for that same reason, an ordinance should also be invalidated if presidential satisfaction in promulgating it is vitiated by mala fide. The third strategy, then, is a hybrid: it equates ordinances with Acts (as in the first instance), but argues in favour of judicial review (as in the second instance). The point here is to narrow the distinction between executive power and legislative power, and to make the latter reviewable on grounds ordinarily reserved for the former. We may refer to this as the 'positive' approach to judicial review of presidential satisfaction.

Of the three, the first strategy is evidently the most conservative. It leaves currently applicable principles of judicial review untouched while incorporating ordinances into its fold. Conversely, the third strategy is the most radical: it seeks to widen the scope of judicial review by adding new grounds. To adopt this strategy is to buy into the U.S. position on legislative motive, particularly as understood in Nelson's fourth phase. The second strategy on this consideration is a median position: Applicable principles are left untouched while expelling ordinances from its purview. However, the second strategy has the implied effect of generating a category of legislative power – call it an 'intermediate legislative power' – that is neither fully executive (e.g., Article 356), nor fully legislative (e.g., Article 245). It is mostly, although not entirely, legislative. It is 'intermediate' because of its office, scope and nature. The power is exercised by the executive; it is limited in scope and is non-deliberative and transient in nature. I will offer a fuller discussion of this concept in general and its Indian version in Article 123 later on. For now, we may turn to the leading decisions on presidential satisfaction to understand the ways in which these three judicial review strategies have been rejected or applied in practice.

D. THE LONG WALK TOWARDS THE INTERMEDIATE

1. Taking the Executive at Its Word: The Original View on Motive

The Supreme Court has mostly remained anchored to the first strategy – that is, the negative approach to judicial review. Two decisions are paradigmatic of this approach. In *Nagaraj v. State of Andhra Pradesh*,[61] Chief Justice Chandrachud held that an ordinance could not 'be invalidated on the ground of non-application of mind'.[62] The power to issue an ordinance was 'not an executive power but [a] power of the executive to legislate'.[63] And because 'transferred malice' was unknown to the field of legislation, an ordinance could not be invalidated on the ground of mala fide intent, either. This view was repeated in *Reddy v. State of Andhra Pradesh*.[64] Armed with an elaborate discussion on the legislative nature of the power involved,[65] the court parroted the obvious conclusion: 'While the courts can declare a statute unconstitutional when it transgresses constitutional limits, they are precluded from inquiring into the propriety of the exercise of the legislative power'.[66]

This refusal to review a president's satisfaction was not a post-Constitution innovation. Rather, the decisions were a straightforward extension of interpretations developed under the 1935 Act and its previous versions. The Judicial Committee in *Bhagat Singh v. The*

[61] AIR 1985 SC 551.
[62] *Id.* at para 31. See *Agarwal v. State of UP* AIR 1956 All 557.
[63] *Id.* at para 31.
[64] AIR 1985 SC 724.
[65] *Supra* n. 18 at para 6 (per Bhagwati J.).
[66] *Supra* n. 20 at para 14. See also *Vishwanath Agarwal v. State of Uttar Pradesh* AIR 1956 All 557; *Prem Narain v. State of UP* AIR 1960 All 205; *Sarju Prasad v. State of UP* AIR 1970 All 571; *Kalyan Bhadra v. Union of India* AIR 1975 Cal. 72; *Fathima v. Ravindranathan* AIR 1975 Ker. 202.

King-Emperor,[67] for example, interpreted the 1915 Act, s. 72, to exclude the governor-general's assessment of emergency from the purview of judicial review. A state of emergency 'is something that does not permit of any exact definition', Viscount Dunedin wrote.[68] Someone had to judge the necessity for drastic action, and that someone could 'be the Governor-General and he *alone*'.[69] Any other view, he felt, 'would render utterly inept the whole provision', especially because emergencies demand immediate action. A fuller view of this exclusionary reasoning was developed in *Jnan Prosanna v. Province of West Bengal*,[70] a case I have previously discussed. The West Bengal Security Act, 1948 (1948 Act), s. 16, authorised the provincial government, on *reasonable* grounds, to preventively detain persons from doing any subversive act was amended by an ordinance. The 'reasonable' requirement was deleted with retrospective effect, thereby restricting judicial review of detention orders. When challenged on the ground that the governor's immediate action was not necessary, Chief Justice Harries was not impressed.[71] 'It appears to me', he said, 'that the Court cannot go into the question whether such circumstances exist as to render it necessary for the Governor to promulgate this Ordinance'.[72] The satisfaction must be of the governor alone, and he found nothing 'to suggest that the Courts would be entitled to question the grounds upon which the Governor was satisfied'.[73]

But Harries C. J. went further; he also rejected the argument that the ordinance was not made in good faith. 'If this Court cannot question the sufficiency of the grounds upon which the Governor was satisfied that urgent legislation was necessary, I think it would be very difficult for any Court to say that the Ordinance was not passed in good faith', he claimed.[74] The ordinance came after the High Court had indicated its willingness to review detention orders and the preamble mentioned that very reason for its promulgation – 'removal of doubts as to the meaning of an important section in the Security Act'. He found nothing mala fide in the government's desire to remove those doubts. Indeed, he accepted the preamble at its face value and, like the U.S. antebellum courts, hesitated to peer into the black box of gubernatorial motive. Consequently, the terms were set. Governors' assessments of the need for immediate action

[67] (1931) 55 Ind. App. 169.

[68] *Id.* at 172.

[69] *Ibid.* (emphasis added). See also *Upendralal v. Narainee Devi* (1931) 58 Ind. App. 169; *King-Emperor v. Benoari Lal Sharma And Others* (1945) 72 Ind. App. 57; *Lakhi Narayan v. State of Bihar* AIR 1950 FC 59.

[70] AIR 1949 Cal. 1.

[71] *Id.* at 69.

[72] *Ibid.*

[73] *Ibid.*

[74] *Id.* at 70.

were final: even motive arguments could not assail their validity. In this sense, when the Supreme Court in *Nagaraj* and *Reddy* offered complete immunity to the president's legislative satisfaction, it had a long tradition of exclusionary reasoning on which to develop that view.

The argumentative structure of these decisions – both pre- and post-Constitution – is consistent with the negative approach outlined earlier. The possibility of judicial review was worked out with an exclusive focus on the legislative nature of the power in Article 123. That it is prefaced by distinct conditions did not matter. For the Supreme Court, then, ordinances are exactly like legislation and, therefore, are subject to identical limitations. The immediate effect of this equivalence is to validate *every* act of presidential satisfaction. As long as parliament is not in session, presidents may whenever, howsoever, and for whatever reasons come to the satisfaction that it is necessary to take immediate action. They may even purposefully create a situation of legislative emergency by dissolving a house in session to promulgate an ordinance, and that, too, the High Courts say, cannot be judicially reviewed.[75]

This thoroughly subjective approach to presidential satisfaction of legislative powers is in contrast to the court's objective approach to presidential satisfaction of executive powers discussed earlier. Indeed, the differences could not be more striking. To recall our previous discussion, judicial review of presidential satisfaction in Article 356 as an exercise of executive power may be read as involving four components. First, as a matter of form, was the president satisfied? Second, was that satisfaction within the 'proper scope' of Article 356? Third, did the president have 'objective materials' on which to make an assessment? And fourth, did the president draw a 'legitimate inference' based on the objective materials? A majority in *Bommai* and later in *Rameshwar Prasad* concluded that all four components were essential to the question of judicial review. With Article 123, however, the court is unwilling to go beyond the first. In other words, any set of facts may count as circumstances that it is 'necessary ... to take immediate action'; any kind of materials may act as a basis for that conclusion and any kind of inference may be drawn out of those materials. Presidential satisfaction in Article 123, in this view therefore, is limitless and courts would not interfere with the president's assessment of legislative urgency.

The negative approach to judicial review, however, sits uneasily with the court's decision on the legality of re-promulgating ordinances in *D. C. Wadhwa* – a case I discussed in Chapter 3. An ordinance, once

[75] *Re K. Veerabhadrayya* AIR 1950 Mad 243.

promulgated, cannot be re-promulgated. That was, in short, the court's conclusion. But Chief Justice Bhagwati left open a small window of possibility. There may be situations, he said, where it may not be possible for the government to introduce and push through in the legislature a bill containing the same provisions as in the ordinance. This may happen especially if the legislature has 'too much legislative business' or 'time at the disposal of the Legislature . . . may be short'.[76] In such cases, presidents (and governors), he thought, may legitimately find that it is necessary to re-promulgate an ordinance. Relying on this exception, the Delhi High Court in *Gyanendra Kumar v. Union of India* upheld a series of ordinances that had been re-promulgated at least once or twice.[77] All ten ordinances were introduced in parliament after it reconvened. But 'other important and urgent business', counsel for the Union of India argued, meant that bills could not be taken up for consideration. The High Court accepted the claim. Based on obvious facts 'that could be taken judicial notice of', Sharma J. concluded that the government had failed to enact the ordinances into law because of 'circumstances beyond [its] control'.[78] And to the extent that re-promulgation fell within the exceptions carved out in *D. C. Wadhwa*, they were neither 'unconstitutional [nor] illegal'.[79]

The negative approach to judicial review along with the *Wadhwa* exception, then, generates a paradox. Whereas presidential satisfaction in its original instance is practically limitless, its re-promulgation triggers a degree of judicial review; judges must decide if there are good reasons for the latter. It is a paradox because if judicial review is possible (and permissible) during *re*-promulgation, why should it be any less possible (or permissible) during promulgation to begin with?[80] Despite the *Wadhwa* exception, the Supreme Court has remained strongly wedded to the negative strategy.

2. *A Sceptical Assessment: Challenges to the Original View*

One notable exception to this general rule, however, is Sujata Manohar J. in her separate opinion in *Singh v. State of Bihar*,[81] where she seems to have adopted the intermediate strategy. In December 1989, the State

[76] *D. C. Wadhwa v. State of Bihar*, AIR 1987 SC 579, 816.

[77] AIR 1997 Del 58.

[78] *Id.* at para 9.

[79] *Ibid.*

[80] See Anil Nauriya, 'Indian Judicial Renascence: The Lines Not Crossed', 22 *Economic and Political Weekly* 239 (1987).

[81] AIR 1998 SC 2288.

of Bihar took over the management and control of non-governmental schools through an ordinance, which it re-promulgated seven times until April 1992. In *Singh*, Manohar J. invalidated all ordinances, including the original one. She began by dissociating ordinances from Acts, focussing on the conditions that make the former distinct. The power to promulgate ordinances has certain safeguards, she said. They are 'not a substitute for regular legislation', of 'limited duration' and must be laid before the assembly when it reassembles.[82] With those exceptions in mind, she turned to the question of judicial review. The state gave no justifications for the immediate action, nor did it have any 'intention of placing any Ordinance before the legislature'.[83] Repeated re-promulgation of the same ordinance, to her, was a ploy to make legislative scrutiny impossible. Accordingly, she concluded that the governor's satisfaction was fraudulent.

This was a remarkable finding: never before had a governor's original legislative satisfaction been invalidated. Extending principles of judicial review – generally reserved for executive power – to ordinances was novel. And Manohar J. was careful to limit her principles to *circumstantially* conditional legislative power only. She showed no willingness to review the exercise of ordinarily conditional legislative power (i.e., Article 245) on similar grounds. Her decision, in that sense, is squarely in sync with the intermediate approach described earlier.

The only other judicial application of the intermediate approach came from the Karnataka High Court in *Hasanabha v. State of Karnataka*.[84] Elections to a local body were held in 1997 in which the ruling party did not secure a majority. The state government introduced an ordinance – Karnataka Agricultural Produce Marketing (Regulation) Ordinance, 1997 – authorising the appointment of three nominated members to every elected committee 'to hold office at the pleasure of the government'. That effectively tilted the verdict in favour of the ruling party. The governor's decision to promulgate the 1997 ordinance after the electoral verdict, petitioners argued, bristled with mala fides. To them, it was designed to achieve ulterior ends rather than remedy any 'real' situation of legislative urgency.

Saldanha J. agreed. To him, the ordinance 'was hopelessly ill-timed', and the mala fide argument had merit.[85] In coming to that conclusion,

[82] *Id.* at para 21.
[83] *Id.* at para 25. See also *A. K. Roy v. Union of India* AIR 1982 SC 710 at para 26–28.
[84] AIR 1998 Kant 91.
[85] *Id.* at para 7.

he, like the judges in Nelson's second period in the United States, was unwilling to grant the governor every benefit of doubt. Describing the ordinance as 'a total and complete sabotage',[86] he rejected the state's claim that it was motivated by a desire to provide representation to those belonging 'to weaker sections and women'. That, to him, was nothing more than an afterthought.[87] Once again, like the judges in Nelson's second and fourth periods, he was willing to draw upon materials other than the express words of the ordinance to assess its underlying motives. The chief minister's admission in the state legislature that the ordinance was necessary 'for purposes of furthering the ruling party's interest' was a testimony to the government's real motives, he said.[88] And for those reasons, the ordinance was invalid. The governor, he claimed, wrongly came to the satisfaction that it was necessary.

This was a clear case of invalidation on grounds of motive; the law was illegal not for what it said, but *when* – and the purposes for which – it was made. The ordinance did not violate provisions of the Constitution. Rather, Saldanha J. pointed out that the government had ample opportunity to alter the composition prior to the elections, implying that if it had been done at a different point in time, the ordinance would have been valid. Like Manohar J. in *Singh*, he stayed firmly anchored to the intermediate approach. The lack of democratic debate and the 'unbridled power to promulgate provision [having] the effect of law' makes it necessary, he said, to scrutinise ordinances with a 'higher degree of care and caution'.[89] This is particularly necessary when ordinances are challenged on grounds of mala fides. In such cases, it is important for the court to 'examine it perhaps with a *higher* degree of meticulousness'.[90]

Both *Singh* and *Hasanabha* are classic applications of the second strategy. They play on the differences between Acts and ordinances while arguing that only the latter is subject to judicial review on grounds of motive, bad faith or non-applicability of mind. It should be parenthetically mentioned that *Hasanabha* was promptly overturned. On appeal, Chief Justice Sethi in the Karnataka High Court reiterated the standard 'principle of interpretation of constitutional law that the legislature, as a body, cannot be accused of passing the law on the ground of *mala fides*'.[91] On the view that the decision was 'a mistake of law', Saldanha J.'s opinion was overturned.

[86] *Id.* at para 6.
[87] *Id.* at para 7.
[88] *Id.* at para 5.
[89] *Id.* at para 10.
[90] *Ibid.* (emphasis added).
[91] *State of Karnataka v. B. A. Hasanabha* AIR 1998 Kant. 210 at para 5.

Some academic commentators have impliedly warmed up to the intermediate approach. Both H. M. Seervai and M. P. Jain, India's leading public law authors, rely on it.[92] Sympathetic to the necessity of judicial review, both present their analysis by disassociating ordinances from Acts. Seervai, for example, emphasizes the executive's discretionary involvement with ordinances while underplaying its legislative character. And because his arguments are built around that emphasis, he is conveniently able to exclude Acts from its purview: 'No law enacted by Parliament can be set aside on the ground that it was passed *mala fide*'.[93] Jain takes a similar position. He is critical of *Reddy*, arguing that the court seemed 'to have gone too far in immunizing an ordinance from judicial review'.[94] It does not seem correct, Jain says, 'to treat an ordinance on all fours with an Act passed by Parliament'.[95] He adds that,

> While it is one thing to say that a validly made ordinance has the same effect as an Act of Parliament, the two – an Ordinance and an Act – are not the same in all respects. The essential difference between the two is that while legislation through Parliament, an elected body, is open and transparent and is subjected to criticism on the floor of the House... making and promulgating an ordinance is purely an executive decision, neither transparent nor open nor subject to any open discussion in a forum.[96]

Therefore, challenging the executive decision on the ground of mala fide 'should always remain a possibility', he said. He commends Saldanha J. in *Hasanabha* and is critical of Chief Justice Sethi who overturned it. But these arguments notwithstanding, the intermediate approach still remains at the margins of public law in India.

How would the intermediate approach change the scope of judicial review? Recall that with the negative approach, the scope of review is limited to the 'formal'. As long as it is the president (in the constitutional sense) who is satisfied about the necessity for immediate action, there is no further review. Adopting the intermediate approach and including mala fide as a ground of review would at the least expand the scope of judicial review to the 'purposive': courts would have to determine if an ordinance is within the proper scope of Article 123. That is to say, courts would have to determine if circumstances 'truly' exist that made it necessary to

[92] H. M. Seervai, *Constitutional Law of India* Vol. III, 2566–2567 (Universal Law, Delhi, 2007); M. P. Jain, *Indian Constitutional Law* 174–175 (LexisNexis, Nagpur, 2009).

[93] Seervai, *Supra* n. 92 at 2566.

[94] Jain, *Supra* n. 92 at 175.

[95] *Ibid.*

[96] *Ibid.*

take immediate action. Consequently, unlike with the negative approach, not all exercises of power under Article 123 would be valid.

In *Krishna Kumar Singh*, Manohar J. concluded that the ordinance and its repeated re-promulgation was primarily designed to circumvent the usual legislative process and, therefore, they were invalid. In *Hasanabha*, Saldanha J. invalidated the ordinance because he concluded that its principal motivation was to undo the effects of an electoral verdict rather than remedy any 'real' situation of emergency. What about our hypothetical BNO? When challenged, judges would similarly have to assess the motives underlying it. Was it promulgated to remedy a 'real' risk of financial collapse and unemployment? Or was it promulgated, say, to protect the pecuniary interests of ministers with significant stakes in the 'failing' banks? To adopt the intermediate will necessarily require judges to wade into these pre-legislative controversies.

It should also be noted that expanding the scope of judicial review in Article 123 to the 'purposive' produces two consequences. First, judges would be required to review presidential satisfaction in Article 123 on some *objective* basis. It would imply that a state of legislative emergency, contrary to Viscount Dunedin in *Bhagat Singh*, supposedly permits an exact definition; the president need not be its sole judge.[97] Second, for the review to be relatively meaningful, expanding the scope of judicial review to the 'purposive', would necessarily require that the 'material' and the 'inferential' be also included. After all, an assessment of urgency is almost impossible without (some) access to the materials on which the original presidential satisfaction was based, and the nature of inferences that led to the conclusion that immediate action was necessary. Therefore, unlike the review of a president's executive satisfaction in Article 356, the review of a president's legislative satisfaction can either be fully subjective or fully objective; a moderately objective review in Article 123 – the kind advocated by the minority in *Bommai* – is *not* a coherent option.

Finally, if the second strategy is at the margins of Indian public law, the third one – the positive approach to judicial review – is still further out. It has barely registered in India. With the possible exception of Ray J. in *Cooper v. Union of India*,[98] the idea has never been judicially proposed or upheld. In *Cooper*, the constitutional validity of the Banking Companies (Acquisition and Transfer of Undertakings) Ordinance, 1969 was challenged on the ground that there was no need for immediate

[97] *Bhagat Singh v. King-Emperor* (1931) 55 IA 169.
[98] AIR 1970 SC 564.

action and that the president wrongly came to the conclusion that an ordinance was necessary. In his dissenting opinion, Ray J. concluded that establishing bad faith or corrupt motive was the only way to challenge presidential satisfaction. Bad faith, he added, 'will destroy *any* action'.[99] If by 'any action' he intended to include both executive and legislative actions, then Ray J. is squarely in sync with the third strategy. It would imply that Acts (and, therefore, ordinances as well) may be invalidated on the ground that it was motivated by animus towards a person or group. India's disinterest in the positive approach is in contrast to the state of the art in the United States where motive arguments are central to many areas of constitutional law, and especially so with regards to statutes alleged to disadvantage African-Americans,[100] restrict unpopular speech or religion,[101] or punish disfavoured individuals.[102] Although differences persist in specific doctrinal areas, the very plausibility of making legislative power subject to mala fide inquiry is no longer in doubt. Therefore, it may be profitable to briefly consider the arguments for doing so here.

Much of the analytical foundation for motive analysis was initially offered by John Ely in 1970 and later reworked by Paul Brest in 1971.[103] Brest argued that motive inquiry, properly understood, 'focuses on the process by which the rule or decision was made; it asks what criteria or objectives the decision-maker took into account'.[104] The substantive decision is not of concern; rather the inquiry merely points out considerations that cannot be taken into account in enacting a given legislation.[105] Even though discerning the sole or dominant reason underlying the choices of a group of legislators is challenging, such rigorous proof, he said, is not essential to motive analysis. He argued that it would suffice

99 *Id.* at para 244 (emphasis added).

100 See *Hunter v. Underwood*, 471 U.S. 222 (1985); Perry, 'The Disproportionate Impact Theory of Racial Discrimination', 125 *University of Pennsylvania Law Review* 540 (1977).

101 See *Lemon v. Kurtzman*, 403 U.S. 602 (1971); *Church of the Lukumi Babalu Aye v. City of Hialeah*, 508 U.S. 520 (1993).

102 Nixon, *Supra* n. 60 *ibid.*

103 John Hart Ely, 'Legislative and Administrative Motivation in Constitutional Law', 79 *Yale Law Journal* 1205 (1970); Paul Brest, 'Palmer V. Thompson: An Approach to the Problem of Unconstitutional Legislative Motive', 1971 *Supreme Court Review* 95 (1971). See also Theodore Eisenberg, 'Disproportionate Impact and Illicit Motive: Theories of Constitutional Adjudication', 52 *New York University Law Review* 36 (1977); Clark, 'Legislative Motivation and Fundamental Rights in Constitutional Law', 15 *San Diego Law Review* 953 (1978); Elena Kagan, 'Private Speech, Public Purpose: The Role of Governmental Motive in First Amendment Doctrine', 63 *University of Chicago Law Review* 413 (1996).

104 Brest, *id.* at 115.

105 *Ibid.*

'to demonstrate that illicit motivation played a non-trivial part in the decision-making process, so that it might have affected the outcome'.[106] This process of teasing out legislators' motives is about drawing inferences based on legislators' actions 'viewed in the context of antecedent and concurrent events and situations' – a process not unlike drawing inferences in other areas of law. Amongst others things, the content of the law, its timing in juxtaposition with some prior event or sequence of events and the maker's statements about the purpose of the law or rule are acceptable ways of reading the mind.[107]

Knowingly or otherwise, Saldanha J. in *Hasanabha* adopted Brest's arguments to partially defend motive analysis in India. Saldanha J. argued that the timing of the ordinance especially in the light of antecedent facts (i.e., the electoral verdict against the ruling party, the chief minister's admission in the state assembly about preserving the ruling party's interest, and most importantly, the incoherency of the legal arguments offered in defence of the ordinance) pointed to one conclusion only: The ordinance was motivated by a desire to undo the legal effects of an election rather than to remedy any 'real' situation of legislative emergency. This motive may not have been the sole or dominant one, but it undeniably played a role in the decision to promulgate the ordinance. Its sheer presence in the balance of considerations, he felt, was sufficient to invalidate the governor's satisfaction.

Unlike Brest, however, Saldanha J. limited himself to ordinances only. Nothing in his decision suggested that Acts may also be reviewed on this basis. That is unsurprising because fully appropriating Brest in India is difficult. The central argument for judicial invalidation of a law on the ground of illicit motive, as Brest admits, hinges on the idea that 'governments are constitutionally prohibited from pursuing certain *objectives*'.[108] The Constitution, in other words, imposes purpose-based limitations on the legislature's power to enact certain legislation. That is to say, *why* a legislature enacted a law matters as much as what it has enacted. But this interpretation of legislative power has never been accepted in India. Starting with *Deo*, the Supreme Court has struck to the view that legislative competence is exclusively a question of power: 'If the legislature is competent to pass a particular law, the motives which impelled it to act are really irrelevant'. Only 'what' matters; 'why' is irrelevant. Until it can be shown that India's Constitution imposes limits on the reasons for which

106 *Ibid.*
107 *Id.* at 124.
108 *Id.* at 116 (emphasis added).

parliament may act, fully appropriating Brest's analysis is analytically challenging.

We now have three alternatives through which to address judicial review in Article 123. To summarise, the negative approach treats Acts and ordinances alike while holding the view that neither should be reviewed on grounds normally applicable to executive power. The intermediate approach treats Acts and ordinances differently while holding the view that only presidential satisfaction of ordinances should be judicially reviewed. Lastly, the positive approach treats both Acts and ordinances alike, but takes the view that both should be reviewed on grounds ordinarily reserved for executive power. Given these options, which one should we adopt? Which one of these options is valid? Hereafter, I will argue that this question cannot be addressed by simply referring to Article 123 for the relevant text is 'agnostic' on the point. That choice must necessarily depend on something outside of the text – something external to it.

E. PRESIDENT'S 'INTERMEDIATE' LEGISLATIVE POWER: INTRODUCING A CONCEPT

In 1975, Article 123 was amended to including the following: 'Notwithstanding anything in this Constitution, the satisfaction of the president mentioned in Clause (1) shall be final and conclusive and shall not be questioned in any Court on any ground'.[109] Three years later, the amendment was deleted. The provision, both in its original and current form, says nothing about judicial review: Article 123, in this respect, is semantically agnostic. Therefore, the validity of the competing strategies cannot be decided simply by referring to the text. And for that reason, arguments proclaiming to derive positions on judicial review from the provision itself, as Seervai and Jain purport to do, appear contrived. They reflect little more than the authors' personal preferences regarding judicial review in Article 123.

Seervai, for example, argues that 'discretionary power conferred on the executive either by the Constitution or by a law, and dependent on the existence of a condition precedent is subject to the jurisdiction of the Courts'.[110] By implication, he concludes, that a president's satisfaction in Article 123 is reviewable. But the claim regarding the reviewability of

[109] § 2, 38th Constitution (Amendment) Act, 1975 (India).

[110] H. M. Seervai, *Constitutional Law of India* Vol. II, 1130 (N.M. Tripathi Private, Bombay, 1968).

discretionary power with conditional precedents is *his* understanding of discretionary power; Article 123 says nothing about it. Elsewhere, he argues that 'the Constitution puts limitations on the president's powers under Article 123 and if the powers are transgressed, e.g., by the promulgation of an Ordinance *mala fide*, the rights of the people are affected illegally'.[111] This is incorrect. Nothing in the *Constitution* limits the president's power to promulgate. If limits exist, they do so because of Seervai's preference for them. Secondly, the reference to 'validity' assumes the existence of some higher principle that can help us arbitrate between the competing strategies. That is unlikely.[112] To the extent that all three strategies satisfy (conventional?) conditions for valid and sound arguments, they are likely equally valid. If that is so, judicial review of presidential satisfaction in Article 123 will largely depend on the strategy one adopts – that is, what one chooses to emphasize (or de-emphasize) in the text. In other words, because the text runs out at this point, effectively the reader must decide the strategy to adopt.

To say that the choice of strategy is textually arbitrary is not to suggest that its validity cannot be judged from any other vantage – albeit somewhat 'external' – point. The history of misuse (the subject of an extended analysis in Chapter 2) and the appropriate level of discretion is one such starting point. The question of judicial review, in large measure, is a question of discretion. Should the executive have wide discretion in promulgating ordinances? Or should such discretion be limited? Depending on one's view of the appropriate level of discretion, some strategies will make more sense than others. The second or third strategy is unambiguously better for those with a preference for limited executive's discretion. Unsurprisingly, Seervai, in making his case for judicial review in Article 123 quickly took refuge in what he saw as a history of abuse.[113] He discussed at length Dr Wadhwa's research in the field that pointed to the executive's frequent use of ordinances with the intent of undermining the legislative process. It is, he writes, 'a sad reflection on the Ministries in power between 1968 and 1981 that they should have started this gross abuse of power, and allowed it to continue. But now that this fraudulent exercise of power has been exposed, it is for the Courts to see that such fraudulent exercise is prevented'.[114] Wadhwa's careful study of the abuse of power under Article 213, he goes on to say, 'shows the need

[111] *Id.* at 1116.

[112] See Duncan Kennedy, *Legal Reasoning: Collected Essays* 87–152 (The Davies Group, Colorado, 2008).

[113] Seervai *Supra* n. 92 at 2566.

[114] *Ibid.*

for extreme vigilance on the part of the Courts because, if this device is not checked, the unwholesome example set by the state of Bihar may be followed by other states'.[115] Later, he chided Chief Justice Chandrachud for his refusal to adjudicate the question of judicial review in *Roy* with a degree of finality.[116] The government, he pointed out, 'had promulgated about 200 Ordinances between 1960 and 1980 of which nineteen had been passed in 1980'.[117] Having regard to this frequent use, 'for a court to allow a large section of our people's rights to be affected by what may turn out to be illegal executive action without redress', he thought, could 'only be described as an unjustified abdication of judicial power'.[118] Jain too, justifies his case for judicial review as a way of deterring executive excesses in the future; challenging the executive decision on the ground of mala fide, he concludes, should always remain a possibility.[119] This possibility of review, he argues, will act as an effective check against executive excesses.

As these arguments readily suggest, a sympathetic reading of judicial review is largely grounded in the belief that the power to promulgate ordinances has been misused, or in the fear that it will be. For Seervai and Jain, misuse, as fact or likelihood, serves as a meta-anvil through which to make sense of the competing strategies. To them, the 'correct' strategy is one that does not preclude a judicial assessment of legislative necessity. But because they prefer to limit the scope of this assessment to ordinances only, the intermediate approach is their obvious ally. To be sure, this manner of accounting for the question of judicial review is not unreasonable, but doing so at least requires an acknowledgement that it is a product of something outside of, or external to, Article 123.

If we are to use the anvil of 'misuse' to make president's satisfaction in Article 123 judicially reviewable, we need a fuller account of intermediate legislative power and the ways in which it is distinct from ordinary legislative power. Legislative power, I would argue, is 'intermediate' when it is exercised by the executive in its *original* capacity. Executive bodies – including the cabinet – frequently make laws that are delegated in nature, but their authority rests on parliamentary approval or some other form of review. With intermediate legislative power, the executive has the power to enact primary legislation; the initial exercise of the power is not dependent on anything else. The concept is particularly useful in demonstrating

[115] *Id.* at 2570.

[116] Seervai *Supra* n. 110 at 1117.

[117] *Ibid.*

[118] *Ibid.*

[119] *Ibid.*

why Acts and ordinances are *not* tied to the same string of legislative power, and expanding the scope of judicial review in one case does not necessarily lead to an expansion in the other case. Currently, because of the court's attachment to the syllogistic template explained earlier, only two options are available: either motive is relevant to *both* Acts and ordinances, or it is irrelevant to both. But interpreting judicial review of presidential satisfaction through the intermediate strategy shows that a third option is possible: motive may be relevant in one instance, but not in another.

Although any number of differences between intermediate and original legislative power may be constitutionally designed, its Indian expression in Article 123, I believe, has the following features. First, its initial exercise is non-deliberative. Parliamentary scrutiny, if any, occurs post-enactment. Second, given the history of misuse, president's assessment of legislative necessity in Article 123, unlike parliament's similar assessment, is potentially open to judicial review. Third, as a product of intermediate legislative power, ordinances are transient. Even though the duration of ordinances is not spelled out directly, their permanence is clearly dependent on future legislative approval. Fourth, if ordinances are not enacted into legislation through normal procedure, they lapse. In such cases, legal effects of ordinances get wiped out retrospectively; it is as if the ordinances never existed. That is the argument I made in Chapter 3. Fifth, even though ordinances and Acts have similar subject-matter scopes, some additional limitations apply to ordinances with respect to retrospective and prospective provisions.

None of these, however, are necessary or sufficient features of intermediate legislative power.[120] These are merely its *Indian* expression and other jurisdictions may define it differently. For example, it is conceivable that intermediate legislative power elsewhere may enforce a strict period of duration, or conversely, provide for indefinite validity. It may impose subject-matter limits, thereby restricting its exercise on matters of, say, taxation or crime. And, contrary to the law in India, intermediate legislative power may, for example, be designed to guarantee legal validity of actions taking under a lapsed ordinance. Some varieties of intermediate legislative power are easily noticeable in the 1935 Act. Under that Act, the governor-general had authority for three distinct types of

[120] For an analysis of what I have referred to as intermediate legislative power in Latin American and European systems, see John Carey and Matthew Shugart (eds.), *Executive Decree Authority* (Cambridge University Press, New York, 1998).

legislation; s. 42, the textual precursor to Article 123, was only one of them. The governor-general, in s. 43, had authority to promulgate ordinances under circumstances that rendered 'it necessary for him to take immediate action for the purpose of enabling him satisfactorily to discharge his functions in so far as he is by or under this Act required in the exercise thereof to act in his discretion or to exercise his individual judgment'. In some matters including defence, ecclesiastics and tribal affairs, the Act conferred independent responsibility on the governor-general and s. 43 was designed to provide legislative authority for these matters when immediate action was necessary. As I discussed in Chapter 1, the term of ordinances under s. 43, even though initially for a period of six months, could be extended for a further period of six months. And contrary to s. 42, the Federal Legislature had no control over it; the Act merely required that such ordinances be laid before parliament. Here, then, is an example of an intermediate legislative power whose features are clearly distinct from Article 123. Both Article 123 and s. 43 share some features – they are premised on the need for 'immediate action'. But they are different in some respects – their terms are clearly different and ordinances under Article 123, unlike s. 43, are subject to a strong form of parliamentary scrutiny post-enactment.

Still another example of intermediate legislative power may be found in s. 44 of the 1935 Act. That provision authorised the governor-general to promulgate something called the Governor-General's Act for performing his discretionary duties under the 1935 Act. Interestingly, the authority to promulgate a Governor-General's Act was not limited to times of emergency; he could do it anytime merely after explaining 'to both Chambers of the Legislature . . . the circumstances which in his opinion [rendered such] legislation essential'. Also, these ordinances, unlike those provided in Article 123 or s. 43, had *permanent* tenure from the very beginning. That is to say, the Governor-General's Acts were like parliamentary legislation; they were valid until repealed by law. These examples reiterate my earlier point that the category of intermediate legislative power has no inherent feature except that it is the exercise of original legislative power by the executive. Its Indian expression in Article 123 has certain features, but they are neither necessary nor sufficient.

Finally, to round up our discussion on judicial review, it is worth noting that two aspects of intermediate legislative power in its Indian expression may be judicially reviewed. In the first instance, judicial review may pertain to the president's *substantive* satisfaction. *Hasanabha* is a classic example. In it, Saldanha J. reviewed the governor's substantive satisfaction that an ordinance amending the results of a local election was necessary. His arguments and reasoning were about the subject matter of the law, its implied effect of undoing the electoral verdict and the motives that may have animated the decision to promulgate that ordinance. But judicial review may also focus on the governor's *procedural* satisfaction. *Krishna Kumar* is a good example of this. There, Manohar J. focussed on the government's apparent disinterest in completing the legalization process. Because an ordinance in Article 123 is transient and requires parliamentary approval in the future to acquire permanence, promulgating it may be procedurally mala fide if the president has no intention of seeking such approval. Without that intent, ordinances can become a cynical practice designed to circumvent the ordinary legislative process and the accountability that comes with it. Manohar J. found the governor wanting in that regard: There was 'no intention of placing any Ordinance before the legislature'.[121] Unlike *Hasanabha*, the focus in *Krishna Kumar* was not on the governor's substantive satisfaction regarding the law. Rather, Manohar J. focussed on the procedural disinterest and the government's apparent intent in undermining the ordinary legislative process. Note that this procedural review – understood as the president's or governor's intention of seeking future parliamentary approval – is unique to intermediate legislative power; for obvious reasons, it does not apply to ordinary legislative power.

What about our hypothetical BNO 2013 then? If understood through the prism of intermediate legislative power, then presidential satisfaction regarding that ordinance, contrary to the current law in India, should be judicially reviewed. If challenged on the ground that the proposed nationalisation was motivated by a desire to protect the pecuniary interests of ministers rather than remedy any 'real' situation of financial emergency, it would fall on judges to assess that claim. As in *Bommai*, judges may be required to address all four components of judicial review discussed earlier – formal, purposive, material and inferential. But because of its distinct analytical grounding, the concept manages to keep parliament's decision to enact a piece of legislation insulated from judicial review. Andthat is its crucial advantage: the concept can explain why ordinances, despite their 'same force and effect' as Acts of parliament, may be subject to different rules of judicial review, or more broadly, may be interpreted to have different features than the latter.

[121] *Supra* n. 97 at para 25.

F. STANDARD OF PROOF: READING PRESIDENTS' MINDS

If the argument so far that the president's authority to promulgate ordinances is a distinct category of legislative power with equally distinct grounds of judicial review is correct, it leaves us with two final questions. First, what level of proof should courts demand in assessing presidential motive? Second, who has the burden of proof? For all the motive analyses in *Hasanabha* and *Kumar*, the decisions had little to say about the standard and burden of proof directly. Both judges assumed some standard – whatever that was – and worked out their conclusions accordingly. We need a clearer statement of the standard of proof and Brest is once again useful here.

Having laid out his defence of motive analyses, Brest suggested that 'the complainant must establish by clear and convincing evidence that an [illicit] objective played an affirmative role in the decisionmaking process'.[122] But parties are not obliged to establish that the objective was the sole or dominant purpose of the law – only that its consideration may have affected the outcome of the process.[123] The decision, in such cases, should simply be invalidated, he argues, but with the possibility that the decision maker readopt the same conditioned 'upon a showing that its readoption is designed to serve entirely legitimate objectives'.[124]

Of the two decisions, *Hasanabha*, I will argue here, adopts Brest whereas *Kumar* rejects it. In *Hasanabha*, the 'clear and convincing' evidence of motive came from the content of the ordinance, its timing (the sequence of events immediately prior to and after its promulgation) and the inconsistencies between the state's purported objectives and the ordinance itself. Nominated members, it was argued, were needed to provide expert supervision to the Agricultural Committees and to provide representation to 'weaker sections and women'.[125] These claims, however, did not square with the original legislation. The need for external expertise seemed superfluous given that the elections were intended to allow a group of agriculturalists, traders and businesspersons to elect *their* representatives.[126] Equally important was the fact that expertise was not a criterion for nomination; the ordinance authorised the state to appoint 'any person' to hold office at its pleasure. Similarly, the second purported objective did not hold up on scrutiny. Representation for

[122] Brest, *Supra* n. 103 at 131.
[123] *Ibid.*
[124] *Ibid.*
[125] *Supra* n. 91 at para 6.
[126] *Ibid.*

weaker sections had already been catered for in the original constitution of the committees and further additions, he concluded, 'would result in reverse discrimination'.[127] Also, the inconsistency between the two objectives was hard to miss. Providing expertise and promoting the interests of so-called weaker sections cannot go together, unless there are sufficient experts amongst the weaker sections, in which case separately promoting their interests is largely unnecessary.

The timing of the ordinance mattered as well. The elections to these committees were in the works for a long period of time. The state government had sufficient opportunity to introduce the requirement of nominated members through ordinary legislation. That they chose to introduce it *after* the publication of adverse election results – from their point of view – suggested that the ordinance was intended for a different purpose.[128] And the chief minister's statements in the legislature, Saldanha J. thought, were a window into the true motives behind the ordinance. While affirming his belief in the democratic norms and electoral process, the chief minister justified the ordinance 'as necessary . . . for purposes of *furthering the ruling party's interest*'.[129] That admission in the light of the surrounding circumstances led to the conclusion that the law was a 'total and complete sabotage' of the electoral process and, therefore, 'downright *mala fide*'.[130] The petitioners had the initial burden of proof of establishing the likelihood of improper motives, which they having discharged, then fell upon the state to rebut. To put it differently, the ordinance was unconstitutional because, contrary to the state's claims, the petitioners succeeded in establishing that circumstances did not exist that made it necessary for the governor to take immediate action.

Kumar, however, is contrary to Brest's position. Manohar J. began with the presumption that re-promulgating an ordinance repeatedly was a 'fraud on the Constitution' – something designed to undermine the ordinary legislative procedure.[131] Consequently, the burden of proof stood reversed. The state had 'not . . . averred that any immediate action was required'.[132] Nor did it explain 'how long the assembly was in session, whether the Ordinance in force was placed before it, or why for a period of two years and four months proper legislation could not be passed'.[133] Absent explanations to that effect, she concluded that the ordinance was invalid.[134] The contrast is sharp. In *Hasanabha*, petitioners had to

[127] *Ibid.*
[128] *Id.* at para 7.
[129] *Id.* at para 5 (emphasis in the original).
[130] *Ibid.*
[131] *Supra* n. 97 at para 25.
[132] *Ibid.*
[133] *Ibid.*
[134] *Ibid.*

provide 'clear and convincing' evidence of improper motives, and the burden was sufficiently high. *Kumar*, however, raises a presumption against the constitutionality of re-promulgated ordinances and – for reasons not entirely explained – imports that into the *first* promulgation. As a result, for Manohar J., ordinances are invalid unless accompanied by proof that the executive intends to seek legislative approval on reassembly of parliament. Petitioners have a limited role in all this. Once basic facts are averred, it is for the state to explain the legislative circumstances that rendered immediate action necessary and its future intent.

Of the two possibilities, *Hasanabha*, it appears, is a better template than anything that has been offered thus far. That approach – of placing the initial burden of establishing by clear and convincing evidence as to the influence of improper motives on the claimants – is consistent with the Supreme Court's preliminary observations in *Roy v. Union of India*.[135] Although the court did not engage with the issue fully, Chief Justice Chandrachud hesitated in placing the entire burden on the executive. 'At least a *prima facie* case must be made out by the challenger to show that there could not have existed any circumstances necessitating the issuance of the Ordinance', he said.[136] But 'every casual or passing challenge to the existence of [such] circumstances', he clarified 'will not be enough to shift the burden of proof '.[137] In other words, although a presumption against the existence of necessary circumstances is not excluded, the initial burden must be discharged by the claimants.

G. CONCLUSION: RETHINKING JUDICIAL REVIEW

In *Reddy v. State of A.P.*,[138] Chief Justice Chandrachud held that 'when the Constitution says that the ordinance making power is legislative power and an ordinance shall have the same force as an Act, an ordinance should be clothed with all the attributes of an Act of legislature carrying with it all its incidents, immunities and limitations under the Constitution'.[139] Ordinances, he added, could not be 'treated as an executive action or an administrative decision'.[140] Implied in this claim is the view that there are only two ways to interpret the status of ordinances: either they are like Acts of parliament or they are executive or administrative orders. In other words, either ordinances are products of original

135 AIR 1982 SC 710.
136 *Id*. at para 29.
137 *Ibid*.
138 AIR 1985 SC 724.
139 *Id*. at para 15.
140 *Ibid*.

legislative power or they are product of delegated legislative power. But the foregoing analysis shows that these are not the only two options available. Ordinances may be understood as products of an intermediate legislative power that has elements of both legislative and executive power, but is clearly distinct from them. Recognising this category offers several advantages. It can explain why ordinances are different from Acts, what makes them different and why they should be treated differently for interpretative purposes. Indeed, once this category is recognised, several of the interpretative challenges surrounding ordinances will begin to look much easier.

In Chapter 3, on a series of analytical matters, I argued that the Supreme Court had erred in adopting the syllogistic template which claims that Acts and ordinances must be interpreted similarly. In this chapter, I have extended that argument to the judicial review of ordinances. A president's decision to promulgate an ordinance, unlike a parliament's decision to enact a statute, should be subject to judicial review. The case for judicial review of presidential satisfaction, however, cannot rest on Article 123 for it is agnostic in this regard. Nor will a straightforward application of current principles applicable in associated areas of presidential satisfaction achieve that objective. Rather, the best case for judicial review depends on recognising a category of intermediate legislative power – one that is neither fully executive nor legislative, but with important characteristics of both.

The concept's analytical purchase, however, goes beyond merely accounting for judicial review of ordinances. Interpreting the president's power to promulgate ordinances as an expression of intermediate legislative power explains why ordinances are unique. That uniqueness can also explain why tying Acts and ordinances to identical effects is an interpretative *choice*. Such interpretations are neither necessary nor inevitable. In fact, identifying ordinances as products of intermediate legislative power provides a philosophical basis on which to reject the syllogistic template. Despite words to the contrary in Article 123, Acts and ordinances should be treated differently because they are fundamentally different things. They have different origins and purposes, and most importantly, are products of different kinds of powers.

5

The Power of No: Presidents, Cabinets and the Making of Ordinances

[The Indian president] has a residual identity separate from cabinet, parliament, and the civilian and military services – an identity beyond government and opposition, beyond partisanship, as representative of the interests of the nation.

Lloyd I. Rudolph and Susan H. Rudolph, 'Redoing the Constitutional Design: From an Interventionist to a Regulatory State' in Atul Kohli (ed.), *The Success of India's Democracy* 141 (Cambridge University Press, Cambridge, 2001).

An elected President notionally represents the collective will of the people, he can use it (and must use it) to temper the occasional excesses of its elected representatives.

Fali Nariman, '"The Silences in Our Constitutional Law": First Durga Das Basu Endowment Lecture 2005', 2 *Supreme Court Cases (Journal)* 15 (2006).

Thus far, by way of analytical arguments, I have defended two claims. First, despite words to the contrary, ordinances in Article 123 do not have the 'same force and effect' as Acts. Second, the president's power to promulgate ordinances is best understood as an intermediate legislative power, one that is neither fully executive, nor fully legislative – but with important elements of both. When combined, the arguments may be rephrased in the following way. The force and effect of Acts and ordinances depend on the kinds of power that bring them into existence. Acts result from the exercise of legislative power; ordinances result from the exercise of intermediate legislative power. Because of that difference, except on limited matters, they do not have the same scope and effect. As I have argued in Chapters 3 and 4, contrary to the Supreme Court's syllogistic template – on matters relating to commencement, prospective and retrospective operation; lapse; 'extraordinary' subject-matter jurisdiction and judicial review – Acts and ordinances are vastly different, and should be so.

In this chapter, I shall demonstrate the applied significance of the argument in its combined form. I shall do so in the context of Article 111 and the president's power to assent to bills:

> When a Bill has been passed by the Houses of Parliament, it shall be presented to the President, and the President shall declare either that he assents to the Bill, or that he withholds assent therefrom.

Further, the provision adds that

> the President may, as soon as possible after the presentation to him of a Bill for assent, return the Bill . . . with a message requesting that they will reconsider the Bill or any specified provisions thereof and, in particular, will consider the desirability of introducing any such amendments as he may recommend in his message, and when a Bill is so returned, the Houses shall reconsider the Bill accordingly, and if the Bill is passed again by the Houses with or without amendment and presented to the President for assent, the President shall not withhold assent therefrom.

The provision, in other words, explains the final step necessary for a bill to become an Act of parliament, and the scope of the president's discretion in that regard. Does the provision apply similarly to ordinances as well? The Supreme Court's syllogistic template would imply that it does. That is to say, ordinances require presidential assent in a similar manner, and the president's discretion with reference to ordinances is no different from his or her discretion with reference to Acts.

My overall objective in this chapter is to show that this claim is incorrect. The president's discretion in Article 111 refers to the exercise of legislative power, and that should have no bearing on his or her power of assenting to – or withholding assent from – ordinances that result from the exercise of a different kind of legislative power. Or, to put it in terms of the combined form earlier, because ordinances result from the exercise of *intermediate* legislative power, a president's constrained discretion in Article 111 should not apply to them. I shall develop this argument in two parts. First, I shall construct an explanation for the implied premise in Article 111 along with references to controversies the provision has endured, and the limited consensus about its meaning today. Second, I shall argue that when applied to ordinances, that limited consensus should not apply.

A. POWER TO ASSENT: CONTROVERSIES AND THE LIMITED CONSENSUS

1. *The Meaning of Silent Words: President's Legislative Powers in India*

The president, by virtue of Article 111, has a say in the legislative process; bills do not become Acts without assent. The Constituent Assembly's Drafting Committee first mooted the idea of presidential assent in India's Constitution. Draft Article 91 read as follows:

> When a Bill has been passed by the Houses of Parliament, it shall be presented to the President, and the President, shall declare either that he assents to the Bill, or that he withholds assent therefrom.
>
> Provided that the President may, not later than six weeks after the presentation to him of a Bill for assent return the Bill if it is not a Money Bill to the House with a message requesting that they will reconsider the Bill or any specific provision thereof, and, in particular, will consider the desirability of introducing any such amendments as he may recommend in his message, and the Houses shall reconsider the Bill accordingly.[1]

Other than giving the president a say in the legislative process, the draft Article did three things. First, it provided for a limited duration within which to exercise that discretionary say: A bill could be returned 'no longer than six weeks' after it was presented to the president. Second, that discretion did not extend to 'Money Bills'. On those matters, the president had no authority to return a bill to parliament for reconsideration. Third, and most importantly, the provision said nothing about the fate of 'reconsidered' bills. In other words, once a bill was reconsidered by parliament and sent to the president for assent, would he or she have discretion to return it again? If so, under the draft article, a permanent back and forth with the two houses would have been possible. As long as the president had some objections to a bill, he or she would have had the authority to return it repeatedly. It was as if the provision envisaged a legislative procedure where both houses and the president had a *co-equal* say in enacting legislation in India.

In the Constituent Assembly, the draft provision generated little controversy. Discussions were limited to a few proposals for amendments.

[1] 'Draft Constitution Prepared by the Drafting Committee' in B. Shiva Rao (ed.), *The Framing of India's Constitution* Vol. III, 517–677, 549 (Universal Law Publishing, New Delhi, 2006).

Dr Ambedkar, for example, proposed that the words 'not later than six weeks' be replaced with the words 'as soon as possible'.[2] Some members objected to it. Diluting the six-week requirement in favour of an amorphous 'as soon as possible', Deshmukh said, would weaken the president's duty to assent.[3] Kamath made a similar point. 'Nobody knows what they mean – what "as soon as" means'. He complained that the phrase was 'vague, purposeless and meaningless' and, therefore, 'should not find a place in the Constitution'.[4] These criticisms notwithstanding, when put to vote, the amendment was adopted. Then there was a proposal from L. N. Mishra to limit the president's discretion with respect to reconsidered bills. He suggested that the following words be added to the proviso: '[I]f the Bill is passed again by the House with or without amendment and presented to the President, the President shall not withhold assent therefrom'.[5] Without these words, the proviso, he felt, was 'incomplete and inconclusive'.[6] The idea received enthusiastic support – and later approved.[7] With these amendments in place, draft Article 91 became Article 111 in the Constitution.

Clearly, the amendments altered the scope of presidential discretion in two respects. Compared to draft Article 91, the amended provision made the president's discretion with reference to time less 'definite'. Earlier, a president had 'no more than six weeks' within which to return a bill to the two houses for consideration. Because of Dr Ambedkar's amendment, the president now must act 'as soon as possible'. Also, the draft article was unclear regarding reconsidered bills: The possibility of repeated vetoes, it seems, was left open. Mishra's amendment brought clarity in that regard. The amended provision made it clear that the president 'shall not withhold assent' from bills that have been reconsidered by the houses. The Constituent Assembly, however, said nothing beyond that and much was left unclear. Members, for example, did not question – or explain – the rationale underlying presidential assent. They simply assumed that the

[2] Constituent Assembly Debates (CAD), Bk. 3. No. VIII, 192 (20 May 1949).

[3] *Id.* at 194.

[4] *Id.* at 195.

[5] *Id.* at 191.

[6] Begum Aizaz Rasul moved a similar amendment, and in defending her proposal, referred to the veto powers of the U.S. President. 'My object in moving this amendment', Rasul said, 'is to do away with [the] ambiguity and to make it clear that the President can return the Bill to Parliament with his suggestions once only . . . In the House of Commons any Bill which has been passed twice by the House of Commons automatically becomes law . . . In the USA, a Bill becomes an Act even if the President vetoes it, provided it is passed by two-thirds majority if the Congress. Some such provision should be made here'. *Id.* at 191.

[7] *Id.* at 195.

president had to have a role. They did not explain why 'as soon as possible' was a clearer directive to the president than 'no later than six weeks'. They gave the president *one* opportunity to engage with the houses, but said nothing about the grounds on which to seek such reconsideration. Most tellingly, the members did not consider the consequences of presidential inaction. In short, Article 111 gave the president a seat at the legislative table, but left a large number of issues unresolved.

2. *'President-in-Parliament': A Reconstructive Exercise*

Almost immediately after the provision came into effect, controversy erupted. Rajendra Prasad, India's first president, came to the view that as the head of the state, his powers were not insignificant. In a letter to Deputy Prime Minister Vallabhbhai Patel, he outlined his general take on presidential powers. 'A reference to the constitution itself shows that there are at least 121 Articles in it apart from the schedules in which the President is mentioned as having to do something or other'. There is no doubt, he added, 'that in most of these matters he has to act according to the advice of the Ministers concerned but I believe the Constitution contemplates that it is open to him to advise ministers not on matters of detail but generally on matters of policy'.[8] Obviously, Prasad did not believe in a ceremonial president; the Constitution, he felt, gave him some – perhaps substantial – discretionary powers.[9] But as India's first prime minister, Nehru thought otherwise. Even though there were several rounds of conflicts on a wide number of issues,[10] the back and forth between Prasad and Nehru was particularly revealing with respect to Article 111. When the prime minister asked for prompt assent to bills, Prasad urged caution. 'I hope, you will concede that when I am asked to sign a document, I must satisfy myself and not sign blindly'.[11]

[8] Rajendra Prasad, 'Prasad to Patel: 27 August 1950' in Valmiki Choudhary (ed.), *Dr. Rajendra Prasad: Correspondence and Select Documents* Vol. XIII, 64–66 (Allied Publishers, New Delhi, 1987).

[9] Almost a year to the day that the Constitution came into effect, Prasad drafted a memorandum explaining at greater length the powers of India's president, as he saw it. See Rajendra Prasad, 'President's Status vis-à-vis Council of Ministers: 24 January 1951' in Valmiki Choudhary (ed.), *Dr. Rajendra Prasad: Correspondence and Select Documents* Vol. XIV, 270–280 (Allied Publishers, New Delhi, 1987).

[10] For a description of some of the issues on which Prasad and Nehru fought over the presidency, see Harshan Kumarasingham, 'The Indian Version of First among Equals – Executive Power during the First Decade of Independence', 44 (4) *Modern Asian Studies* 709–751 (2010).

[11] *Supra* n. 8 at 76–77. On the president's constitutive role in the parliamentary process, see also S. S. Khera, 'The President in Parliament' in S. L. Shakdher (ed.), *The Constitution*

The first round of battle on the question of the president's legislative discretion took place over the Bihar Zamindari Abolition Bill. In July 1950, Prasad wrote to Nehru questioning elements of the bill and signalling his reluctance to sign in. The cabinet pondered over the matter and decided that the compensation scheme provided for in the bill was fair.[12] Prasad persisted. He wrote to Nehru again asking that it be delayed so that the relevant ministries could reconsider his 'strong convictions' on the matter.[13] But when Nehru threatened to resign, he gave in. He assented to the bill, along with a comment noting his disagreement. The second – and more protracted – battle came in September 1951 when Nehru confirmed his intention to reform Hindu personal law. Initially, the plan was to enact an omnibus bill dealing with almost all aspects of family law including marriage, divorce, succession, inheritance, property and women's rights. Prasad immediately made known his objections to the bill, suggesting to Nehru that he reserved the 'right to examine on its merits' and take measures 'consistent with the dictates of [his] conscience'.[14] Alarmed by the likelihood of presidential 'obstruction' to a set of reforms dear to him, the prime minister replied the same day.

> These are serious matters of great constitutional importance. They might involve a conflict with the President on the one side and the Government and Parliament on the other. They would inevitably raise the question of the President's authority and powers to challenge the decision of the Government and of Parliament... In our view the President has no power or authority to go against the will of Parliament in regard to a Bill that has been well considered by it and passed. The whole conception of constitutional government is against any exercise by the President of any such authority.[15]

This is not an apposite place to develop a detailed account of presidential powers in India's Constitution.[16] But certain things are worth pointing

and the Parliament in India: The Twenty-Five Years of the Republic 118–127 (National Publishing House, New Delhi, 1976).

[12] Glanville Austin, *Working a Democratic Constitution* 83 (Oxford University Press, New Delhi, 1999).

[13] *Ibid.*

[14] *Supra* n. 9 at 104–106.

[15] *Id.* at 106–107.

[16] The scope of presidential powers in India's Constitution still remains relatively unsettled. Important questions are yet to be answered. For a sense on the literature on the matter, see, e.g., K. M. Munshi, *The President under the Indian Constitution* (Bharatiya Vidya Bhawan, Bombay, 1967); Jashwant B. Mehta, *Presidential System: A Better Alternative?* (N. M. Tripathi, Bombay, 1979); Anirudh Prasad, *Presidential Government or Parliamentary Democracy* (Deep and Deep, New Delhi, 1981); Vasant Sathe, *Two Swords In*

out. Constitutionally speaking, Nehru was obviously incorrect. His characterisation of the dispute as one between 'the President on one side and the Government and the Parliament on the other' turned several constitutional provisions on their heads. In India's Constitution, the president has a dual character. He or she is, at once, the executive head of the state (by virtue of Article 53)[17] and a *constitutive* organ of parliament (by virtue of Article 79).[18] Because parliament is made up of the president, the Upper House and the Lower House, it makes little sense to talk about 'the President on one side . . . and the Parliament on the other'. After all, there is no parliament without the president. Nehru's second point was equally suspect. 'The President', in his view, had 'no power or authority to go against the will of Parliament'. But by virtue of being a constitutive organ of parliament, the president has authority to do two things. First, under Article 86(2), the president has the authority to 'intervene' in parliamentary proceedings: She or he may 'send messages to either House of Parliament, whether with respect to a Bill then pending in Parliament or otherwise'.[19] In such cases, the houses 'shall consider' any such matter 'with all convenient despatch'. Second, Article 111 gives the president limited authority to go against the will of both houses. When presented with a bill that has been passed by both houses, the president may reserve it for assent. There is, as we have seen before, no timeline within which

One Scabbard: A Case for Presidential Form of Parliamentary Democracy (NIB Publishers, New Delhi, 1989); A. G. Noorani, *The Presidential System: The Indian Debate* (Sage, New Delhi, 1989); B. L. Hansaria, *Does India Need a New Constitution?* (Eastern Law House, Calcutta, 1998); Naunihal Singh, *A System of Governance: Parliamentary or Presidential* (Anmol Publishers, New Delhi, 2008).

[17] Constitution of India, Article 53(1) ('The executive power of the Union shall be vested in the President and shall be exercised by him either directly or through officers subordinate to him in accordance with this Constitution').

[18] The literature on presidential powers has mostly overlooked – or at times discounted – the significance of this arrangement. See, e.g., D. N. Banerjee, 'The Indian Presidency', 26(1) *Political Quarterly* 70 (1955); B. A. V. Sharma and N. M. Valecha, 'The Indian President', 33(1) *Political Quarterly* 59 (1962); Editorial, 'A Plea for the Study of Power of the President of India', 12 *Journal of Indian Law Institute* 400 (1970); Henry W. Holmes, 'Power of the Indian President: Myth or Reality?' 12 *Journal of Indian Law Institute* 367 (1970); V. S. Deshpande, president, 'His Power and Their Exercise', 13 *Journal of Indian Law Institute* 326 (1971). For an introductory analysis along the lines I have suggested here, see M. V. Pylee, 'The President under the Constitution' in S. L. Shakdher (ed.), *The Constitution and the Parliament in India: The Twenty-Five Years of the Republic* 105–117 (National Publishing House, New Delhi, 1976).

[19] Constitution of India, Article 86(2) ('The President may send messages to either House of Parliament, whether with respect to a Bill then pending in Parliament or otherwise, and a House to which any message is so sent shall with all convenient despatch consider any matter required by the message to be taken into consideration'.).

to grant such assent. But the president is also authorised to return the bill to the two houses requesting that it be reconsidered. Therefore, in expressing his desire to 'examine [the Hindu Code Bill] on its merits', Prasad had the Constitution on his side.[20] His threats, however, never came to fruition.

Legally, Nehru won the battle over the presidency when he lined up leading lawyers including Sir Alladi Krishnaswami Aiyar[21] and Attorney General M. C. Setalvad to make the case against presidential powers.[22] By selectively emphasising the issue of executive power and the primacy of the cabinet in such matters, both Aiyar and Setalvad, separately came to the conclusion that the president has no independent powers in the Constitution.[23] Setalvad, for example, took the view that:

> The President under [India's] Constitution has no prerogatives personal or otherwise. In this respect his position as compared to that of the British monarch is weaker . . . The fact that the President unlike the King is elected to his office for a term makes no difference to this position. The election is merely a method for the choice of the constitutional executive head.[24]

An elaborate electoral procedure was dismissed as a 'mere method', and the implications of the president as a constitutive organ of parliament barely received attention.

Politically, Nehru won the battle when he secured a massive mandate in the first-ever general elections in 1952. Prasad had consistently taken the view that Nehru did not have electoral legitimacy to initiate reforms that were – as he saw it – controversial, far-reaching and discriminatory.[25] But that decisive electoral verdict left Prasad with no other grounds on which to assert his views. He gave in. The Hindu Code Bill was broken up into smaller parts, and enacted in a staggered manner throughout the next five years.[26]

The next major controversy involving Article 111 came more than four decades later when President Zail Singh refused assent to what became known as the Postal Bill, 1986. Egged on by Rajiv Gandhi's government,

[20] *Supra* n. 9 at 107–108. See also Ram Gopal, *Undemocratic Elements in the Indian Constitution* 161–162 (Somaiya Publications, Bombay, 1977).

[21] *Id.* at 280–282.

[22] *Id.* at 283–286.

[23] Both of their analyses heavily focussed on the executive side of issues, and I believe, did not sufficiently explore the implications of the president's legislative powers.

[24] *Supra* n. 9.

[25] *Supra* n. 10.

[26] Reba Som, 'Jawaharlal Nehru and the Hindu Code: A Victory of Symbol over Substance', 28(1) *Modern Asian Studies*, 169–172 (1994).

both houses of parliament passed a bill authorising the central and state governments to 'intercept, detain or dispose of' any postal article or class of postal articles in the interests of public safety or tranquillity, the security of India or on the occurrence of any public emergency.[27] When it reached the president's desk, Singh refused to do anything. In his memoirs, he claimed – not implausibly – that the bill 'undermined the Constitution's fundamental freedoms'.[28] On two occasions, he informally suggested certain changes to it.[29] Nothing came of those efforts, and he simply sat on the matter.

The legality of such a course of action depends on the options deemed available under Article 111. Clearly, there are two choices: The president may assent or return a bill to the houses, seeking reconsideration. But is there a third choice – namely, to do nothing? Singh perhaps thought so, but his inaction, Glanville Austin argues, amounted to a 'pocket veto', something the author believes 'is not envisaged in the Constitution'.[30] Is this third option inconsistent with the language of Article 111? Recall that the provision as originally drafted gave the president no more than a definite period of 'six weeks' to assent to a bill. That was changed to a more nebulous 'as soon as possible' at Dr Ambedkar's behest. Nor is there any provision that *deems* assent to have been granted after a specified period.[31] But whether lawful or otherwise, Zail Singh's third option eventually prevailed. He sat on the bill for the rest of his presidential term, and his successor, R. Venkatraman, took more than two years to return it for reconsideration. By then, appetite for the bill was lost. It languished in the Upper House for nearly twelve years and was finally withdrawn by the Vajpayee government in March 2002.[32]

The most recent controversy involving Article 111 had to do with the Office of Profit Bill, 2006, the facts of which I have already mentioned on several occasions. Once the ordinance-related part of the controversy died down, the two houses of parliament hurriedly enacted an amendment

[27] *Supra* n. 12 at 512.

[28] Zail Singh, *Memoirs of Giani Zail Singh: The Seventh President of India* 276 (Har-Anand Publications, New Delhi, 1997).

[29] *Ibid.*

[30] *Supra* n. 12 at 513.

[31] See, e.g., Constitution of the Republic of Singapore, Article 22H (4) ('For the purposes of this Article, where, on the expiration of 30 days after a Bill has been presented to the President for his assent, the President has neither signified the withholding of his assent to the Bill nor referred the Bill to a tribunal pursuant to Article 100, the President shall be deemed to have assented to the Bill on the day immediately following the expiration of the said 30 days'.).

[32] Anon, 'Postal Office Bill Withdrawn' *Times of India*, 16 March 2002.

to the Parliament (Prevention of Disqualification) Act, 1959[33] to shield forty members of parliament from possible disqualification for allegedly holding offices of profit. The bill, amongst others, declared that the chairperson of the National Advisory Council – a post previously held by Mrs Sonia Gandhi; chairpersons of trusts, public or private; and offices of chairperson, president, vice-president or secretary of governing bodies of duly registered societies to be exempt from disqualification. Most egregiously, the amendment was to have retrospective effect, thereby immunising members who were perhaps already in violation of the law. It was, as Rajeev Dhawan put it, 'an entirely opportunistic Bill'.[34] Pratap Mehta went further. To him, it was a 'constitutional travesty that licensed and exonerated the flouting of law'.[35] The bill, he argued, was solely intended to let incumbents off the hook rather than achieve a rational objective. Unsurprisingly, when it reached President A. P. J. Kalam, he took his time. He consulted with constitutional experts and wrote back to the two houses, suggesting that the bill be reconsidered in the context of the 'settled interpretation of the expression "Office of Profit" in Article 102 of the Constitution, and the underlying constitutional principles therein'.[36] In particular, he requested that three issues be addressed:

(i) Evolution of generic and comprehensive criteria which are just, fair and reasonable and can be applied across all States and Union Territories in a clear and transparent manner;
(ii) The implication of including for exemption the names of offices the holding of which is alleged to disqualify a member and in relation to which petitions for disqualification are already under process by competent authority; and
(iii) Soundness and propriety of law in making the applicability of amendment retrospectively.[37]

Dr Manmohan Singh's government, however, chose not to pay heed to those suggestions. The bill was re-enacted and returned to the president for assent. This was new. Never before in the last fifty-six years was a

[33] 10 of 1959.
[34] Shankar Kumar, 'Over to the Prez' *Sahara Times*, 5 August 2006. Similarly, senior lawyer Fali Nariman described it as a 'lawless law'. See Seema Mustafa and Venkatesh Kesari, 'Profit Bill a Blatant Bid to Save MPs' *Asian Age*, 2 June 2006.
[35] Pratap Mehta, 'Checks and Balances' *Indian Express*, 1 June 2006.
[36] Anon, 'Office-of-profit Bill not Big Enough for Kalam' *Hindustan Times*, 31 March 2006.
[37] President Kalam's statement to the two houses is quoted in V. Venkatesan, 'A Rare Return' *Frontline*, 23(12), (June 30) 2006.

president confronted with a 'returned' bill. And a question arose: Does President Kalam have the constitutional authority to simply sit on the matter, thereby exercising an implied veto? Prima facie, the language of Article 111, gravitates against that possibility. The provision says that 'if the Bill is passed again by the Houses with or without amendment and presented to the President for assent, the President *shall not* withhold assent therefrom'. Inaction, it seems, is not an option, at least regarding 'returned' bills.[38] Presumably, Kalam knew this all along. After more than a fortnight of tantalising suspense, he relented.[39] He made – what he later described as – the 'toughest' decision of his presidential term and signed into law a bill he conscientiously believed was arbitrary and, possibly, unconstitutional.[40]

President Kalam's thoughtful conduct resolved the immediate controversy, but it brought old questions back into focus. What precisely are the legislative powers of India's president? How far can he or she go? What can he or she do in exercise of such powers? Many of these questions remain unresolved. It is unclear, for example, if the president has authority to exercise an implied veto. Although the case against an implied – or pocket – veto is stronger in the case of a 'returned' bill, the matter, I believe, is not free from doubt. However, after more than six decades of constitutional governance, three things should be clear regarding Article 111. First, in assenting to a bill, a president exercises *independent* judgment, and does not act as a surrogate. A cabinet cannot dictate how the president should act.[41] Second, in the exercise of that judgment, the

[38] Noorani in his usual over-the-top analysis concluded that President Kalam's refusal to assent to a returned bill would be a 'constitutional crime'. A. G. Noorani, 'No, Mr. President' *Hindustan Times*, 25 July 2006.

[39] Anon, 'OOP Bill gets Kalam OK, Experts Say Can be Contested' *Indian Express*, 19 August 2006.

[40] Anon, 'P M Nair: "Kalam Erred on Office of Profit Bill"' *Times of India*, 22 April 2008. The constitutionality of the Parliament (Prevention of Disqualification) Amendment Act, 2006 was later upheld by the Supreme Court in *Consumer Education and Research Society v. Union of India* (2009) 9 SCC 648.

[41] See also K. Subba Rao, *Some Constitutional Problems* 288–289 (University of Bombay, Bombay, 1970). In his *Sir Chimanlal Setalvad Law Lectures*, Judge Subba Rao took the view that presidential discretion regarding assent is 'implicit' in Article 111. ('The President has power to give assent or not to give assent... Should he, in giving or withholding his assent, act upon the advice of the Ministry? The condition of the assent of the President is a device to give the House an opportunity to reconsider the provisions of a bill, if in his opinion they are against public interests or against constitutional provisions, whether mandatory or directory. If he is bound to act on the advice of the Prime Minister in this regard, what purpose does it serve? The Council of Ministers controls the majority of the Parliament, pilots the bills and secures their

president has authority to send a bill back for reconsideration. Third, if both houses return a bill to the president, he or she cannot, at the very least, formally send it back for a second time. In short, the president has authority to independently assess a bill, and seek reconsideration *once*. If returned, it cannot be sent back again. But why, one might ask, does the president have authority to interfere with the 'will of the people'?

Parliament, I mentioned before, is made up of the president, the Upper House and the Lower House, and they represent different things. To understand why the president has a say on legislative matters, one must understand where the president stands in this arrangement. Electorally speaking, in some respects, the president's representative legitimacy is closer to the members of the Upper House, who – like the president – are indirectly elected.[42] But in other respects, the president transcends both houses. The Lower House is made up of directly elected members from particular constituencies. They, therefore, can at best claim to represent their respective *constituencies*.[43] Similarly, the Upper House is made up of indirectly elected members from particular states. They, therefore, can at best claim to represent their respective *states*.[44] But as the *only* nationally – albeit indirectly – elected official in the Constitution, the president has a (limited) form of representative legitimacy that is unavailable to members of either house. The president, even if notionally, represents the

passage through the House. The power to assent is not intended to give a chance to the Executive to withdraw the bill after it has been passed. On the other hand if the bill has passed against the Cabinet's wishes the Ministry has to resign and the said power is not intended to save the Ministry from resignations. It is therefore implicit in the said power that it is intended to be exercised by the President in his discretion. In other words, he is not bound to accept the advice of the Council of Ministers'.) Not everyone agrees. Justice Krishna Iyer, for example, takes the view that presidents and governors must be guided by the advice of the cabinets in decisions regarding bills. See Krishna Iyer, *The Indian Presidency* 72, 78–79 (Deep and Deep Publications, New Delhi, 1988) ('If every bill can be considered by the President, sitting as a Third Chamber, with no time limit for assent or refusal, the legislative process and the Cabinet's claim to commanding position [will] stand stultified'.).

42 Constitution of India, Article 54 ('The President shall be elected by the members of an electoral college consisting of: (a) the elected members of both Houses of Parliament; and (b) the elected members of the Legislative Assemblies of the States'.).

43 Constitution of India, Article 81(1) ('[T]he House of the People shall consists of: (a) not more than five hundred and thirty members chosen by direct election from territorial constituencies in the States'.).

44 Constitution of India, Article 80(4) ('The representatives of each State in the Council of States shall be elected members of the Legislative Assembly of the State in accordance with the system of proportional representation by means of the single transferable vote'.).

people in a 'national capacity' and in that sense, transcends both houses.[45] In some ways, therefore, India's parliament is a representative troika: constituencies (the Lower House), states (the Upper House) and 'the nation' (the president) are part of it.[46] Therefore, when Article 111 authorises the president to return bills to the two houses for reconsideration, it impliedly gives each of the three representatives, at the first instance, an equal say in enacting legislation. Presidential intervention, therefore, is not an interference with the 'will of the people', but its realisation.[47]

However, Article 111 does something more. It says that 'if the Bill is passed again by the Houses with or without amendment and presented to the President for assent, the President shall not withhold assent therefrom'. The provision, in other words, elevates the role of the two houses in the second instance. Once the representatives of the constituencies and the states reconsider a piece of legislation and in their collective (i.e., majority) wisdom enact it for the second time, the president must go along with it. Presumably, underlying this arrangement is the idea that when compared to the president, the two houses, at least in theory, enjoy a greater degree of representative proximity, numeric strength and deliberative superiority. Constituencies and states are electorally 'closer' to the people; they are greater in number and required to engage in parliamentary (i.e., public) deliberation. Their collective will, therefore, trumps presidential objection. It is because of this that the president, I would argue, is not authorised to return a bill back to the two houses for a second time. That much is not in doubt. Whatever else may be unclear about Article 111, it is fairly beyond dispute that the president in exercising his or her *legislative* powers cannot formally return a bill to the two houses for a second time.

This normative reconstruction of Article 111 and the role of the president in the legislative scheme of things, it should be pointed out, runs against the current state of the art in India. Although the provision has not been the subject of serious judicial interpretation, stray observations suggests that some judges regard the president's role in legislative affairs as a British gloss without constitutional significance. In his concurring opinion in *Shamsher Singh v. State of Punjab*,[48] V. R. Krishna Iyer J.

45 *Supra* n. 39 at 275.

46 This is not to suggest that the three organs represent different things. Each organ represents the people, but does so in a different (territorial) capacity.

47 See also P. B. Mukharji, *Critical Problems of the Indian Constitution* 13–17 (University of Bombay, Bombay 1967).

48 AIR 1974 SC 2192.

took the view that presidential assent in India must be understood in the way assent is understood in the United Kingdom.[49] The monarch is bound to give assent to parliamentary bills and the refusal to do so – on the ground that she personally disapproves of a bill or that it was intensely controversial – would be unconstitutional.[50] This, he claimed, 'holds good for the President and the Governor in India'.[51] This is not an appropriate place for a detailed critique of Krishna Iyer's J. opinion in *Shamsher Singh*. Suffice it to say, however, that the observations are largely the product of a refusal to take constitutional provisions seriously. First, India's presidency is *not* the equivalent of the British monarchy: It is not an inherited office. In fact, the concurring opinion does not consider the significance of the indirectly elected national office in any way. Second, British constitutional conventions cannot override written provisions of India's Constitution. Although such conventions may enlighten our understanding of the texts, they cannot determine the latter's meaning. Put differently, provisions – not conventions – come first. But the structure of Krishna Iyer's J. opinion makes it clear that he had little interest in the Constitution's text. Rather, he was interested in what India's Constitution would look like once British conventions were imported into it. His views, however, did not find any mention in the majority opinion written by Chief Justice A. N. Ray, and to that extent, we do not have the benefit of a serious judicial analysis of presidential assent in India.

Now that we have a preliminary understanding of the principle embedded in Article 111 and ways in which president's legislative powers are limited, let us return to ordinances and assent. To what extent, if at all, does Article 111 apply to ordinances? If the Supreme Court's syllogistic template is to hold, it would imply that Article 111 applies to ordinances in the same manner as acts. Therefore, a president may return an ordinance to the cabinet once, but not for a second time. In the rest of this chapter, I will argue that this view is incorrect. Because the president exercises intermediate legislative power in promulgating ordinances, the limits imposed by Article 111 do not apply. To put it provocatively, a president, therefore, may return an ordinance *as many times* as he or she chooses. This question of ordinances and assent is best discussed in two parts. First, the threshold question: Does Article 111 apply to ordinances? Second, if so, to what extent does it apply?

49 *Id.* at para 153.
50 *Ibid.*
51 *Ibid.*

B. THE CONSENSUS UNDONE: ORDINANCES AND INTERMEDIATE LEGISLATIVE POWER

Let us turn to the first question. Does Article 111 apply to ordinances? In other words, is presidential assent in Article 111 necessary for ordinances to become law? That this question should be posed after more than sixty years of consistent – and unchallenged practice – may strike readers as strange, if not worse. But it is worth pointing out that the 'textual' hurdles in making Article 111 applicable to ordinances are not insignificant. To understand why that is so, consider Article 123: 'An Ordinance promulgated under this article shall have the same force and effect as an *Act of Parliament*'. An Act, when it exists, has certain legal properties, and Article 123(2) compares the status of an ordinance to an Act, suggesting that both have the 'same force and effect'. Article 111, in contrast, deals with *bills* and describe how they become Acts: 'When a Bill has been passed by the Houses of Parliament, it shall be presented to the President, and the President shall declare either that he assents to the Bill, or that he withholds assent therefrom'. The provision is antecedent to an Act; one has to get past Article 111 before one may discuss an Act and its legal effects. Articles 123 and 111, in other words, refer to different things. The former assumes that an Act exists and explains the effect of ordinances with references to Acts. The latter explains how an Act comes into existence and, in particular, the final hurdle that must be overcome for a set of enacted provisions to qualify as an Act. Applying conditions in Article 111 to ordinances, therefore, would amount to giving them the same effect as bills, not Acts – an outcome entirely contrary to Article 123. For that reason, Article 111, I would argue, does not apply to ordinances: Matters relating to assent and presidential discretion in such cases must be resolved, as far as possible, by referring to Article 123.

Distancing Article 123 from the effects of Article 111 may lead to the following question: Why is there no provision on assent to ordinances? This question, I believe, rests on an incomplete understanding of Article 111 and its differences with Article 123. With respect to bills, a separate provision on assent is required because of the enacting procedure and the role parliamentary constituents play in that process. The Lower House, Upper House and the president, as I mentioned before, make up India's parliament. Because the deliberative and voting functions are generally reserved for the two houses, the additional step of assent helps secure presidential concurrence, thereby ensuring that all three constituents agree on an Act. But Article 123 is different. It authorises the president – to the exclusion of the two houses – to promulgate ordinances that have the 'same force and effect' as Acts. With the deliberative and voting requirements done away with, the president in promulgating an ordinance acts alone. And given the involvement of a single office, an additional provision on assent is unnecessary: Assent is built into the very act of promulgating an ordinance. A president, after all, cannot promulgate an ordinances unless he or she 'assents' to its promulgation.

What I have argued thus far is that there are two kinds of assent in India's Constitution. Assent of the first kind is tied to the exercise of parliament's legislative power; it is explicitly provided for in Article 111. Here, legislation is enacted by the two houses, and presidential assent becomes relevant after that. Then there is assent of the second kind (implicitly included in Article 123) that is tied to the exercise of intermediate legislative power (i.e., the president's power to promulgate ordinances). Here, 'legislation' is drawn up by the cabinet, and presidential assent becomes relevant after that. It is at this point of assent that the other question of discretion arises. In Article 111, the president does not have the discretion to formally return a bill to the houses for a second time. In Article 123, how far should that discretion extend? In other words, how many times, if at all, should the president be able to return a draft ordinance to the cabinet? That is the question to which I shall now turn.

The representative mandate of cabinets is significantly different from that of the two houses taken together. Therefore, an analysis of discretionary powers involving ordinances and assent, it seems, must be informed by an understanding of the ways in which the representative mandate of cabinets and houses differ. In India, cabinets – as I mentioned in Chapter 2 – generally speaking, can only be of four kinds: (1) single-party majority, (2) single-party minority, (3) coalition majority and (4) coalition minority. But the tenure of these cabinets can be further broken down into three periods: (1) after a cabinet is sworn in, but before it proves its majority; (2) while a cabinet is in office, having proved its majority and (3) while a cabinet is in office as a caretaker one, which may be because of resignation, a no-confidence motion or the completion of tenure.

This categorisation, however, is subject to one exception. Thus far, presidents have not asked single-party majority cabinets to prove their majority after taking office. Presumably, the assumption is that such cabinets have the requisite numbers, and a confidence motion is an unnecessary formality. Accordingly, Nehru, for example, was not required to

TABLE 5.1. *List of prime ministers and ordinances promulgated after losing a trust vote*

Prime Minister	Period	Dates	Ordinances
C. Charan Singh	Before trust vote	28.07.79 – 20.08.79	–
	After resigning	21.08.79 – 13.01.80	7
V. P. Singh	Before trust vote	02.12.89 – 21.12.89	–
	After resigning	07.11.90 – 09.11.90	–
K. Chandra Shekhar	Before trust vote	10.11.90 – 16.11.90	–
	After resigning	07.03.91 – 20.06.91	6
P. V. Narasimha Rao	Before trust vote	21.06.91 – 15.07.91	–
	After resigning	11.05.96 – 15.05.96	–
A. B. Vajpayee	Before trust vote	16.05.96 – 28.05.96	–
	After resigning	29.05.96 – 31.05.96	–
H. D. Deve Gowda	Before trust vote	01.06.96 – 12.06.96	–
	After resigning	12.04.97 – 20.04–97	–
I. K. Gujral	Before trust vote	21.04.97 – 22.04.97	–
	After resigning	29.11.97 – 18.03.98	13
A. B. Vajpayee	Before trust vote	19.03.98 – 28.03.98	–
	After resigning	17.04.99 – 12.10.99	3

prove his majority in 1952, 1957 or 1962. Nor was Mrs Indira Gandhi asked to prove her majority in 1966, 1971 or 1980. Therefore, with respect to single-party cabinets, it is safe to say that only two periods are relevant: (1) while a cabinet is in office because of its majority and (2) while a cabinet is in office after resigning or losing majority (i.e., as a caretaker cabinet). Also, in some cases, even coalition minority cabinets were exempt from proving their majorities in the Lower House. For example, A. B. Vajpayee was not asked to prove his majority in October 1999 because the NDA and its associates had the numbers to command a majority.[52] This was also true of Dr Manmohan Singh when he was sworn in as the leader of a coalition minority in May 2004.[53]

Table 5.1 makes two things clear. Thus far, cabinets have never promulgated ordinances before securing a trust vote in parliament. However, on several occasions, cabinets have promulgated ordinances *after* losing

[52] As before, I characterise the government as a 'coalition minority' because not all coalition partners were part of the government. Some of the parties, despite being part of the coalition, only extended 'outside' support. That is to say, they were part of the alliance, but not part of the government.

[53] In both of these cases, I label the government as a 'minority' because some of the partners of the coalition merely provided outside support without participating in the government.

a trust vote or resigning in the knowledge that it would lose such a vote. I. K. Gujral's cabinet has the most egregious record. In the four months as a caretaker cabinet, it promulgated as many as thirteen ordinances. Of these, eleven were cases of re-promulgation.[54] Charan Singh and K. Chandra Shekhar are not far behind, with as many as seven and six ordinances respectively. Finally, Vajpayee recommended three ordinances while serving as a caretaker prime minister.

Charan Singh's ordinances included, amongst others, a prohibition on strikes by the employees of the Reserve Bank of India,[55] changes to company law[56] and the creation of a new offence.[57] Similarly, Chandra Shekhar, as a caretaker prime minister, relied on the ordinance-making powers to make changes to the law on criminal procedure[58] and more brazenly, to extend the life of the dreaded Terrorist and Disruptive Activities Act, 1987 by two years.[59]

Because they were promulgated after the governments lost their confidence motions, these ordinances, by definition, cannot claim a representative mandate. They involved no deliberation or voting and came from cabinets that had clearly lost their majorities. Why, then, should the president be bound by a cabinet's recommendation to promulgate an ordinance if it is returned to him or her a second time? Recall that in Article 111, the president must back off from the initial objections if the two houses reiterate their collective wisdom and assert that a piece of legislation is necessary. Implicit in this arrangement is the idea that the two houses have a greater representative appeal and, therefore, can effectively veto a president's objections the second instance. But ordinances are different. A president by virtue of being the only nationally – albeit indirectly – elected official, I would argue, has enough representative 'width' to *retain* his or her objections to an ordinance even if it is recommended for a second time. This is especially true when ordinances are recommended by cabinets that have categorically lost majority

54 See, e.g., The Representation of People (Amendment) Ordinance, 1997 (23 of 1997); The Finance (Second Amendment) Ordinance, 1997 (24 of 1997); The Merchant Shipping (Amendment) Second Ordinance, 1997 (27 of 1997); The Prasar Bharti (Broadcasting Corporation of India) (Amendment) Second Ordinance, 1997 (29 of 1997); The Essential Commodities (Special Provisions) Second Ordinance, 1998 (1 of 1998).

55 The Reserve Bank of India (Maintenance of Services) Ordinance, 1979 (4 of 1979).

56 The Companies (Amendment) Ordinance, 1979 (9 of 1979).

57 The Prevention of Blackmarketing and Maintenance of Supplies of Essential Commodities Ordinance, 1979 (10 of 1979).

58 The Code of Criminal Procedure (Amendment) Ordinance, 1991 (4 of 1991).

59 The Terrorist and Disruptive Activities (Prevention) Amendment Act, 1991 (5 of 1991).

support in parliament, or are yet to prove their majorities in the Lowe House.[60]

But the argument, it seems, should have a far-wider application, including in cases when cabinets enjoy working majorities. There are several reasons for this. First, majority for a cabinet only implies a majority in the Lower House of parliament. There is no guarantee – or requirement – that a cabinet also enjoys the support of a majority in the Upper House. Second, even in cases where a cabinet does have a working majority in both houses of parliament, it does not follow that an ordinance necessarily enjoys majority support. Third, members of the cabinet may not even be members of either house. In such cases, they cannot claim any degree of representative legitimacy.[61] An ordinance, in that sense, reflects the 'will of the cabinet', not the 'will of both houses of parliament'. And therein lies the crucial difference. A president, in Article 111, is bound by the 'will of both houses' at the second instance, presumably because of the latter's representative proximity, numeric strength and deliberative superiority. A cabinet, however, cannot claim these qualities to the same extent as the two houses. To put it differently, constitutional bodies that bring legislation into existence are different from bodies that bring ordinances into existence. For that reason, a president, I would argue, need not give way to a cabinet's legislative desires merely because it is recommended for a second time.[62]

What does all this mean in practical terms? Consider these facts. In March 1996, the Tenth Lok Sabha had come to a close all but in name. Seeking to gain what seemed like an unfair advantage, the Narasimha Rao

[60] Even though thus far there are no cases of ordinances being promulgated prior to a cabinet securing a majority vote, note that there are no temporal limits in Article 123.

[61] Constitution of India, Article 75(5) ('A Minister who for any period of six consecutive months is not a member of either House of Parliament shall at the expiration of that period cease to be a Minister'.).

[62] *Supra* n. 39 at 290–291. Judge Subba Rao came to a similar conclusion, but by a different analysis. He argued that if 'the President is bound to accept the advice of the Ministry in the matter of ordinances it may lead to abuse of power.... That he does not act automatically on advice is clear as under the Article he shall be "satisfied" that the circumstances exist which render it necessary for him to take immediate action. The expression "satisfaction" is a mental process. It involves the consideration of the pros and cons of the question. The President may take the advice of the Government, but he has to be satisfied and not the Cabinet. This construction will put a salutary check on the arbitrary action of the Cabinet or on its abuse of power'. Even though Subba Rao does not address the issue of repeated refusals directly, it follows from his interpretation of Article 123. If it is the president who must be satisfied as to the circumstances that make an ordinance necessary, there is no question of the president being bound by the cabinet's advice merely because the ordinance is presented for a second time.

cabinet placed two ordinances before President Shankar Dayal Sharma for promulgation. One was to shorten the period of poll campaigns from three weeks to two weeks and the other to extend reservations in public employment to Dalit Christians. Opposition parties immediately decried the move, and in meetings with the president, made their objections clear.[63] Whereas some characterised it as a 'misuse', others described the proposal as 'undemocratic and unethical'.[64] President Sharma sent it back, adding that 'independent of the relative intrinsic merits of the ordinances proposed, promulgating these ordinances would appear to be inappropriate and contrary to the canons of constitutional propriety in view of circumstances existing at this particular juncture'.[65] Rao's cabinet backed off, and decided not to press the matter further.

What if the cabinet had sent the ordinance back to the president? If the Supreme Court's syllogistic template is correct, a president must treat the ordinance no differently than a bill sent back to him under Article 111. In other words, President Sharma would have been bound to promulgate it, or at least would not have the authority to return it to the cabinet for a second time. My argument here is that presidents have no such compulsion: President Sharma, if he so chose, could have returned the ordinance as many times as he wanted. This is because Article 111 is irrelevant to questions regarding ordinances. It deals with the president's legislative power, and in the exercise of such power, a president competes with the two houses of parliament for a say on legislative matters. When the latter reaffirm that a piece of legislation is needed, the president, by virtue of the position's limited representative appeal, must give way. But ordinances are different: They do not have the qualities that lend legitimacy to acts of parliament. When a president promulgates an ordinance based on Article 123, he or she exercises intermediate legislative power, and competes with the *cabinet* – not the two houses.[66]

[63] Anon, 'Ordinance Move Assailed' *Times of India*, 17 March 1996.

[64] *Ibid.* See also Anon, 'President Declines Assent to Ordinances' *Times of India*, 20 March 1996.

[65] Fali Nariman, '"The Silences in Our Constitutional Law": First Durga Das Basu Endowment Lecture 2005', 2 *Supreme Court Cases (Journal)* 15 (2006). See also Subhas Kipekar, 'Promulgation of Ordinance Now Not Right: Sharma' *Times of India*, 21 March 1996. Many quickly hailed his decision. Speaking to the *Times of India*, a senior politician commented that the president's refusal 'to sign the two ordinances … marks the setting of a very high standard in the approach to an important period in our political history. It is an approach that has regard for freedoms as well as the discipline entailed by an advanced parliamentary democracy'.

[66] The issue of comparative representative appeal should not be exaggerated. Governors, after all, have no representative appeal and, if pushed too far, would imply that they do not have authority to return ordinances for a second time.

C. CONCLUSION

Under Article 111, a president cannot formally return a bill to the two houses for a second time. That much is not in doubt. In this chapter, I have argued that that consensus regarding bills should not apply to ordinances. When a president assents to a bill, he or she exercises legislative power. A bill, at least in theory, reflects certain representative, numeric and deliberative qualities. And it is the presence of those qualities that partly explains why a president cannot formally return it for a second time. But when a president promulgates an ordinance, he or she exercises intermediate legislative power. Such an ordinance, by definition, lacks the qualities that give a bill its elevated status. And for that reason, presidents, I would argue, must treat ordinances differently from Acts. Therein lies the applied significance of the argument I have defended in this book. Acts and ordinances result from the exercise of different kinds of legislative power. Therefore, except on very limited matters, they do not have the 'same force and effect'. As such, Article 123 does not mean what it says.

Conclusion: 'Edwardian' Reading of Ordinances

Article 123 – and its state equivalent, Article 213 – in India's Constitution are useful examples of what Carey and Shugart refer to as constitutional decree authority (CDA).[1] Two requirements are essential for CDA. First, the authority to promulgate decrees must be directly provided for in a Constitution. This is unlike situations where the Constitution merely authorises parliament to further delegate core legislative function to the executive. Carey and Shugart refer to this latter arrangement as 'delegated decree authority' (DDA).[2] Second, decrees should enjoy similar status as Acts of parliament. Ordinances in India's Constitution satisfy both requirements. Presidents are authorised to promulgate them directly. And by virtue of Article 123(2), they have the 'same force and effect' as Acts.

But this CDA is not an 'emergency power' through which executives may suspend civil liberties or take over state and local administration in times of internal unrest or external threat. As explained in Chapter 1, such powers are separately provided for in the Constitution. With ordinances, a president must merely be satisfied that 'circumstances exist that render it necessary for him to take immediate action'. Other substantive conditions are irrelevant. Therefore, Articles 123 and 213 are examples of 'standard' – not emergency – CDA.[3]

This classification can be further refined. Textually speaking, ordinances in India are examples of provisional decree authority: They come into effect immediately, but are not permanent. Ordinances must be properly legislated into Acts of parliament before the expiry of six weeks from the day both houses come back to session. Otherwise, they 'cease to

[1] John M. Carey and Matthew Soberg Shugart, 'Calling Out the Tanks or Filling Out the Forms?' in John M. Carey and Matthew S. Shugart (eds.), *Executive Decree Authority* 1–29, 13 (Cambridge University Press, Cambridge, 1998).

[2] *Ibid.*

[3] *Id.* at 14.

operate'.[4] But there are good reasons to suggest that the Indian arrangement has effectively mutated into prototypical decree authority.

The preceding chapters offered three levels of arguments. I argued in Chapter 1 that there are no good reasons to provide for ordinances in the Constitution. Both empirically and normatively, arguments about the need for such a mechanism fail. Many legal systems function perfectly well without ordinances. Dr Ambedkar's 'necessary evil' claim is not borne out empirically, whereas Seervai's 'ordinances must exist alongside provisions for judicial review' argument is not borne out normatively. But other reasons also invite caution.

First, ordinances militate against the idea that ordinary (or primary) legislation to be so called must satisfy basic representative, numeric and deliberative qualities. Because they are enacted by cabinets rather than parliaments, by definition, numeric or deliberative preconditions do not apply initially. Their representative quotient is also limited. Article 123 elevates the 'will of the cabinet' to the status of legislation proper, and arguably does so in ways that are inconsistent with elementary demands of the rule of law. Second, ordinances offer improper incentives to cabinets. Recall that ordinances may be promulgated only when either of the two houses is not in session. In other words, ordinances are meant to remedy situations of legislative urgency that make parliamentary legislation difficult to achieve. But when turned on its head, this mechanism incentivises cabinets to keep parliament *from* functioning. The reasoning is simple. It is far easier to legislate without parliament than through it. But this is possible only if either house of parliament is not in session. Cabinets, however, enjoy complete discretion to decide when parliament should be in session.[5] As a result, exercising that discretion to keep parliament out of – rather than in – session makes more sense; cabinets have much to gain from a non-functioning parliament. Third, because ordinances offer an easy way out of a legislative logjam, parties in office have little, if any, incentive to negotiate on legislative issues. Ordinances, in other words, make legislative intransigence *more* likely. Conversely, they

[4] I say 'textually speaking' because as I have argued in Chapter 3 in detail, the Supreme Court has effectively written off this 'cease to operate' requirement. As a result, even if the cabinet fails to convert an ordinance into an Act, its effects remain permanently valid.

[5] This, of course, is subject to the constitutional requirement that the houses of parliament must meet once every six months. Constitution of India, Article 85(1) ('The President shall from time to time summon each House of Parliament to meet at such time and place as he thinks fit, but six months shall not intervene between its lasting sitting in one session and the date appointed for its first sitting in the next session').

render parliamentary opposition to legislation ineffective: No matter the situation, cabinets always have a way out, at least temporarily. Taken together, these arguments suggest that the story of India's progressively poor, almost abysmal, parliamentary functioning cannot be understood without a good grasp of ordinances – both the mechanism per se and how it has been used. And meaningful reform of parliament cannot be achieved without reforming the provision for ordinances.

The second level of argument concerns India's empirical record. In my view, a collection of 'political' and interpretative reasons are needed to make sense of the persistent reliance on ordinances in India. On the political side of the equation, three things are worth highlighting. As I argued in Chapter 2, precedents, parliamentary performances and the personalities involved are all part of India's ordinance story. The precedential reasons began with Prime Minister Nehru himself. In the early years of the republic, he adopted a lax attitude towards Article 123 and, in particular, towards what counted as 'immediate action' in that provision. When Speaker G. V. Mavalankar warned against it, his concerns were brushed aside. Nehru nationalised the life insurance business through an ordinance and promulgated a special national security law for the State of Manipur. Cabinets, since then, have never looked back. Indira Gandhi's socialist agenda was almost entirely implemented through ordinances, and successive cabinets from across the political spectrum have taken to them to enact legislation relating to national security. Secondly, the point about parliamentary performances is an empirical one. There is a statistically significant correlation between the decline in parliamentary performance (measured by the number of days in session and sitting) and the number of ordinances. But the issue of causation remains debatable. It is not readily clear if poor parliamentary performance has compelled cabinets to resort to ordinances or, conversely, if the mechanism for ordinances has led to a poor parliamentary record. As I argued previously, the latter possibility cannot be dismissed out of hand. Thirdly, ordinances are related to political personalities and their attitude towards parliament. The more that prime ministers view parliament as a cumbersome institution – or still worse, have contempt for it – the more likely ordinances will flourish. In Chapter 2, I explained the difference between these two attitudes, with an outline of the different ways in which this latter contempt may be expressed.

India's empirical record, it should be noted, offers interesting parallels and contrasts with Latin American and European jurisdictions. I shall emphasize three aspects here. The first point has to do with numbers. Latin

American and European jurisdictions (with the exception of France) have struggled to control the rate of ordinances,[6] and they are far greater than the 615 ordinances India has had so far. In Argentina, four presidents between 1983 and 2001 issued as many as 315 decrees.[7] In neighbouring Brazil, four presidents between 1989 and 2000 issued 5,537 decrees, including 571 original ones.[8] The numbers are equally large in Russia.[9]

The second point has to do with slippage. Although ordinances in India are textually limited only to circumstances that render it 'necessary for [the president] to take immediate action', things have been different in practice. As I described in Chapter 2, the mechanism has been used to promulgate both important and trivial ordinances, including those that could not conceivably be regarded as requiring 'immediate action'. Starting with Nehru, Indian prime ministers refused to take the constitutional text – and the constraints therein – seriously. In this respect, they have much in common with their presidential counterparts in Latin America. Take Rubio and Goretti's verdict about decrees in Argentina, for example. They 'have been used and misused', the authors argue. 'In some cases the emergency was real; in others there were only particularistic needs, and in others the putative emergency was merely a vehicle for Menem to exercise personal discretion'.[10]

The view from Brazil is no different. As the first president under Brazil's new Constitution, José Sarney 'did not take seriously the constitutional requisites of "urgency and relevance" which were intended to limit the use of the decree'.[11] His first decree in 1988 'protected certain fishes from being captured during their reproductive cycle and imposed fines on the fishermen who violated the new rules',[12] but in invoking his decree

[6] For a discussion on why France has had relatively few decrees, see John Huber, 'Executive Decree Authority in France' in John M. Carey and Matthew S. Shugart (eds.), *Executive Decree Authority* 233–253 (Cambridge University Press, Cambridge, 1998).

[7] Gabriel L. Negretto, 'Government Capacities and Policy Making by Decree in Latin America: The Cases of Brazil and Argentina', 37(5) *Comparative Political Studies* 531–562, 554 (2004).

[8] *Ibid.* at 543.

[9] See Oleh Protsky, 'Ruling with Decrees: Presidential Decree Making in Russia and Ukraine', 56(5) *Europe Asia Studies* 637–660, 658 (2004).

[10] Delia Ferreira Rubio and Matteo Goretti, 'When the President Governs Along: The Decretazo in Argentina 1989–93', in John M. Carey and Matthew S. Shugart (eds.), *Executive Decree Authority* 33–61, 51 (Cambridge University Press, Cambridge, 1998).

[11] Timothy Power, 'The Pen Is Mightier than the Congress: Presidential Decree Power in Brazil' in John M. Carey and Matthew S. Shugart (eds.), *Executive Decree Authority* 197–233, 204 (Cambridge University Press, Cambridge, 1998).

[12] *Ibid.* at 205.

power for a relatively unimportant purpose, 'Sarney treated the constitutional language trivially, and Congress, perceiving a fair accompli, went along with him'. Like in India, the early disregard for the 'urgency and relevance' clause quickly 'became institutionalized' and evolved into a parallel legislative mechanism.[13]

The third point is about the substantive focus of decrees. In India, ordinances have been used to regulate a large number of substantive issues, but there are three broad topics that involve the systematic use of ordinances. Two of them – nationalisation of the economy and regulating national security affairs – are relevant for comparative purposes. In India, ordinances were used to nationalise vast swathes of the economy; Jawaharlal Nehru initially – and later on, his daughter, Indira Gandhi – were the protagonists of this socialist affair. But in Latin America and Eastern Europe, the reverse was true: Economic ordinances were systematically used to *deregulate* the economy and reduce the role of government in economic affairs. Amongst others, Carlos Menem in Argentina, José Sarney and Fernando Collor de Mello in Brazil, Alberto Fujimori in Peru and Boris Yeltsin in Russia extensively relied on decrees to implement free-market policies in the midst of the economic crisis that swept the two continents in the late 1980s and early 1990s.[14]

With respect to national security, however, India's experience is more typical. As I described in the Introduction, decree power (of varying kinds) was used in several jurisdictions to regulate matters concerning crime and criminal procedure. Yeltsin, for example, gave law enforcement agencies significant new powers through a decree in 1994. Titled 'On urgent measures to protect the population from banditry and other forms of organized violence', the decree gave Russian authorities, amongst other things, sweeping search powers, authorised the use of evidence obtained in such searches as 'proof of guilt' in any subsequent criminal trial and empowered authorities to look through the business and financial records of such suspects.[15] Incidentally, none of these required any prior court

[13] *Id.*

[14] This determined use of decrees to set the economy in order led to the argument about 'delegative democracy'. See Guillermo O'Donnell, 'Delegative Democracy' 5(1) *Journal of Democracy* 55–69 (1994); Paul Kubicek, 'Delegative Democracy in Russia and Ukraine' 27(4) *Communist and Post-Communist Studies* 423–441 (1994). See also Adam Przeworski, *Democracy and the Market: Political and Economic Reforms in Eastern Europe and Latin America* (Cambridge University Press, Cambridge, 1991).

[15] Scott Parrish, 'Presidential Decree Authority in Russia, 1991–1995' in John M. Carey and Matthew S. Shugart (eds.), *Executive Decree Authority* 62–103, 84 (Cambridge University Press, Cambridge, 1998).

approval. The decree was roundly condemned (including by members of the Duma), but they could not cobble together a sufficient majority to override Yeltsin's veto.[16] Similarly, in Peru, Fujimori relied on his DDA to introduce radical counterinsurgency measures that threatened civil liberties and democratic governance. His decrees, amongst other things, made all citizens eligible for conscription, required them to supply any information requested to fight terrorism, redefined treason and mandated prison sentences for publishing or broadcasting any information pertinent to national defence deemed secret by the government.[17] These measures were staunchly opposed by legislators of all political stripes, and they eventually succeeded in enacting a piece of legislation that imposed significant restraints on the president's power to govern by decrees.[18] Similar to India, however, legislators in Russia and Peru rarely succeeded in repealing or amending specific decrees through the chambers, or compelling presidents to themselves introduce substantive changes to those measures.[19]

The third level of argument in this book is about constitutional interpretation, and the role courts have impliedly played in encouraging ordinances. Consider Article 123 and the 'controls' included therein. Two conditions must be satisfied before the provision may be invoked: 1) Either house of parliament must not be in session and 2) the president must be satisfied that circumstances exist that render it necessary to take immediate action. After promulgation, a different control applies: Unless properly enacted into law by parliament, an ordinance 'ceases to exist'. But based on a syllogistic piece of reasoning that grants Acts and ordinances comparable standing, courts have systematically immunised each of these controls from the purview of judicial review. As I discussed in Chapter 3, in *Re Kalyanam Veerabhadraya*,[20] the Madras High Court came to the conclusion that cabinets have complete discretion to bring

[16] *Id.*

[17] Gregory Schmitt, 'Presidential Usurpation or Congressional Preference? The Evolution of Executive Decree Authority in Peru' in John M. Carey and Matthew S. Shugart (eds.), *Executive Decree Authority* 104–141, 137 (Cambridge University Press, Cambridge, 1998).

[18] See Law of Parliamentary Control over the Normative Acts of the President of the Republic (Law 25, 397). This legislative victory eventually proved pyrrhic. This legislation perhaps contributed in large measure to Fujimori's ultimate decision to shut down Congress and call out the tanks.

[19] One notable exception in India was the Prevention of Corruption Ordinance, 2001 (9 of 2001). The Vajpayee cabinet was compelled to introduce several important changes before it was enacted into law in an extraordinary session of the two houses in 2002.

[20] AIR 1950 Mad 243.

legislative sessions to a close. In other words, a cabinet may prorogue either house of parliament at any time for any reason. Indeed, a cabinet may do so solely to make an ordinance constitutionally possible and even in such cases, courts will avoid reviewing the matter. The same is true of the next control: presidential satisfaction. As I discussed in Chapter 4, in *Nagaraj v. State of Andhra Pradesh*[21] – and several cases thereafter – the Supreme Court has taken the view that presidential satisfaction in Article 123 is not judicially reviewable. In other words, the cabinet is the *sole* judge of circumstances that are necessary to take immediate action. A legislative emergency is whatever the cabinet says it is. Likewise, the final control also has been undone. Article 123(2) clarifies that a lapsed ordinance must 'cease to exist'. And yet, as I analysed in Chapter 3, starting with *Bhupendra Bose v. State of Orissa*[22] – and consistently thereafter – the Supreme Court has taken the view that legal effects of all transactions initiated or completed while an ordinance was in force become *permanently* valid. Failed ordinances have no legal costs, and cabinets, therefore, are free to promulgate ordinances indiscriminately. If they succeed in turning an ordinance into an Act of parliament, cabinets obviously succeed. But even if an ordinance fails, it still 'succeeds'. When read together, these cases demonstrate how immunity from judicial review has also encouraged a lax attitude amongst cabinets. It is in this sense that both political and interpretative reasons are necessary to understand the nature of ordinances in India.

Where do we go from here? The most efficient solution, as I mentioned before, is to acknowledge the extent to which ordinances have eaten into the vitals of India's legislative arrangement and do away with them. Deleting Article 123 and its state counterpart in Article 213 is the best way forward. That, however, is unlikely to happen. Cabinets across the political spectrum are far too invested in this convenient arrangement. In fact, any serious recommendation for deleting Article 123 (and Article 213) is likely to generate legions of self-serving arguments for retaining them. A more modest way forward may be to introduce a set of reforms that will restore a sense of urgency to ordinances. Ordinances are not legislation by just another means: They are special, involve urgent circumstances and are limited in several respects. This view has fallen off our constitutional psyche, and it needs to regain appeal. In the rest of this Conclusion, I will briefly sketch out three reforms that, I believe, will help us best achieve that objective.

[21] AIR 1985 SC 551.

[22] AIR1962 SC 945.

First, reconsider the convention of publicising ordinances. In the early part of the twentieth century, a convention of addressing the nation on the promulgation of an ordinance developed in British India. Even though the practice was not always common, it was at least honoured in important cases. On several occasions, governor-generals publicly explained their rationale for introducing ordinances. After independence, the practice continued for a while. The prime minister or relevant cabinet ministers made it a point to address the nation on the promulgation of an ordinance. As I discussed in Chapter 2, Finance Minister C. D. Deshmukh made an extensive broadcast to the nation after the Life Insurance (Emergency Provisions) Ordinance, 1956[23] was brought into effect.[24] Similarly, Indira Gandhi – in a national broadcast over All India Radio – explained her rationale for nationalising banks and the benefits, she felt, would accrue to the nation.[25] By the early 1980s, however, that limited practice was lost. Cabinet ministers since then have never felt it necessary to explain extraordinary laws to the people. This may partly have to do with the normalisation of ordinances, both in our understanding of the mechanism and the sheer volume of them.

With two specific changes, the convention of addressing a nation on the promulgation of an ordinance is worth reviving. It must be consistently practised: *every* ordinance – not merely 'important' ones – must be explained. But any such address must also include an explanation as to *why* an ordinance was necessary. Because there are no such expectations today, ordinances are rarely publicised. In the limited cases when they are publicised, the debate almost immediately veers towards the merits of the provisions as opposed to the need for an ordinance in the first place. This is where publicising reasons for an ordinance may be useful. Such a requirement will at least compel the cabinet to spell out its reasons for an ordinance, and throw light on its understanding of what constitutes 'immediate action' in Article 123. When stated publicly and clearly, such justifications will invariably invite scrutiny, both from opposition parties and the general public. And this public back-and-forth about the very need for an ordinance has the potential to revive awareness about its extraordinary nature.[26]

[23] 1 of 1956.

[24] Anon, 'Insurance Firms "Misused" Power and Privilege' *Times of India*, 20 January 1956

[25] Anon, 'Indira Explains New Scheme', *Times of India*, 20 July 1969.

[26] If necessary, a constitutional justification for publicising ordinances can easily be found. As I described in Chapter 3, 'rule of law' requires, at the very least, that people be aware

Second, reconsider the constitutional status of ordinances. Article 123(2) says that ordinances have the 'same force and effect' as Acts of parliament. This has led the Supreme Court to tie both Acts and ordinances to the same string of legislative power, and adopt a syllogistic template in interpreting the latter. As a result, any controversy regarding the force and effect of ordinances is usually resolved by referring to the force and effect of Acts. As I discussed in detail in Chapter 3, conceptualising ordinances in this manner creates several hurdles. Take, for example, retrospective effect. Can an ordinance enjoy retrospective effect? Or, more specifically, can an ordinance enjoy retrospective effect from a point in time when both houses of parliament were in session? In addressing this matter, courts looked at Acts to the exclusion of everything else. They said that because Acts can have unlimited retrospectivity (except in some cases), ordinances must have the same. That such a view effectively turns ordinances into a parallel legislative mechanism did not matter. Similarly, consider the legal effect of a lapsed ordinance. Article 123(2)(b) says that an ordinance that does not become an Act of parliament 'ceases to exist'. By equating ordinances to temporary Acts, courts have repeatedly taken the view that legal effects of all actions initiated or completed during the pendency of an ordinance become permanently valid. That such an interpretation effectively authorises the cabinet to permanently undo validly enacted piece of legislation did not matter.

These challenges, I believe, stem from a misunderstanding about ordinances and the mechanism of promulgating them. Article 123 is not a self-contained provision: It draws from, relies upon and stands within a family of provisions in the Constitution. Therefore, any meaningful assessment of Article 123 requires an understanding of the 'provisional tree' – and the ways in which that provision stands together with its agnates. But the Supreme Court's syllogistic template fails to do that. As I described in Chapter 2, the template raises Article 123 to a heuristic absolute and thereby fails to account for the range of architectural limits – provisional, principled and pragmatic – that run through it. When taken into account, these limits suggest that the power to promulgate ordinances is best understood as an exercise of *intermediate* legislative power – a novel category that is neither fully legislative nor fully executive, but contains important components of both. Intermediate legislative

of the laws to which they are subjected. Because ordinances do not involve any public deliberation, post-promulgation, some degree of publicising is essential if Article 123 is to be practised in a way consistent with the most elementary demands of the rule of law.

power stands in contradistinction to the existing categories of constituent, legislative and delegated powers. As I explained in Chapter 4, it may be defined as the exercise of original legislative power by the executive, and once we understand ordinances through this lens, interpretative challenges regarding their force and effect disappear.

Why would the interpretative challenges disappear? Currently, Acts and ordinances are tied to the same string of legislative power. As a result, expanding the scope of judicial review in one case leads to an expansion in the other case. Consider, once again, the issue of retrospectivity. Acts, generally speaking, may have unlimited retrospectivity. A syllogistic approach suggests that ordinances must also allow for unlimited retrospectivity. But once we acknowledge that ordinances are products of a different kind of legislative power, it becomes possible to treat the two differently. Ordinances may have limited retrospectivity, whereas Acts may have an unlimited one. Similarly, reasons for promulgating ordinances may be judicially reviewed, whereas Acts may be excluded from such review. Apart from its interpretative utility, this new category can account for ordinances in a way that is consistent with the legislative scheme in India's Constitution. As I argued in Chapter 4, equating ordinances with Acts and conferring permanent validity on actions taken under a lapsed ordinance turns India's legislative arrangement upside down. It authorises the cabinet to permanently repeal laws enacted by parliament, thereby privileging executive Acts over parliamentary legislation. But relying on intermediate legislative power to understand the origin of ordinances makes a more consistent outcome possible. Ordinances are not the equivalent of temporary Acts and, therefore, a lapsed ordinance, unlike a temporary Act, cannot produce permanent effects. Consequently, if an ordinance lapses, it ceases to have effect *as if it never existed*. Approaching the matter in this way restores the proper hierarchy of Acts over ordinances, and ensures that failed ordinances do override the stated will of parliament.

If correct, the argument about intermediate legislative power suggests that ordinances are 'inferior' to Acts. The suggestion is hardly novel. Almost 400 years ago, Sir Edward Coke offered a similar formulation in the *Case of Proclamations*.[27] When asked how far English monarchs could rely on their prerogative powers to make law independent of the two houses, he rendered an opinion limiting the extent of such powers. 'The King cannot change any part of the common law, or statute law,

[27] (1611) 12 Co. Rep. 74.

or the customs of the realm', he said. Nor can he 'create any offence by his prohibition or proclamation, which was not an offence before, for that [is] to change the law, and to make an offence which was not'.[28] However, 'the King out of his province, and to prevent dangers, which it will be too late to prevent afterwards', Coke said, may prohibit a thing that is already punishable by law, fine and imprisonment, such that 'will aggravate the offence if it to be afterwards committed'.[29] For Edward Coke, then, ordinances were something *less* than law proper. Vertically, they were neither part of common law, statute law or custom in England; horizontally, they could only achieve limited things.

The concept of intermediate legislative power that I have defended in this book essentially has an Edwardian structure. However, some caveats must be added. This form of legislative power, by definition, is vertically inferior to parliamentary Acts: Ordinances or proclamations do not have the same qualities that lend legitimacy to Acts. But, horizontally speaking, ordinances have no inherent qualities: They may or may not be inferior to Acts. Edward Coke, for example, took the view that regal proclamations had subject-matter limits. They could only be used for limited purposes. In this respect, Indian ordinances are clearly different. Except in some extraordinary situations, there are no subject-matter limits: 'If and so far as an Ordinance under this article makes any provision which Parliament would not under this Constitution be competent to enact, it shall be void'.[30] Unlike in England, an ordinance in India *can* create new offences, alter punishments, impose taxes, expropriate property or confer statutory rights. However, as I argued in Chapters 3 and 4, given the Constitution's legislative arrangement, ordinances cannot do certain things. It is in this sense that they do not have the 'same force and effect' as Acts of parliament.

Third, the urgency of ordinances may be revived by incorporating a proviso in Article 123 that was rejected in the Constituent Assembly. Currently, ordinances do not affect parliament's legislative schedule: Article 123(2) merely says that an ordinance must be properly enacted into law no later than six weeks from the date of reassembly of the two houses. Because the provision does not set a date for parliament to reassemble, it allows for the possibility that an ordinance may be in force for an inordinate period of time. In the Constituent Assembly, K. T. Shah was

[28] *Ibid.*

[29] *Ibid.* See also Esther Cope, 'Sir Edward Coke and Proclamations, 1610' 15(3) *American Journal of Legal History* 215–221 (1971).

[30] Constitution of India, Article 123(3).

worried by this possibility. 'We must leave no room for any doubt as to the maximum length of time during which the Presidential Ordinance can remain in operation', he said.[31] Building on this, Mahboob Ali Baig suggested that parliament be brought back to session immediately after the promulgation of an ordinance. 'When Parliament can be called at once within a week or ten days, I do not see any reason', he said, 'why we should allow an opportunity to delay calling Parliament in order to decide whether the ordinance promulgated should continue'.[32] The suggestion, however, was never debated, and for reasons unknown to us, the Assembly decided not to link ordinances to changes in the parliamentary calendar. Given that ordinances in their current form do not impose any institutional constraints, the suggestion of an 'automatic trigger' is worth reconsidering. That is to say, the promulgation of an ordinance must automatically require a special session of parliament within a relatively short period of time. With transport connectivity vastly superior to the state of affairs in 1949, there is no reason why 700-odd persons cannot gather in the nation's capital on short notice. This 'inconvenience' of additional parliamentary sessions will refocus attention on the mechanism per se while possibly reducing the number of ordinances significantly.

Taken together, these three reforms have the potential to restore a sense of urgency to our understanding of ordinances in India and ways in which they deviate from and thereby compromise the ordinary legislative controls that lend legitimacy to parliamentary Acts. But this analysis, as I mentioned in the Introduction, comes with a serious limitation. It says almost nothing about ordinances at the state level and the more-or-less similarly worded provision in Article 213. Unfortunately, research on this aspect of ordinances – including primary data and basic analysis – is rather scanty and something that demands immediate attention.

[31] Constituent Assembly Debates (CAD), Bk. 3. No. VIII, 208 (23 May 1949).
[32] *Id.* at 213.

Bibliography

BOOKS

Adams, George Burton (1921), *The Constitutional History of England*, New York: H. Holt.

Agnihotri, V. K. (2004), *Handbook on the Working of Ministry of Parliamentary Affairs*, New Delhi: Ministry of Parliamentary Affairs.

Allan, T. R. S. (2001), *Constitutional Justice: A Liberal Theory of the Rule of Law*, Oxford: Oxford University Press.

Allen, C. K. (1945), *Law and Orders*, London: Stevens and Sons.

Amos, Maurice (1930), *The English Constitution*, London: Longmans, Green and Co.

Anand, C. L. (2008), *Constitutional Law and History of Government of India*, New Delhi: Universal.

Anson, Sir William (1886), *The Law and Custom of the Constitution*, Oxford: Clarendon Press.

Austin, Glanville (1999), *Working a Democratic Constitution*, New Delhi: Oxford University Press.

Baker, John Hamilton (2002), *An Introduction to English Legal History*, Ohio: Butterworths/LexisNexis.

Banerjee, Anil Chandra (1961–1965), *Indian Constitutional Documents 1757–1939*, Calcutta: A. Mukherjea and Co.

Beatt, David M. (2004), *The Ultimate Rule of Law*, Oxford: Oxford University Press.

Benichou, Lucien (2000), *From Autocracy to Integration: Political Developments in Hyderabad State 1938–1948*, Chennai: Orient Longman.

Bennion, Francis (2008), *Bennion on Statutory Interpretation*, London: LexisNexis.

Blackstone, Sir William and Thomas Cooley (1871), *Commentaries on the Law of England*, Chicago: Callahan and Cockcroft.

Chakrabarty, Bidyut (2006), *Forging Power: Coalition Politics in India*, New Delhi: Oxford University Press.

Choudhary, Valmiki (ed.) (1987), *Dr. Rajendra Prasad: Correspondence and Select Documents* Vol. XIII, New Delhi: Allied Publishers.

Constituent Assembly Debates (1949), New Delhi: Lok Sabha Secretariat.
Dicey, A. V. (1959), *An Introduction to the Study of the Law of the Constitution*, New Delhi: Universal Law Publishing.
Donald, David and Jean Baker, et al. (2001), *The Civil War And Reconstruction*, New York: W. W. Norton.
Dworkin, R. (1985), *A Matter of Principle*, Cambridge: Harvard University Press.
Elton, G. R. (1955), *England Under the Tudors*, London: Methuen and Co.
Engineer, Asghar Ali (1987), *The Shah Bano Controversy*, Delhi: Ajanta Publishers.
Eskridge, William N. (1994), *Dynamic Statutory Interpretation*, Cambridge: Harvard University Press.
Fuller, L. (1964), *The Morality of Law*, New Haven: Yale University Press.
Goldsworthy, Jeffrey Denys (1999), *The Sovereignty of Parliament: History and Philosophy*, New York: Oxford University Press.
Government of India (1996), *Presidential Ordinances 1950–1996*, New Delhi: Lok Sabha Secretariat.
Government of India (2004), *Manual of Parliamentary Procedures in the Government of India*, New Delhi: Ministry of Parliamentary Affairs.
Government of India (2009), *Handbook for Members of Lok Sabha*, 15th ed., New Delhi: Lok Sabha Secretariat.
Graves, Michael A. R. (1985), *Early Tudor Parliaments: Crown, Lords and Commons, 1485–1603*, New York: Longman.
Halsbury's Laws of England, 3rd ed., Vol. 36 (1961), London LexisNexis.
Halstead, T. J. (2007), *Congressional Research Service Report for Congress, Presidential Signing Statements: Constitutional and Institutional Implications, available at*: http://www.fas.org/sgp/crs/natsec/RL33667.pdf (visited on 31 August 2011).
Hansaria, B. L. (1998), *Does India Need a New Constitution?* Calcutta: Eastern Law House.
Haskins, George Lee (1948), *The Growth of English Representative Government*, London: Oxford University Press.
Heinz, Robert (1976), *The Proclamations of the Tudor Kings*, Cambridge: Cambridge University Press.
Holdsworth, Sir William (1936), *A History of English Law*, London: Methuen and Co.
Hughes, Paul L. and Robert F. Fries (1959), *Crown and Parliament in Tudor-Stuart England: A Documentary Constitutional History, 1485–1714*, New York: Putnam.
Jain, M. P. (2009), *Indian Constitutional Law*, Nagpur: LexisNexis.
Jayal, Niraja and Pratap Mehta (eds.) (2010), *Oxford Companion to Politics in India*, New Delhi: Oxford University Press.
Kannabiran, Kalpana and Ranbir Singh (eds.) (2008), *Challenging the Rule(s) of Law: Colonialism, Criminology and Human Rights in India*, New Delhi: Sage.
Kapur, Devesh and Pratap Mehta (eds.) (2007), *Public Institution in India*, New Delhi: Oxford University Press.
Kashyap, Subhas (2004), *Our Parliament*, New Delhi: National Book Trust.

Kashyap, Subhas (2006), *Parliamentary Procedure: Law, Privileges, Practice and Precedents*, Delhi: Universal Publishers.
Keith, A. B. (1969), *A Constitutional History of India 1600–1935*, New York: Barnes and Noble.
Kemp, Betty (1959), *King and Commons 1660–1832*, London: St. Martin's Press.
Kennedy, Duncan (2008), *Legal Reasoning: Collected Essays*, Colorado: The Davies Group.
Kohli, Atul (ed.) (2001), *The Success of India's Democracy*, Cambridge: Cambridge University Press.
Krishnaswamy, Sudhir (2010), *Democracy and Constitutionalism in India*, New Delhi: Oxford University Press.
Lapsley, Gaillard Thomas (1951), *Crown, Community and Parliament in the Later Middle Ages; Studies in English Constitutional History*, Oxford: B. Blackwell.
Lijphart, Arend (1992), *Parliamentary Versus Presidential Government*, Oxford: Oxford University Press.
Lyon, Bryce Dale (1980), *A Constitutional and Legal History of Medieval England*, New York: Norton.
Maitland, F. W. (1908), *The Constitutional History of England*, Cambridge: Cambridge University Press.
Manor, James (ed.) (1994), *Nehru to the Nineties: The Changing Office of Prime Minister in India*, London: Hurst and Co.
Maxwell, Peter Benson (1991), *On the Interpretation of Statutes*, Colorado: Fred Rothman.
Mehra, Ajay K. and Gert W. Kueck (2003), *The Indian Parliament: A Comparative Perspective*, Delhi: Konark Publishers.
Mehta, Jashwant B. (1979), *Presidential System: A Better Alternative?* Bombay: N. M. Tripathi.
Ministry of Parliamentary Affairs (2010), *Statistical Handbook*, New Delhi: Government of India.
Morris-Jones, W. H. (1957), *Parliament in India*, London: Longmans, Green and Co.
Mukherjea, A. R. (1983), *Parliamentary Procedure in India*, New Delhi: Oxford University Press.
Munshi, K. M. (1967), *The President under the Indian Constitution*, Bombay: Bharatiya Vidya Bhawan.
Nehru, Jawaharlal (1936), *India and the World*, London: George, Allen and Unwin.
Nehru, Jawaharlal (1940), *Towards Freedom*, New York: Jones Day.
Nikolenyi, Csaba (2009), *Minority Governments in India: The Puzzle of Elusive Majorities* (London, Routledge).
Noorani, A. G. (1989), *The Presidential System: The Indian Debate*, New Delhi: Sage.
Noorani, A. G. (2004), *The Trial of Bhagat Singh: Politics of Justice*, New Delhi: Oxford University Press.
Panandiker, V. A. Pai and Ajay K. Mehra (1996), *The Indian Cabinet: A Study in Governance*, Delhi: Konark Publishers.

Patnaik, Raghunath (1996), *Powers of the President and Governors of India*, New Delhi: Deep and Deep Publications.

Peerenboom, Randall (ed.) (2004), *Asian Discourses of Rule of Law*, London: Routledge.

Plucknett, Theodore (1956), *A Concise History of Common Law*, Boston: Little, Brown and Co.

Pollard, Albert Frederick (1964), *The Evolution of Parliament*, New York: Russell and Russell.

Prakash, Surya (1995), *What Ails India's Parliament*, New Delhi: Harper Collins.

Prasad, Anirudh (1981), *Presidential Government or Parliamentary Democracy*, New Delhi: Deep and Deep.

Raj, Hans (1989), *Executive Legislation in Colonial India 1939–1947*, New Delhi: Anamika Prakashan.

Rao, B. Shiva (ed.) (2006), *The Framing of India's Constitution*, New Delhi: Universal Law Publishing.

Raz, Joseph (1979), *The Authority of Law: Essays on Law and Morality*, Oxford: Oxford University Press.

Russell, Conrad (1971), *The Crisis of Parliament: English History 1509–1660*, Oxford: Oxford University Press.

Sampford, Charles (2006), *Retrospectivity and the Rule of Law*, Oxford: Oxford University Press.

Sathe, S. P. (2002), *Judicial Activism in India*, New Delhi: Oxford University Press.

Sathe, Vasant (1989), *Two Swords in One Scabbard: A Case for Presidential Form of Parliamentary Democracy*, New Delhi: NIB Publishers.

Saxena, K. S. and Anil Gupta (eds.) (1985), *Indian Democracy: Recent Trends and Issues*, New Delhi: Anmol Publications.

Sayles, George, O. (1974), *The King's Parliament of England*, New York: W. W. Norton.

Seervai, H. M. (1968), *Constitutional Law of India*, Bombay: N.M. Tripathi Private.

Seervai, H. M. (2007), *Constitutional Law of India*, Delhi: Universal Law.

Shaman, Jeffrey M. (2001), *Constitutional Interpretation: Illusion and Reality*, Westport, CT: Greenwood Press.

Shankar, B. L. and Valerian Rodrigues (2011), *The Indian Parliament: A Democracy at Work*, New Delhi: Oxford University Press.

Shourie, Arun (2007), *The Parliamentary System*, New Delhi: ASA Rupa.

Singh, Mahendra Prasad and Anil Mishra (eds.) (2004), *Coalition Politics in India: Problems and Prospects*, New Delhi: Manohar.

Singh, Naunihal (2008), *A System of Governance: Parliamentary or Presidential*, New Delhi: Anmol Publishers.

Singh, Zail (1997), *Memoirs of Giani Zail Singh: The Seventh President of India*, New Delhi: Har-Anand Publications.

Stubbs, William (1875), *The Constitutional History of England in Its Origin and Development*, Oxford :Clarendon Press.

Stubbs, William (1896), *The Constitutional History of England*, Oxford: Clarendon Press.

Tamanaha, Brian (2004), *On the Rule of Law: History, Politics, Theory*, Cambridge: Cambridge University Press.

Thompson, Faith (1953), *A Short History of Parliament 1295–1642*, Minneapolis: University of Minnesota Press.

Tremblay, Luc (1997), *The Rule of Law, Justice and Interpretation*, Montreal: McGill-Queen's University Press.

Unger, Roberto (1976), *Law in Modern Society*, New York: Free Press.

Wadhwa, D. C. (1983), *Re-promulgation of Ordinances: A Fraud on the Constitution of India*, Pune: Gokhale Institute of Politics and Economics.

Wadhwa, D. C. (2008), *Endangered Constitutionalism: Documents from a Supreme Court Case*, Pune: Gokhale Institute of Politics and Economics.

Walker, Clive and James Broderick (2006), *The Civil Contingencies Act 2004: Risk, Resilience and the Law in the United Kingdom*, Oxford: Oxford University Press.

Warren, Gordon H. (1981), *Fountain of Discontent: The Trent Affair and Freedom of the Seas*, Boston: Northeastern University Press.

Weber, Max (trans. from German by Edward A. Shils and Henry Finch) (1949), *The Methodology of the Social Sciences*, New York: Free Press.

Wilkinson, Bertie (1964), *Constitutional History of England in the Fifteenth Century*, New York: Barnes and Noble.

ARTICLES

'Draft Constitution Prepared by the Drafting Committee' in B. Shiva Rao (ed.), *The Framing of India's Constitution* Vol. III, 517–677, 549 (Universal Law Publishing, New Delhi, 2006).

Adair, E. R., 'The Statute of Proclamations', *English Historical Review*, 32(125), (1917), p. 34.

Agarwal, Arun, 'The Indian Parliament', in *Public Institution in India*, Devesh Kapur and Pratap Mehta (eds.) (2007). New Delhi: Oxford University Press, p. 77.

Amnesty International, 'Briefing on the Armed Forces (Special Powers) Act, 1958, Asa 20/025/2005', *available at*: http://web.amnesty.org/library/pdf/ASA200252005ENGLISH/$File/ASA2002505.pdf.

Anil Kalhan, Gerald P. Conroy, Mamta Kaushal and Sam Scott Miller, 'Colonial Continuities: Human Rights, Terrorism, and Security Laws in India', 20 *Columbian Journal of Asian Law* (2006–2007).

Anon, '165 Firms Will Be Affected' *Times of India*, 20 January 1956.

Anon, 'Afroze Finally Gets a Taste of Freedom' *Times of India*, 10 April 2002.

Anon, 'Afroze Is the First to be Booked Under POTO in State' *Times of India*, 9 March 2002.

Anon, 'Afroze Was Part of Al Quida Hit Squad' *Times of India*, 28 March 2002.

Anon, 'Army's Help to be Sought if Necessary' *Times of India*, 4 June 1958.

Anon, 'Bail Suspects Could be Released after Court Ruling' *BBC News*, 29 June 2011, *available at*: http://www.bbc.co.uk/news/uk-13957873 (visited on 31 August 2011).

Anon, 'Banking Ordinance is Challenged' *Times of India*, 22 July 1969.

Anon, 'Centre Takes Over Forty Six "Sick" Mills' *Times of India*, 1 November 1972.
Anon, 'C. R. Doubts Validity of Ordinance' *Times of India*, 19 July 1969.
Anon, 'Earlier in Day, BJP Spelt Out Her Office of Profit' *Indian Express*, 23 March 2006, *available at*: http://www.indianexpress.com/news/earlier-in-day-bjp-spelt-out-her-office-of-profit/1040/0.
Anon, 'Emergency Powers Ordinance May be Withdrawn' *Times of India*, 9 August 1957.
Anon, 'Fighting Naga Rebels: Aid of Armed Forces' *Times of India*, 7 June 1958.
Anon, 'Fourteen Top Banks are Nationalised' *Times of India*, 20 July 1969.
Anon, 'Getting Away with Murder: 50 Years of the Armed Forces Special Powers Act' *Human Rights Watch*, August 2008, *available at*: http://www.hrw.org/legacy/backgrounder/2008/india0808/india0808webwcover.pdf.
Anon, 'Government to Rush Bill Rendering P. and T. Strike Illegal' *Times of India*, 4 August 1957.
Anon, 'Govt. Assumes Emergency Powers to Prevent Strikes' *Times of India*, 8 August 1957.
Anon, 'Govt. Ordinance: NDA Lodges Protest with Kalam' *Rediff News*, 23 March 2006, *available at:* http://www.rediff.com/news/2006/mar/22profit1.htm (visited on 21 November 2011).
Anon, 'Govt. Powers POTO through Joint Session' *Times of India*, 27 March 2002.
Anon, 'Govt. to Manage Coking Coal Mines' *Times of India*, 17 October 1971.
Anon, 'Hasty Decision' *Times of India*, 21 January 1956.
Anon, 'Human Rights Body to be Set Up' *Times of India*, 30 September 1993.
Anon, 'Human Rights Panel a "Fraud on People"' *Times of India*, 8 December 1993.
Anon, 'India and the War: Paper Currency Reserve' *Times of India*, 15 December 1916.
Anon, 'Insurance Firms "Misused" Power and Privilege' *Times of India*, 20 January 1956.
Anon, 'Insurance Nationalisation Helps Plan' *Times of India*, 21 January 1956.
Anon, 'Life Insurance to be Nationalised with Immediate Effect' *Times of India*, 20 January 1956.
Anon, 'Loss to Foreign Markets' *Times of India*, 20 January 1956.
Anon, 'No Discussion on Ordinance in Cabinet' *Times of India*, 23 March 2006.
Anon, 'Office-of-profit Bill not Big Enough for Kalam' *Hindustan Times*, 31 March 2006.
Anon, 'OOP Bill gets Kalam OK, Experts Say Can be Contested' *Indian Express*, 19 August 2006.
Anon, 'Ordinance Issued on Non-Coking Coal Mines' *Times of India*, 31 January 1973.
Anon, 'Ordinance on Near-Extinct Rs. 1 Note Survives Seven Decades' *Deccan Herald*, 12 September 2010, *available at*: http://www.deccanherald.com/content/95919/ordinance-near-extinct-rs1-note.html (visited on 31 August 2011).

Anon, 'P. and T. Stand Explained' *Times of India*, 9 August 1957.
Anon, 'Paper Currency Act: Proposed Amendment' *Times of India*, 11 January 1916.
Anon, 'Paper Currency Reserves Increased by 12 Crores' *Times of India*, 15 November 1916.
Anon, 'Parliament Disruption Main Pool of Opposition: Vice President' *Indian Express*, 2 February 2011, *available at*: http://www.indianexpress.com/news/parliament-disruption-main-tool-of-opposition-vice-president/745252/0.
Anon, 'Parliament Okays Rights Bill' *Times of India*, 23 December 1993.
Anon, 'P M Nair: "Kalam erred on Office of Profit Bill"' *Times of India*, 22 April 2008.
Anon, 'Police Get Sweeping Powers to Fight Terror' *Times of India*, 17 October 2001.
Anon, 'Postal Office Bill Withdrawn' *Times of India*, 16 March 2002.
Anon, 'Posts and Telegraphs Strike Called Off' *Times of India*, 9 August 1957.
Anon, 'POTO Promulgated with Amendment's' *The Tribune*, 1 January 2002 *available at*: http://www.tribuneindia.com/2002/20020101/nation.htm#3 (visited on 16 November 2011).
Anon, 'POTO Receives President's Nod for Second Time' *Times of India*, 1 January 2002.
Anon, 'President Revokes Ordinance' *Times of India*, 13 August 1957.
Anon, 'Protest Against Essential Services Emergency Bill' *Times of India*, 4 August 1957.
Anon, 'Public Prosecutor Says Police Didn't Consult Him about POTO Charges' *Times of India*, 27 March 2002.
Anon, 'Public Safety Ordinance: Preventive Purpose' *The Straits Times*, 1 May 1929.
Anon, 'Report of the Committee, Headed by Justice (Retd) B. P. Jeevan Reddy, to Review the Armed Forces (Special Powers) Act 1958', *available at*: http://www.hindu.com/nic/afa/afa-part-iv.pdf.
Anon, 'Sonia as NAC Head Is Pseudo-Constitutional Power Centre: BJP' *Indian Express*, 30 March 2010.
Anon, 'Sonia Resigns from Lok Sabha, NAC' *Business Line*, 24 March 2006.
Anon, 'Strike Decision Stands' *Times of India*, 7 August 1957.
Anon, 'The Die Is Cast' *Times of India*, 21 July 1969.
Anon, 'Tighter Control of Banks: Bill in Parliament Likely' *Times of India*, 18 July 1969.
Anon, 'Top Fourteen Banks Are Nationalised' *Times of India*, 20 July 1969.
Anon, 'To Right Wrongs' *Times of India*, 4 October 1993.
Anon, 'Transfer of India Securities Held by the Nizam Banned' *Times of India*, 2 July 1948.
Anon, 'UF Circles Hail Bank Nationalisation' *Times of India*, 20 July 1969.
Anon, 'Uproar in Parliament over Ordinance "Shielding" Sonia' *Hindustan Times*, 22 March 2006.
Anon, 'Viceroy's Action: Public Safety Ordinance' *Times of India*, 15 April 1929.
Anon, 'Viceroy to Issue Ordinance: Address to Legislature' *Times of India*, 13 April 1929.

Anon, 'Vital Stats: Legislative Activity in Parliament', *available at*: http://www.prsindia.org/parliamenttrack/vital-stats/legislative-activity-in-parliament-2008-421/ (visited on 16 November 2011).

Ayyangar, N. Gopalswami and Alladi Krishnaswami Ayyar, 'Memorandum on the Principles of the Union Constitution', in *The Framing of India's Constitution*, B. Shiva Rao (ed.) (2006), New Delhi: Universal Law Publishing, p. 540.

Banerjee, D. N., 'The Indian Presidency', *Political Quarterly*, 26(1), (1955), p. 70.

Baxi, Upendra, 'Introduction', in *Endangered Constitutionalism: Documents from a Supreme Court Case*, D. C. Wadhwa (ed.) (2008), Pune: Gokhale Institute of Politics and Economics.

Baxi, Upendra, 'Rule of Law in India', in *Asian Discourses of Rule of Law*, Randall Peerenboom et al. (eds.) (2004), London: Routledge, p. 328.

Bhatnagar, Rakesh, 'All Eyes on the Supreme Court to Resolve Gujarat Tangle' *Times of India*, 26 August 2002.

Bradley, Curtis A. and Eric A. Posner, 'Presidential Signing Statements and Executive Power', *Constitutional Commentary* 23(3), (Winter 2006), p. 307.

Brest, Paul, 'Palmer V. Thompson: An Approach to the Problem of Unconstitutional Legislative Motive', *Supreme Court Review*, 1971 (1971), p. 95.

Chandra, Shailaja, 'Abolish MCI, Councils' *The Pioneer*, 3 September 2009.

Chasie, Charles and Sanjoy Hazarika, 'The State Strikes Back: India and the Naga Insurgency', *Policy Studies*, 52 (2009), *available at*: http://www.eastwestcenter.org/fileadmin/stored/pdfs/ps052.pdf.

Clark, 'Legislative Motivation and Fundamental Rights in Constitutional Law', *San Diego Law Review*, 15 (1978), p. 953.

Cottrell, Jill, 'Re-Promulgation of Ordinances in India: A Note', *The International and Comparative Law Quarterly*, 37(4), (October 1988), p. 1044.

Craig, Paul P., 'Formal and Substantive Conceptions of the Rule of Law: An Analytical Framework', *Public Law* (1997), p. 467.

Dalal, Sucheta, 'Confusion Compounded' *Times of India*, 5 July 1992.

Dalal, Sucheta, 'Decontrol without a Framework' *Times of India*, 2 June 1992.

Dalal, Sucheta, 'Ordinance Likely on Powers of SEBI' *Times of India*, 15 January 1992.

Dalal, Sucheta, 'SEBI Clueless on Ordinance' *Times of India*, 20 February 1992.

Deshpande, V. S., 'President, His Power and Their Exercise', *Journal of Indian Law Institute*, 13 (1971), p. 326.

Dhawan, Rajeev, 'Protecting the Bureaucracy' *The Hindu*, 7 March 2003.

Driedger, Elmer A., 'Statutes: Retroactive Retrospective Reflections', *Canadian Bar Review*, 56 (1978), p. 268.

Editorial, 'A Plea for the Study of Power of the President of India', *Journal of Indian Law Institute*, 12 (1970), p. 400.

Eisenberg, Theodore, 'Disproportionate Impact and Illicit Motive: Theories of Constitutional Adjudication', *New York University Law Review*, 52 (1977), p. 36.

Ely, John Hart, 'Legislative and Administrative Motivation in Constitutional Law', *Yale Law Journal*, 79 (1970), p. 1205.

Fallon, Richard H., 'The Rule of Law as a Concept in Constitutional Discourse', *Columbia Law Review*, 97(1), (1997), p. 1.
Finn, John E., 'Sunset Clauses and Democratic Deliberation: Assessing the Significance of Sunset Provisions in Antiterrorism Legislation', *Columbia Journal of Transnational Law*, 48 (2010), p. 442.
Fisch, Jill E., 'Retroactivity and Legal Change: An Equilibrium Approach', *Harvard Law Review*, 110 (1997), p. 1056.
Gersen, Jacob E., 'Temporary Legislation', *University of Chicago Law Review*, 74 (2007), p. 247.
Graetz, Michael J., 'Retroactivity Revisited', *Harvard Law Review*, 98 (1985), p. 1820.
Hewitt, Vernon and Shirin M. Rai, 'Parliament', in *Oxford Companion to Politics in India*, Niraja Jayal and Pratap Mehta (eds.) (2010), New Delhi: Oxford University Press.
Holmes, Henry W., 'Power of the Indian President: Myth or Reality?' *Journal of Indian Law Institute*, 12 (1970) p. 367.
Jaitley, Arun, 'POTO Pin-Up' *Times of India*, 13 December 2001.
Jeffrey, Robin, 'The Prime Minister and the Ruling Party', in *Nehru to the Nineties: The Changing Office of Prime Minister in India*, James Manor (ed.) (1994), London: Hurst and Co.
Jehangir, Cowasji, 'Ordinance Is Undemocratic' *Times of India*, 21 January 1956.
Jha, Prem Shankar, 'Coalition Politics and Economic Decision-Making', in *Coalition Politics in India: Problems and Prospects*, Mahendra Prasad Singh and Anil Mishra (eds.) (2004), New Delhi: Manohar.
Jinks, Derek P., 'The Anatomy of an Institutionalized Emergency: Preventive Detention and Personal Liberty in India', *Michigan Journal of International Law*, 22 (2001), p. 311.
Julian P. Boyd et al. (eds.) (1958), *The Papers of Thomas Jefferson XV*, 'The Federalist' No. 26 (Alexander Hamilton), available at: http://thomas.loc.gov/home/histdox/fed_26.html (visited on 16 November 2011).
Kagan, Elena, 'Private Speech, Public Purpose: The Role of Governmental Motive in First Amendment Doctrine', *University of Chicago Law Review*, 63 (1996), p. 413.
Kamal Kabra, 'Nationalisation of Life Insurance in India', *Economic and Political Weekly* 21(47), (22 November 1986), p. 2045.
Khomne, Ranjit, 'Afroze Likely to be Booked under POTO' *Times of India*, 3 January 2002.
Khomne, Ranjit, 'Cases under POTO Will Stay Even if the Bill Is Defeated' *Times of India*, 22 March 2002.
Kumar, Shankar, 'Over to the Prez' *Sahara Times*, 5 August 2006.
Kumarasingham, Harshan, 'The Indian Version of First among Equals – Executive Power during the First Decade of Independence', *Modern Asian Studies*, 44(4) (2010), p. 709.
Laws, Sir John, 'The Constitution: Morals and Rights', *Public Law* (1996), p. 622.
Madhukar, C. V., 'House This for Debate?' *The Indian Express*, 3 January 2007.
Malhotra, Inder, 'Run Over the Banks' *Indian Express*, 10 July 2009.

Margulies, Peter, 'Judging Terror in the "Zone Of Twilight": Exigency, Institutional Equity and Procedure after September 11', *Boston University Law Review*, 84 (2004), p. 383.

Mehdudia, Sujay, 'President Kalam Signs Office of Profit Bill, *The Hindu*, 19 September 2006, *available at*: http://www.hindu.com/2006/09/19/stories/2006091922020300.htm.

Mehta, Pratap, 'Checks and Balances' *Indian Express*, 1 June 2006.

Ministry of Home Affairs Office Order No. 11011/97/2004-NE-III, 19 November 2004.

Munzer, Stephen, 'A Theory of Retroactive Legislation', *Texas Law Review*, 61 (1983), p. 425.

Muralidharan, Sukumar, 'BJP and Friends' *Frontline*, 15(1), 10–23 January 1998.

Mustafa, Seema and Venkatesh Kesari, 'Profit Bill a Blatant Bid to Save MPs' *Asian Age*, 2 June 2006.

Nagasaila, D. and V. Suresh, 'Repromulgation of POTO: Is It Legal?' *Economic and Political Weekly*, 37(5), (2002), p. 371.

Nariman, Fali, '"The Silences in Our Constitutional Law": First Durga Das Basu Endowment Lecture 2005', *Supreme Court Cases (Journal)*, 2 (2006), p. 15.

Nauriya, Anil, 'Indian Judicial Renascence: The Lines Not Crossed', *Economic and Political Weekly*, 22(6), (7 February 1987), p. 239.

Nelson, Caleb, 'Judicial Review of Legislative Purpose', *New York University Law Review*, 83 (2008), p. 1784.

Noorani, A. G., 'No, Mr. President' *Hindustan Times*, 25 July 2006.

Noorani, A. G., 'Supreme Court and Ordinances', *Economic and Political Weekly*, 22(9), (1987), p. 357.

Omvedt, Gail, 'Parliamentary System in India: Issues and Suggestions', *Indian Journal of Political Science*, 33(3–4), (1999), p. 4.

Pandey, A. P., 'Hundred Years of Ordinances in India: 1861–1961', *Journal of Indian Law Institute*, 10 (1968), p. 259.

Peerenboom, Randall, 'Human Rights and Rule of Law: What's the Relationship?' *Georgetown Journal of International Law*, 36(4), (2005), p. 809.

Perry, 'The Disproportionate Impact Theory of Racial Discrimination', *University of Pennsylvania Law Review*, 125 (1977), p. 540.

Prasad, Rajendra, 'Prasad to Patel: 27 August 1950' in *Dr. Rajendra Prasad: Correspondence and Select Documents*, Valmiki Choudhary (ed.) Vol. XIII, 1987, New Delhi: Allied Publishers, p. 64.

Prasad, Rajendra, 'President's Status vis-à-vis Council of Ministers: 24 January 1951' in *Dr. Rajendra Prasad: Correspondence and Select Documents*, Valmiki Choudhary (ed.) Vol. XIV, (1987), New Delhi: Allied Publishers, p. 270.

Principles relating to the Status of National Institutions (The Paris Principles) (48/134 of 20 December 1993), *available at*: http://www2.ohchr.org/english/law/parisprinciples.htm.

Rajeev Dhavan, 'Op-Ed, Terrorism by Ordinance' *The Hindu*, 1 October 2004, *available at*: http://www.hindu.com/2004/10/01/stories/2004100104781000.htm.

Ramakrishnan, Venkitesh, 'A Masterstroke' *Frontline* 23(6), 25 March–07 April 2006, *available at*: http://hindu.com/fline/fl2306/stories/20060407007212900.htm.

Ramkrishnan, V., 'All for Survival' *Frontline*, 15(8), 11–24 April, 1998.

Rau, B. N., 'Memorandum on the Union Constitution', in *The Framing of India's Constitution*, Vol. 2, B. Shiva Rao (ed.) (2006), New Delhi: Universal Law Publishing.

Ray, Amal, 'From a Constitutional to an Authoritarian System of Government: Interactions Between Politics and the Constitution in India', *Journal of Commonwealth and Comparative Politics*, 25(3), (1987), p. 275.

Rosenfeld, Michel, 'Constitutional Adjudication in Europe and the United States: Paradoxes and Contrasts', *International Journal of Constitutional Law*, 2 (2004), p. 633.

Rudolph, Lloyd I. and Susan H. Rudolph, 'Redoing the Constitutional Design: From an Interventionist to a Regulatory State' in *The Success of India's Democracy*, Atul Kohli (ed.) (2001), Cambridge: Cambridge University Press, p. 141.

Sharma, B. A. V. and N. M. Valecha, 'The Indian President', *Political Quarterly*, 33(1), (1962), p. 59.

Sibal, Kapil, 'Politics of POTO: Nothing Anti-National about Dissent' *Times of India*, 16 November 2001.

Singh, Ujjwal Kumar, 'Penal Strategies and Political Resistance in Colonial and Independent India', in *Challenging the Rule(s) of Law: Colonialism, Criminology and Human Rights in India*, Kalpana Kannabiran and Ranbir Singh (eds.) (2008), New Delhi: Sage, p. 226.

Som, Reba, 'Jawaharlal Nehru and the Hindu Code: A Victory of Symbol over Substance', *Modern Asian Studies*, 28(1), (1994), p. 169.

Sorabjee, Soli, 'Decision of the Supreme Court in S. R. Bommai v.. Union of India', *Supreme Court Cases (Journal)*, 3 (1994), p. 1.

South Asia Human Rights Documentation Centre, 'Armed Forces Special Powers Act: A Study in National Security Tyranny', *available at*: http://www.hrdc.net/sahrdc/resources/armed_forces.htm.

Subramaniam, Samantha, 'The Long View: AFSPA's Bitter Roots' *New York Times*, 21 November 2011 *available at*: http://india.blogs.nytimes.com/2011/11/21/the-long-view-afspas-bitter-roots/#more-8705.

Torri, Michelguglielmo, 'Factional Politics and Economic Policy: The Case of India's Bank Nationalization', *Asian Survey*, 15(12), (December 1975), p.1.

Travis, Alan, 'Court Ruling 'A Disaster,' Say Police' *The Guardian*, 29 June 2011, *available at*: http://www.guardian.co.uk/politics/2011/jun/29/bail-ruling-theresa-may-considers-emergency-legislation (visited on 31 August 2011).

Travis, Alan, 'Court Ruling Leaves Police Powerless to Enforce Bail Conditions' *The Guardian*, 1 July 2011, *available at*: http://www.guardian.co.uk/uk/2011/jul/01/police-powerless-enforce-bail-conditions?intcmp=239 (visited on 31 August 2011).

Travis, Alan, 'Emergency Law to Overturn Court Ruling on Police Bail' *The Guardian*, 30 June 2011, *available at*: http://www.guardian.co.uk/uk/2011/jun/30/emergency-law-bail-ruling?intcmp=239 (visited on 31 August 2011).

Varadarajan, Sidharth, 'Reject POTO in Toto' *Times of India*, 14 November 2001.
Venkataraman, R., 'To Stop Office-of-Profit Axe, UPA Gets Ordinance' *Indian Express*, 21 March 2006.
Venkatesan, V., 'A Rare Return' *Frontline*, 23(12), 30 June 2006.
Venkatesan, V., 'POTO and a Stand-Off' *The Frontline*, 22 December 2001, *available at*: http://www.hindu.com/fline/fl1826/18260190.htm (visited on 16 November 2011).
Waldron, Jeremy, 'The Concept and the Rule of Law', *Georgia Law Review*, 43(1), (2008), p. 1.

STATUTES (INCLUDING CONSTITUTIONS, ACTS AND ORDINANCES)

38th Constitution (Amendment) Act, 1975 (India).
Abducted Persons (Recovery and Restoration) Amendment Ordinance, 1951 (7 of 1951).
Administration of Evacuee Property (Amendment) Ordinance, 1950 (27 of 1950).
Armed Forces (Assam and Manipur) Special Powers Ordinance, 1958 (1 of 1958).
Armed Forces (Jammu and Kashmir) Special Powers Act, 1990 (21 of 1990).
Armed Forces (Jammu and Kashmir) Special Powers Ordinance, 1990 (3 of 1990).
Armed Forces (Miscellaneous Provisions) Ordinance, 1950 (8 of 1950).
Armed Forces (Punjab and Chandigarh) Special Powers Act, 1983 (34 of 1983).
Armed Forces (Punjab and Chandigarh) Special Powers Ordinance, 1983 (9 of 1983).
Armed Forces (Special Powers) Continuance Act, 1964 (9 of 1964).
Armed Forces (Special Powers) Continuance Ordinance, 1956 (1 of 1954).
Armed Forces (Special Powers) Continuance Ordinance, 1964 (1 of 1964).
Armed Forces Special Powers (Jammu and Kashmir) Ordinance, 1990 (3 of 1990).
Asian Refractories Limited (Acquisition of Undertaking) Ordinance, 1971 (13 of 1971).
Banking Companies (Acquisition and Transfer of Undertaking) Ordinance, 1969 (8 of 1969).
Banking Companies (Acquisition and Transfer of Undertaking) Ordinance, 1970 (3 of 1970).
Banking Notes (Declaration of Holdings) Ordinance, 1946 (II of 1946).
Barsi Light Railway Company (Transferred Liabilities) Ordinance, 1953 (7 of 1953).
Bengal Cotton Gambling Ordinance, 1912.
Bengal Criminal Law (Amendment) Ordinance, 1924 (I of 1924).
Bengal Criminal Law (Amendment) Ordinance, 1930 (I of 1930).
Bombay Public Security Measures Act (Delhi Amendment) Ordinance, 1948 (XIV of 1948).
Building and Other Construction Workers (Regulation of Employment and Conditions of Service) Ordinance, 1995 (14 of 1995).
Burma Notes Ordinance, 1942 (XXVIII of 1942).
Burn Company and Indian Standard Wagon Company (Nationalization) Ordinance, 1976 (8 of 1976).

Calcutta Tramways Company (Taking over of Management) Amendment Ordinance, 1971 (10 of 1971).
Caltex (Acquisition of Shares of Caltex Oil Refining) Limited Ordinance, 1976 (15 of 1976).
Capital Issues (Control) Repeal Ordinance, 1992 (9 of 1992).
Central Vigilance Commission Ordinance, 1998 (15 of 1998).
Central Vigilance Commission Ordinance, 1999 (4 of 1999).
Chandigarh Disturbed Areas Ordinance, 1983 (6 of 1983).
Chota Nagpur Tenancy Act, 1908 (VI of 1908).
Civic Guards Ordinance, 1940 (VIII of 1940).
Civil Contingencies Act, 2004 c. 36 (UK).
Coal Mines (Nationalization) Amendment Ordinance, 1976 (3 of 1976).
Coal Mines (Nationalization) Ordinance, 1976 (3 of 1976).
Coal Mines Provident Fund and Miscellaneous Provisions (Amendment) Ordinance, 1996 (5 of 1996).
Coal Mines (Taking over of Management) Ordinance, 1973 (1 of 1973).
Coinage Ordinance, 1940 (IV of 1940).
Coking Coal Mines (Emergency Provisions) Ordinance, 1971 (12 of 1971).
Commercial Intercourse with Enemies Ordinance, 1914 (VI of 1914).
Constitution of India, 1949.
Constitution of Singapore, 1963.
Constitution of the Democratic Socialist Republic of Sri Lanka, 1978.
Constitution of the Islamic Republic of Pakistan, 1973.
Constitution of the People's Republic of Bangladesh, 1971.
Cotton Excise Duty (Suspension) Ordinance, 1925 (I of 1925).
Currency Ordinance, 1940 (IV of 1940).
Defence of India Ordinance, 1962 (4 of 1962).
Delhi Administration (Amendment) Ordinance, 1977 (6 of 1977).
Delhi Evacuee Property (Supplementary) Ordinance, 1947 (XXIII of 1947).
Delhi Refugees Registration Ordinance, 1947 (XXIV of 1947).
Dentists (Amendment) Ordinance, 1992 (14 of 1992).
Depositories Ordinance, 1995 (11 of 1995).
Displaced Persons (Claims) Continuance Ordinance, 1952 (5 of 1952).
Displaced Person (Institution of Suits) Ordinance, 1948 (XVIII of 1948).
Dramatic Performances Ordinance, 1876.
East Punjab Public Safety (Amendment) Ordinance, 1951 (5 of 1951).
Emergencies Act, 1985 (Canada).
Emergency Legislation Continuance Act, 1915 (I of 1915).
Enemy Trading Ordinance, 1916 (V of 1916).
Essential Commodities (Special Provisions) Amendment Ordinance, 1992 (12 of 1984).
Essential Service (Maintenance) Ordinance, 1941 (XI of 1941).
Essential Service (Prevention of Strikes) Ordinance, 1951 (1 of 1951).
Essential Services Maintenance Bill, 1957
Essential Services Maintenance Ordinance, 1957 (5 of 1957).
Excess Profit Tax Ordinance, 1943 (XVI of 1943).
Exchange of Prisoners Ordinance, 1948 (VI of 1948).

Export of Saltpetre Ordinance, 1861.
Export of Saltpetre Ordinance, 1862.
Federal Constitution of Malaysia, 1957.
Foreign Exchange Regulation (Amendment) Ordinance, 1951 (10 of 1951).
Foreign Exchange Regulation (Amendment) Ordinance, 1969 (6 of 1969).
Foreigners (Amendment) Ordinance, 1914 (VII of 1914).
Foreigners Ordinance, 1914 (III of 1914).
General Insurance (Emergency Provisions) Ordinance, 1971 (6 of 1971).
Goa, Daman and Diu (Administration) Ordinance, 1962 (2 of 1962).
Gold Coinage Ordinance, 1918 (II of 1918).
Gold (Import) Ordinance, 1917 (III of 1917).
Gold Ordinance, 1920 (III of 1920).
Government of India Act, 1915.
Government of India Act, 1919 (9 and 10 Geo. 5, Ch 101).
Government of India Act, 1935 (26 Geo. 5 and 1 Edw. 8, Ch 2).
High Court (Seals) Ordinance, 1950 (13 of 1950).
High Denomination Bank Notes (Demonitisation) Ordinance, 1946 (III of 1946).
Hindu Succession Act, 1956 (30 of 1956).
Import and Export of Goods Ordinance, 1916 (IV of 1916).
India and Burma (Emergency Provisions) Act, 1940 (3 and 4 Geo. 6, Ch. 33).
Indian Air Force Volunteer Reserve (Discipline) Ordinance, 1939 (VII of 1939).
Indian Army (Amendment) Ordinance, 1948 (XIX of 1948).
Indian Copper Corporation (Taking over of Management) Ordinance, 1972 (4 of 1972).
Indian Councils Act, 1861.
Indian Evidence Act, 1872.
Indian Income Tax (Amendment) Ordinance, 1945 (X of 1945).
Indian Income-Tax (Amendment) Ordinance, 1950 (Ordinance 28 of 1950).
Indian Independence Act, 1947 (10 and 11 Geo. 6, Ch. 30).
Indian Iron and Steel Company (Acquisition of Shares) Ordinance, 1976 (10 of 1976).
Indian Iron and Steel Company (Taking over of Management) Ordinance, 1972 (6 of 1972).
Indian Medical Council (Amendment) Ordinance, 1992 (13 of 1992).
Indian Paper Currency (Amendment) Ordinance, 1916 (I of 1916).
Indian Paper Currency (Amendment) Ordinance, 1917 (II of 1917).
Indian Paper Currency (Amendment) Ordinance, 1918 (III of 1918).
Indian Paper Currency Ordinance, 1918 (I of 1918).
Indian Press and Unauthorised News Sheets and Newspapers Ordinance, 1930 (X of 1930).
Indian Press Ordinance, 1930 (II of 1930).
Indian Railways Act, 1890 (9 of 1890).
Indian Royal Navy (Powers of Command) Ordinance, 1943 (XVII of 1943).
Indian Tariff (Amendment) Ordinance, 1950 (30 of 1950).
Industrial Disputes (Amendment) Ordinance, 1951 (9 of 1951).
Industrial Disputes (Amendment) Ordinance, 1995 (12 of 1995).

Industrial Disputes (Banking Companies) Commencement of Decision Ordinance, 1954 (7 of 1954).
Influx from Pakistan (Control) Amendment Ordinance, 1950 (22 of 1950).
Influx from West Pakistan (Control) Ordinance, 1948 (XVII of 1948).
Ingress into India Ordinance, 1914 (V of 1914).
Interim Constitution of Nepal, 2007.
Jayanti Shipping Company (Acquisition of Shares) Ordinance, 1971 (14 of 1971).
Judicial Commissioner's Courts Ordinances, 1950 (14 of 1950).
Konkan Passenger Ships (Acquisition) Ordinance, 1973 (4 of 1973).
Lahore Conspiracy Case Ordinance, 1930 (III of 1930).
Laxmirattan and Atherton West Cotton Mills (Taking over of Management) Ordinance, 1976 (11 of 1976).
Life Insurance (Emergency Provisions) Ordinance, 1956 (1 of 1956).
Madras Hereditary Village Offices Act, 1895.
Madras Maintenance of Public Order Act, 1947 (1 of 1947).
Madras Ordinance, 1949 (1 of 1949).
Maintenance of Internal Security Act, 1971 (5 of 1971).
Maintenance of Internal Security (Amendment) Ordinance, 1974 (11 of 1974).
Maintenance of Internal Security (Amendment) Ordinance, 1975 (4 of 1975).
Maintenance of Internal Security (Amendment) Ordinance, 1976 (5 of 1976).
Maintenance of Internal Security (Fourth Amendment) Ordinance, 1975 (22 of 1975).
Maintenance of Internal Security Ordinance, 1971 (5 of 1971).
Maintenance of Internal Security (Second Amendment) Ordinance, 1975 (7 of 1975).
Mangrol and Manavader (Administration of Property) Ordinance, 1948 (XXII of 1948).
Manipur University Ordinance, 2005 (II of 2005).
Martial Law Ordinance, 1919 (I–IV of 1919).
Martial Law Ordinance, 1921 (II of 1921).
Martial Law Ordinance, 1930 (VIII of 1930).
Merchant Shipping (Acceding States) Ordinance, 1948 (XXVIII of 1948).
Metal Corporation of India (Acquisition of Undertaking) Ordinance, 1966 (10 of 1966).
Metal Corporation of India (Nationalisation and Miscellaneous Provisions) Ordinance, 1976 (12 of 1976).
Military Safety (Power of Detention) Ordinance, 1944 (IV of 1944).
National Commission for Backward Classes Ordinance, 1993 (23 of 1993).
National Commission for Minority Educational Institutions Ordinance, 2004 (6 of 2004).
National Institute of Pharmaceutical Education and Research (Second) Ordinance, 1998 (9 of 1998)
National Security (Amendment) Ordinance, 1984 (5 of 1984).
National Security (Amendment) Ordinances, 1987 (3 of 1987).
National Security (Amendment) Ordinances, 1988 (4 of 1988).
National Security (Second Amendment) Ordinance, 1984 (6 of 1984).

National Security Ordinance, 1980 (11 of 1980).
National Tax Tribunal Ordinance, 2003 (3 of 2003).
Naval Force (Miscellaneous) Provisions Ordinance, 1950 (21 of 1950).
Pakistan Military Personnel Amnesty Ordinance, 1948 (I of 1948).
Parliament (Prevention of Disqualification) Amendment Act, 2006 (31 of 2006).
Parliament (Prevention of Disqualification) Ordinance, 1950 (12 of 1950).
Parliamentary Proceedings (Protection of Publication) Repeal Ordinance, 1975 (25 of 1975).
Patents (Amendment) Ordinance, 1994 (13 of 1994).
Pension Fund Regulatory and Development Authority Ordinance, 2004 (8 of 2004).
Police and Criminal Evidence Act, 1984.
Prevention of Terrorism (Amendment) Second Ordinance, 2001 (12 of 2001).
Prevention of Terrorism Ordinance, 2001 (9 of 2001).
Preventive Detention (Amendment) Ordinance, 1950 (20 of 1950).
Protection of Human Rights Act, 1993.
Protection of Human Rights Ordinance, 1993 (30 of 1993).
Public Safety Ordinance, 1929 (I of 1929).
Public Safety Ordinance, 1948 (XXIV of 1948).
Punjab Disturbed Areas Ordinance, 1983 (5 of 1983).
Punjab Legislature Regulation of Procedure in Relation to Financial Business Ordinance, 1968 (1 of 1968).
Punjab Municipal Corporation Act, 1976
Railways (Employment of Members of Armed Forces) Ordinance, 1965 (4 of 1965).
Regulation of Meetings Ordinance, 1907 (I of 1907).
Repealing Ordinance, 1946 (I of 1946).
Representation of People (Amendment) Ordinance, 1956 (8 of 1956).
Saurashtra (Abolition of Local Sea Customs Duties and Imposition of Port Development Levy) Repealing Ordinance, 1952 (4 of 1952).
Securities and Exchange Board of India Ordinance, 1992 (5 of 1992).
Securities (Hyderabad) Ordinance, 1948 (XVI of 1948).
Sick Textile Undertakings (Nationalization) Ordinance, 1974 (12 of 1974).
Sick Textile Undertaking (Taking over of Management) Ordinance, 1972 (9 of 1972).
Silver (Import) Ordinance, 1917 (IV of 1917).
Statute of Proclamations, 1539.
Supply and Prices of Goods Ordinance, 1950 (26 of 1950).
Swadeshi Cotton Mills Company Limited (Acquisition and Transfer of Undertakings) Ordinance, 1986 (5 of 1986).
Tea Companies (Acquisition and Transfer of Sick Tea Units) Ordinance, 1985 (3 of 1985).
Terrorist Affected Areas (Special Courts) Ordinance, 1984 (9 of 1984).
Terrorist and Disruptive Activities Act, 1985 (31 of 1985).
Terrorist and Disruptive Activities (Prevention) Amendment Ordinance, 1985 (4 of 1985).

Terrorist and Disruptive Activities (Prevention) Amendment Ordinance, 1987 (2 of 1987).
Terrorist and Disruptive Activities (Prevention) Amendment Ordinance, 1991 (5 of 1991).
Building and Other Construction Workers (Regulation of Employment and Conditions of Service) Act, 1996 (27 of 1996).
Essential Commodities (Special Provisions) Amendment Ordinance, 1993 (1 of 1993).
Jayanti Shipping Company (Taking over of Management) Ordinance, 1966 (4 of 1966).
National Security (Amendment) Ordinances, 1987 (3 of 1987).
Securities and Exchange Board of India Ordinance, 1992 (5 of 1992).
Supreme Court and High Court Judges (Conditions of Service) Amendment Ordinance, 1996 (7 of 1996).
The Terrorist Affected Areas (Special Courts) Ordinance, 1984 (9 of 1984).
Transfer of Detained Persons Ordinance, 1949 (XVI of 1949).
Travancore-Cochin Appropriation (Vote on Account) Ordinance, 1956 (4 of 1956).
Treaty of Peace (Austria) Ordinance, 1920 (IV of 1920).
Treaty of Peace (Hungary) Ordinance, 1921 (I of 1921).
Treaty of Peace Ordinance, 1920 (I of 1920).
Unauthorised News Sheets and Newspapers Ordinance, 1930 (VII of 1930).
University Grants Commission Act, 1956 (3 of 1956).
Unlawful Activities (Prevention) Amendment Ordinance, 2001 (12 of 2001).
Unlawful Activities (Prevention) Amendment Ordinance, 2004 (2 of 2004).
Unlawful Activities (Prevention) Ordinance, 1964 (6 of 1966).
Unlawful Association Ordinance, 1930 (IX of 1930).
Victoria State Emergency Act, 2005 (LI of 2005).
War Injuries Ordinance, 1941 (VII of 1941).
War Risks (Goods) Insurance Ordinance, 1940 (IX of 1940).
Women's Auxiliary Corps Ordinance, 1942 (XIII of 1942).

CASES

K. Roy v. Union of India AIR 1982 SC 710.
Agarwal v. State of UP AIR 1956 All 557.
Ahmed Khan v. Emperor AIR 1948 Lah. 120.
Allstate Ins. Co. v. Abbott, 495 F.3d 151 (5th Cir. 2007).
Barium Chemicals Ltd. v. Company Law Board AIR 1967 SC 295.
Bhagat Singh and Others v. The King-Emperor (1931) 55 Ind. App. 169.
Bhupendra Bose v. State of Orissa AIR 1962 SC 945.
Bommai v. Union of India (1994) 3 SCC 1.
British Railways Board Appellants v. Pickin (1974) AC 765.
Chakardharpur Biri and Tobacco Merchants' Association and Others v. State of Bihar 1973 TaxLR 2132.
Church of the Lukumi Babalu Aye v. City of Hialeah, 508 U.S. 520 (1993).

D. C. Wadhwa v. The State of Bihar AIR 1987 SC 579.
Deo v. State of Orissa, (1954) 1 SCR 1.
DiMa Corp. v. Town of Hallie, 185 F.3d 823 (7th Cir. 1999).
Dutt v. Union of India AIR 2004 SC 1295.
Edinburgh v. Wauchope (1842) VIII Clark and Finnelly 710.
Emperor v. Sreekant Pandurang Ketkar A.I.R. 1943 Bom. 169.
Fathima v. Ravindranathan AIR 1975 Ker. 202.
Gyanendra Kumar v. Union of India AIR 1997 Del 58.
Hasanabha v. State of Karnataka AIR 1998 Kant. 91.
Hirji Laxmidas v. Fernendez (1945) F.L.J. 119.
Hollinshead v. Hazleton (1916) 1 AC 428.
Hubli Electricity Co. Ltd. v. Province of Bombay L.R. (1948) 76 Ind. App. 57.
Hunter v. Underwood, 471 U.S. 222 (1985).
Indira Nehru Gandhi v. Raj Narain A.I.R. 1975 SC 2299.
In Re K. Veerabhadrayya AIR 1950 Mad 243.
In Re Velayudm 1950 (1) M.L.J. 508.
J.K. Jute Mills Co. v. State of Uttar Pradesh AIR 1961 SC 1534.
Jnan Prosanna v. Province of West Bengal AIR 1949 Cal. 1.
Kalyan Bhadra v. Union of India AIR 1975 Cal. 72.
Kartar Singh v. Punjab (1994) 3 SCC 569.
Kerala v. People's Union for Civil Liberties (2009) 8 SCC 46.
Kesavananda Bharati v. State of Kerala (1973) 4 SCC 225.
King-Emperor v. Benoari Lal Sharma and Others (1945) 72 Ind. App. 57.
Krishna Kumar Singh v. State of Bihar AIR 1998 SC 2288.
Labrador Co. v. The Queen (1893) AC 104.
Lakhi Narayan v. State of Bihar AIR 1950 FC 59.
Lakhi Narayan Das v. The Province of Bihar [1949] F.C.R. 693.
Laxmibai v. State of M.P. AIR 1951 Nagpur 94.
Lee v. Bude (1870–1871) LR 6 CP.
Leigh v. Kent 3 TR 362.
Lemon v. Kurtzman, 403 U.S. 602 (1971).
M.P.V. Sundararamier and Co. v. State of Andhra Pradesh (1958) SCR 1422, 1460.
Mahanta v. State of Assam AIR 1999 Gau 32.
Maneka Gandhi v. Union of India AIR 1978 SC 597.
Mathura Prasad Singh and Others v. State of Bihar AIR 1975 Pat 29.
Naga People's Movement for Human Rights v. Union of India A.I.R 1998 SC 431.
Nagaraj v. State of Andhra Pradesh AIR 1985 SC 551.
Nayar v. Union of India AIR 2006 SC 3127.
Nixon v. Administrator of General Services., 433 US 425 (1977).
Prabhakar Kondaji Bhapkar v. Emperor AIR 1944 Bom. 119.
Prem Chand Jain v. R. K. Chhabra (1984) 2 SCR 883.
Prem Narain v. State of UP AIR 1960 All. 205.
Q. v. Salford Magistrates' Court and Paul Hookway [2011] EWHC 1578 (Admin).
R. v. Wells 4 Dowl. 562.

Rajasthan v. Union of India (1977) 3 SCC 592.
Rameshwar Prasad v. Union of India (2006) 2 SCC 1.
R. C. Cooper v. Union of India 1970 (3) SCR 550.
Re Kalyanam Veerabhadraya AIR 1950 Madras 243.
Reddy v. State of Andhra Pradesh AIR 1985 SC 724.
Reference by President (No. 1 of 2002) (2002) 8 SCC 237.
R. K. Garg v. Union of India (1982) 1 SCR 947.
S. Krishnan v. The State of Madras AIR 1951 SC 301.
Sambamurthy v. A.P. (1987) 1 SCR 879.
Sarju Prasad v. State of UP AIR 1970 All. 571.
Satwant Singh Sawhney v. Assistant Passport Officer AIR 1967 SC 1836.
Sib Nath Banerjee v. King-Emperor AIR 1943 Cal. 344.
Singh v. State of Bihar AIR 1998 SC 2288.
Smithfield Foods, Inc. v. Miller, 367 F.3d 1061 (8th Cir. 2004).
State of Andhra Pradesh v. McDowell and Co. AIR 1996 SC 1627.
State of Karnataka v. B. A. Hasanabha AIR 1998 Kant. 210.
State of Karnataka v. Union of India and Others AIR 1978 SC 68.
State of Punjab v. Satya Pal Dang AIR 1969 SC 903.
Steavenson v. Oliver 151 E.R. 1024.
Sudhakar v. A.P. AIR 2006 SC 3385.
T. Venkata Reddy v. State of A.P. AIR 1985 SC 724.
The United Provinces v. Atiqa Begum 1940 F.C.R. 110 (F.B.).
Tukino v. Aotea District Maori Land Board (1941) AC 308.
United Motors India Ltd. v. State of Bombay (1953) 55 Bom LR 246.
United States v. O'Brien 391 U.S. 367 (1968).
Upendralal v. Narainee Devi (1931) 58 Ind. App. 169.
Venkata Reddy v. State of A. P. AIR 1985 SC 724.
Village of Arlington Heights v. Metropolitan Housing Development Corporation 429 U.S. 252 (1977).
Vishwanath Agarwal v. State of Uttar Pradesh AIR 1956 All. 557.
Warren v. Windle 102 E. R. (K. B.) 578.
White v. Boot 2 TR. 274.
Wicks v. Director of Public Prosecutions (1947) AC 362.

DICTIONARIES

Black's Law Dictionary, 9th ed. (2009), St. Paul, MN: West.
Cambridge Advanced Learner's Dictionary, 3rd ed. (2008), Cambridge: Cambridge University Press.
Longman Dictionary of Contemporary English, 4th ed. (2003), Essex: Pearson Education Limited.
Macmillan English Dictionary, 2nd ed. (2007), Oxford: A and C Black Publishers Limited.
New Oxford Dictionary of English (2001), New York: Oxford University Press.
Osborn's Concise Law Dictionary, 11th ed. (2009), London: Sweet and Maxwell/Thomson Reuters.
Oxford Dictionary of Law, 5th ed. (2002), Oxford: Oxford University Press.

The Essential Law Dictionary, 1st ed. (2008), Illinois: Sphinx Publication.
West's Encyclopaedia of American Law, 2nd ed. (2005), Detroit: Thomson/Gale.

REPORTS

Law Commission of India, 32nd Report on Section 9 of The Code of Criminal Procedure 1973 (May 1967).
Law Commission of India, 60th Report on the General Clauses Act, 1897 (May 1974).

Index